Reynold Hillenbrand
The Reform of the Catholic Liturgy and the Call to Social Action

Robert Tuzik

HillenbrandBooks

Chicago / Mundelein, Illinois

REYNOLD HILLENBRAND: THE REFORM OF THE CATHOLIC LITURGY AND THE CALL TO SOCIAL ACTION © 2010 Archdiocese of Chicago: Liturgy Training Publications, 3949 South Racine Avenue, Chicago IL 60609; 1-800-933-1800, fax 1-800-933-7094, e-mail orders@ltp.org. All rights reserved. See our Web site at www.LTP.org.

Hillenbrand Books is an imprint of Liturgy Training Publications (LTP) and the Liturgical Institute at the University of Saint Mary of the Lake (USML). The imprint is focused on contemporary and classical theological thought concerning the liturgy of the Catholic Church. Available at bookstores every where, or through LTP by calling 1-800-933-1800 or visiting www.ltp.org. Further information about the **Hillenbrand Books** publishing program is available from the University of Saint Mary of the Lake/Mundelein Seminary, 1000 East Maple Avenue, Mundelein, IL 60060 (847-837-4542), on the Web at www.usml.edu/liturgicalinstitute, or e-mail litinst@usml.edu.

Printed in the United States of America.

Library of Congress Control Number: 2009933061

ISBN 978-1-59525-030-8

HRH

This book is dedicated to His Eminence Francis Cardinal George, OMI, Archbishop of Chicago, and the priests of the Archdiocese of Chicago, who have carried on the work of liturgical renewal and social justice to which Msgr. Reynold Hillenbrand dedicated his life.

Contents

Preface

The contribution of Msgr. Reynold Hillenbrand to the liturgical movement in the United States captures the hopes, dreams, ideals, and theology of the liturgical movement in the United States. The life and work of Reynold Hillenbrand will introduce the reader to many of our liturgical pioneers and social justice activists, both clerical and lay. Their work helped prepare a whole generation of Church leaders, who embraced the renewal of the Church's liturgy and life after the Second Vatican Council.

Reynold Hillenbrand was the product of a devout German family. He had the good fortune of growing up in a liturgically and socially active community, St. Michael's Parish on the North side of Chicago. St. Michael's was known for its emphasis on active participation in the liturgy and the Church's mission to establish a more just social order. The influence of a parish community in encouraging vocations to the priesthood and an active involvement of the laity in the mission of the church is one of the great lessons we can draw from this study of Hillenbrand's life and work.

At St. Mary of the Lake Seminary, Reynold Hillenbrand received the typical scholastic education in philosophy and theology that was common to U.S. priests in the first half of the twentieth century. At the same time, Hillenbrand's brilliant intellect kept him growing in and open to the new insights in theology and pastoral practice gained from the research of biblical, patristic, and liturgical scholars. These insights combined with the directives for renewal of the life of the Church and the social order gave Hillenbrand a perspective and a zeal that was most engaging. Hillenbrand spoke to the hopes and dreams of so many in the Church. It is no wonder that he was often called on to be a speaker at national conventions and gatherings of the specialized lay apostolate.

If you want to trace the development of the liturgical movement in the twentieth century, especially paying attention to the encouragement and directives given by every Pope from Pius X to Pius XII, then the study of Hillenbrand's life and work will meet that goal. Hillenbrand's writings quote every major Encyclical and papal pronouncement regarding the need for full, conscious, active participation in the liturgy. While he tended to absolutize three encyclicals (*Quadragesimo Anno, Mystici Corporis,* and *Mediator Dei*), he nonetheless demonstrated the importance of taking direction from the Holy Father in prioritizing his work in the Church and the world.

If you want an introduction to the major institutions promoting liturgical and social renewal, then the study of Hillenbrand's life and work is what you need. Hillenbrand was the Keynote speaker at the very first National Liturgical Week, which was held in Holy Name Cathedral in Chicago. He was a member of and leader in the St. Jerome Society, the Vernacular Society, the Liturgical Conference, the Young Christian Students, the Young Christian Workers, and the Christian Family Movement. He supported groups like CISCA (Chicago Interstudent Catholic Action), the Grail, Summer Schools of Social Action and Liturgy for Priests, the first Summer School of Liturgy at the University of Notre Dame, and the Archdiocesan Liturgical Commission in Chicago.

If you are curious about who were the leaders of the liturgical and social action movements in the United States, then the study of the life and work of Reynold Hillenbrand will solve your curiosity. Hillenbrand knew practically every famous liturgical pioneer and social justice activist in the country. He was involved with so many great leaders: Virgil Michel, Martin Hellriegel, Gerald Ellard, H. A. Reinhold, Godfrey Diekmann, Michael Mathis, Maurice Lavanoux, Dom Ermin Vitry, Dorothy Day, Peter Marin, Catherine DeHuech Doherty, John Ryan, Francis McGowan, John Egan, and Pat and Patti Crowley, to name just a few. In the pages of this book you will discover who these leaders were and find references for further study of the works of these inspired people of faith.

Unfortunately, sickness and the passing of years led Hillenbrand to lose his influence both in liturgical renewal and with the specialized lay apostolate. Hillenbrand stubbornly held to a synthesis of scholastic theology, Cardijn methodology (see, judge, act), and directives from the past (given in *Quadragesimo Anno, Mystici Corporis,* and *Mediator Dei*). He could not accept the eclectic approach to theology found in the documents of Vatican II. In addition, the liturgical excesses (celebrating Mass without vestments, using new and unapproved Eucharistic Prayers, interchanging the roles of lay ministers with the priest celebrant, an unwillingness to sing anything in Latin, and so on) of some liturgical experiments after Vatican II made him question what he had accomplished with his life. Yet, to his dying breath he was convinced that liturgy must be connected with daily life, empowering Jesus' apostles to build a just social order in our world.

The Archbishops and priests of the Archdiocese of Chicago have had a long history of providing leadership to liturgical renewal and social action in the United States. Our current Archbishop, His Eminence Francis Cardinal George, OMI, has continued this work, serving for nine years as the representative of the United States Conference of Catholic Bishops with the International Commission on English in the Liturgy, for over ten years as a member of the Congregation for Divine Worship and the Discipline of the Sacraments and its Vox Clara Subcommittee, two years as Chairman of the Bishop's Committee on the Liturgy, and, most recently, as President of the United States Conference of Catholic Bishops. In 2000, Cardinal George founded the Liturgical Institute at the University of St. Mary of the Lake. Liturgical leadership has truly been a strong emphasis in the ministry of the Archbishops of Chicago for many generations.

One of Cardinal George's first pastoral letters, *Dwell in my Love*, addressed the challenge of racism and prejudice in Chicago and the nation. Cardinal George supports the work of Priests for Justice, a group of Chicago priests concerned with the rights of immigrants to our country. The Cardinal is very concerned that the Church make its voice heard in local organizations, which affect the quality of life in community. Social justice and respect for life is often mentioned in Cardinal George's writings and talks as a way to live out the commitment we make in the liturgy to carry on Jesus' work in the world. I am certain that Hillenbrand would have been a great supporter of the work of our current Archbishop. The Archbishop and priests of Chicago are truly committed to carrying on the great work of social reconstruction that is at the heart of our mission as Church.

It is with a deep sense of gratitude to so many outstanding Archbishops, Auxiliary Bishops, and priests from Chicago that I humbly dedicate this book. I am happy to call myself a priest of the Archdiocese of Chicago. We have accomplished a great deal in Chicago and beyond, since the days of Reynold Hillenbrand. My hope is that the publication of this book will keep the fires burning for still more progress in liturgical renewal and social justice, for much of what Reynold Hillenbrand believed and taught is still useful in the life of the Church today.

—Rev. Robert L. Tuzik, PHD

Acknowledgments

Many people have contributed to the successful completion of this book. I am deeply grateful to Professor James F. White, whose strong guidance and encouragement were the deciding factors in my completing this work. I must also acknowledge the gracious and thoroughly professional assistance I received from the staff of the Notre Dame Archives, who daily encouraged me and guided me through Hillenbrand's large collection of personal papers. In addition, I am indebted to the staff of the Feehan Memorial Library at the University of St. Mary of the Lake, who provided me with the necessary assistance in locating materials pertinent to Hillenbrand's years as a student and rector at the Seminary.

I have received the support of numerous priests and laity, who have offered me their wise counsel regarding Hillenbrand's numerous activities. I want to acknowledge the guidance of Michael Ahlstrom, Steven Avella, Gerard Broccolo, Richard Butler, Thomas Conley, Daniel Coughlin, Godfrey Diekmann, John Egan, John Hayes, Frederick Hillenbrand, Harry Koenig, John Lodge, Joseph O'Connell, Thomas Raftery, Mark Searle, Gloria Sieben, Edward Siedlecki, Michael Weston, William White, and Richard Wojcik. In addition, I want to thank my classmates and friends at the University of Notre Dame, who gave me their insights and encouragement throughout the years of writing. Finally, I want to thank the late, Joseph Cardinal Bernardin, without whose support I would not have been able to attend the University of Notre Dame.

Abbreviations

CFM   *Christian Family Movement*

CMRH   *Msgr. Reynold Hillenbrand Collection*

CMRH no./no.   *Box number/file number by which one can locate material*
               from CMRH

CYO   *Catholic Youth Organization*

LTP   *Liturgy Training Publications*

NCWC   *National Catholic Welfare Conference*

ODW   *Office for Divine Worship*

UNDA   *University of Notre Dame Archives*
               University of Notre Dame
               Notre Dame, Indiana

USCC   *United States Catholic Conference*

YCS   *Young Christian Students*

YCW   *Young Christian Workers*

Part I

The Historical Evolution

Chapter 1

The Formation of a Liturgical Pioneer: 1905–1931

FAMILY, PARISH, THE POPES, AND GERMAN THEOLOGY

Reynold Henry Hillenbrand's grandparents emigrated to the United States from Southern Germany in the mid nineteenth century.[1] They settled in the largely German farm community of East Bristol, Wisconsin. Eventually, Reynold's father George moved from Wisconsin to Chicago, Illinois in order to study dentistry at Northwestern University. In 1901 George received his doctorate and married Eleanor Schmidt from his home town of Bristol. That same year George and Eleanor moved to Chicago, where they joined St. Michael's parish, the largest German Catholic parish on Chicago's near North side.

Reynold Hillenbrand was born on July 19, 1904, in Chicago, Illinois. He was the second of nine children born to George Hillenbrand and Eleanor Schmitt.[2] Throughout his life, Reynold Hillenbrand would enjoy a close relationship with his relatives in Chicago as well as in Wisconsin, where two of his uncles, Henry Schmitt and Frederick Hillenbrand, were priests of the Archdiocese of Milwaukee.

---

1. Hillenbrand's maternal great-grandfather, Joseph Schmitt, emigrated to the United States in 1845 from Aschfeld, Unterfranken in Bavaria. Hillenbrand's paternal grandfather, Ernest Hillenbrand, emigrated to the United States in the early 1860s also from Bavaria. Msgr. Frederick Hillenbrand, retired pastor of St. Mary's Church and Reynold's older brother, related these facts to this author in an interview at St. Mary's Church, Evanston, Illinois, April 29, 1986.

2. The nine children born to George and Eleanor were Frederick (1902), Reynold (1904), Harold (1906), George (1908), Eugene (1910), Charles (1912), Magdaline (1914), Eleanor (1916), and Helen (1919).

REV. C. RUDOLPH C.SS.R.

ST. MICHAEL'S CHURCH, CHICAGO, ILL. 1852

Saint Michael's parish in Chicago's Old Town neighborhood, like many German parishes, had a strong sense of social justice. St. Michael's was also known for its rich liturgical and devotional traditions and strong music program. Hillenbrand would later take this formation to his own efforts in uniting liturgy and social justice. *Archdiocese of Chicago.*

The Hillenbrands were active members of St. Michael's parish, which was organized in 1852 to serve the needs of German Catholics living around North Avenue and Larrabee Street.[3] Hillenbrand received a traditional German Catholic education during his eight years at St. Michael's Grammar School and his one year at St. Michael's High School. St. Michael's had a high degree of social consciousness, as is evidenced by its publication of a weekly newspaper, the *Weltbuerger*, and by its support of the bilingual magazine, *Central-Blatt and Social Justice*.[4]

St. Michael's served as a site for the meetings of numerous voluntary associations, which were sponsored by the German Central Verein.[5] These associations were organized according to mutual interest, age, sex, and occupation.[6] Originally formed in 1854 to defend Catholics against the attack of free masonry and its claim to be the "universal religion of humanity," the German Central Verein sought to organize Catholic benevolent societies promoting the involvement of Catholics in public life and the defense of the rights of Catholic immigrants coming to the United States. It enjoyed the approval of the Holy See for its strict adherence to Catholic doctrine, especially as it applied to social justice and the rights of workers.

In *The Conservative Reformers: German American Catholics and the Social Order*, Philip Gleason makes the assertion: "if one wishes to understand the involvement of the German American Catholics with the social question, the Central-Verein is indisputably the place to

3. See Harry C. Koenig, Ed., *A History of the Parishes of the Archdiocese of Chicago, Vol. I* (Chicago: Archdiocese of Chicago, 1980), pp. 631–638. "At the time of the golden jubilee of the founding of St. Michael parish, which was celebrated on Oct. 19, 1902, approximately 2,000 families belonged to the parish and 1,950 children were enrolled in the parish school."

4. See Philip Gleason, *The Conservative Reformers, German-American Catholics and the Social Order* (Notre Dame: University of Notre Dame Press, 1968), pp. 3–4: "*Central-Blatt and Social Justice* also gave sympathetic attention to the liturgical movement long before liturgical reform became popular."

5. See Philip Gleason, *The Conservative Reformers*, and Colman J. Barry, *The German Church and German Americans* (Milwaukee: Bruce Publishing Company, 1953) for additional information on the work of the Central Verein in the U.S.

6. See Stephen J. Shaw, *Chicago's Germans and Italians, 1903–1939: the Catholic Parish as a Way-Station of Ethnicity and Americanization* (Chicago: University of Chicago, 1981), pp. 102–103: "The earliest societies were founded on the basis of occupation, sex, and interest . . . . Many clubs were mutual-interest societies, the most important being the Verein für Künst und Wissenschaft (Association of Art and Science).

begin."[7] In my opinion, Hillenbrand's later involvement with Catholic Action groups such as the Young Christian Workers was influenced by his early exposure to the associations which were organized by the German Central Verein.

The Central Bureau that coordinated the voluntary associations was located in Chicago. Frederick P. Kenkel, the director of the social reform program of the Central Bureau from 1908–1952, was baptized at St. Michael's and was a well-known figure to the people of this parish. Kenkel fostered the idea that there was a connection between the organic conception of society and a deeper appreciation of the liturgy in numerous articles that appeared in the bilingual magazine, *Central Blatt and Social Justice.*[8] Since Hillenbrand's family subscribed to *Central Blatt and Social Justice,* Hillenbrand may have read some of Kenkel's articles, thus developing in him an early interest in the connection between liturgy and social justice. However, Hillenbrand never quoted Kenkel or his magazine in any lecture or writing. Hence, there is no solid evidence to prove the extent to which Hillenbrand was influenced by the publications and the ideals of the Central Verein.

Liturgically, St. Michael's was known for elaborate ceremonies, a strong commitment to music and singing, and a vibrant devotional life. At the annual parish mission (retreat), German missionaries would stress the importance of baptism, confession, and frequent reception of Holy Communion.[9] Processions to mark important feasts such as Corpus Christi or events such as First Communion, Sunday evening vespers, sermons in German (in 1914 English first began to be used), Forty Hours Devotion before the beginning of each Lent, and daily

---

7. Gleason, pp. 5–6. Gleason's thesis is that one cannot understand the quest for social reform in the United States without studying the history of German American Catholics. By analyzing the efforts of German immigrants to adjust to American society one uncovers many of the themes (the evils of individualism, materialism, spiritual disunity, etc.) and goals (the workers' right to organize, a corporate social order based on an organic conception of society, active participation in the liturgy, etc.) that later became synonymous with the social action and liturgical movements. A excellent study of the social thought of the Central Verein is found in Sr. Mary Liguori Brophy's book, The Social thought of the German Roman Catholic Central Verein, Washington, D.C.: Catholic University of America Press, 1941.

8. See *Central Blatt and Social Justice,* Vol. XIV (Jan.-Mar., 1922), pp. 323–26, 259–60, 396–98; Vol. XVIII (May, 1925), pp. 58–59.

9. See Jay P. Dolan, Ed., *The American Catholic Parish, A History from 1850 to the Present, Vol. II* (New York: Paulist Press, 1987), pp. 308–317 on German parish life.

Interior of Saint Michael's parish in Chicago' Old Town neighborhood. *Photo © James Morris.*

Benediction preserved both the traditions of the congregation's beloved Germany and modeled the more active type of participation which Hillenbrand later associated with the liturgical movement.[10]

German Catholic resistance to adopting the English language and American customs was beginning to weaken during Hillenbrand's grammar school education (1910–1918). The fact that St. Michael's introduced an English sermon at the high Mass in 1914 indicated a partial Americanization of the parish.[11] Hillenbrand's future education at St. Mary of the Lake Seminary would be heavily influenced by the growing trend among Catholic bishops to create a truly American clergy independent of the need for European priests to serve in ethnic parishes. This need to establish an American clergy might also account for some of the isolation of the United States Church from developments in the European Church.

Hillenbrand grew up in a Church still reacting to Leo XIII's condemnation of Americanism on January 22, 1899 in the encyclical *Testem Benevolentiae*. According to Leo XIII, the underlying principle behind Americanism was the conviction that in order to attract new converts and achieve harmonious relations with other groups, "the

---

10. Joseph O'Connell, Professor of Art at the College of St. Benedict, in an interview with the author on April 1, 1988, at the College of St. Benedict, described the rich liturgical life at St. Michael's parish. (O'Connell lived in St. Michael's parish and knew Hillenbrand as a young man.) However, Hillenbrand never spoke about the liturgy at St. Michael's in any lecture or writing. Thus, there is no solid evidence for claiming any additional influence of St. Michael's on Hillenbrand's love for the liturgy.

11. See Colman J. Barry, *The Catholic Church and German Americans* (Milwaukee: Bruce Publishing Company, 1953), p. 119: On August 17, 1888, Archbishop John Ireland of St. Paul defined Americanization as "the filling up of the heart with love for America and her institutions."

Church should shape her teachings more in accord with the spirit of the age and relax some of her ancient severity and make some concessions to novel ideas."[12] Even though Hillenbrand eventually adopted the novel idea (at the time)of a "Mystical Body" ecclesiology as the basis of his synthesis on liturgy and social action, Hillenbrand was definitely advocating ideas that many people, educated with the traditional, hierarchical definition of church, found strange or even dangerous. To some people this biblical understanding of Church (where those of the priesthood of the baptized and the ordained both offered the sacrifice of the Mass) sounded like a Protestant rejection of the hierarchical notion of Church that they had grown up with and believed was infallible doctrine.

What saved Hillenbrand from being branded a radical in some of his viewpoints was a strong loyalty to the teachings of the Popes. During the first half of the twentieth century, the church was led by a series of very popular popes. Leo XIII (1878–1903) became the champion of the worker. St. Pius X (1903–1914) promoted frequent Communion, first Communion at the age of reason (about seven), and active participation in the liturgy. Pius XI (1922–1939) challenged the laity to participate in Catholic Action and in the liturgy.

In *The American Catholic Experience,* Jay P. Dolan reminds us that during this period radio (and eventually television) brought the papacy closer to home.

> The deaths and elections of popes became front-page news and table talk. Such popularity reinforced the Pope's position as monarch in the church.[13]

The publicity surrounding the deaths of Pius X and Benedict XV during Hillenbrand's grammar school and high school years must have awakened in him an early interest in papal teachings. If some of Hillenbrand's ideas on creating a more just social order were considered radical by his contemporaries, Hillenbrand could always quote Pius X's motto on the need "to restore all things in Christ."[14]

---

12. Charles de T'Seraclaes & Maurice F. Egan, *The Life and Labors of Pope Leo XIII* (New York: Rand, McNally, & Company, 1903), p. 305. See John Cogley and Roger Van Allen, *Catholic America,* (New York: Sheed and Ward, 1986), p. 62.

13. Dolan, *The American Catholic Experience,* p. 387.

14. Of all the Popes who lived during Hillenbrand's lifetime, Pius X is one of his favorites and is often quoted in Hillenbrand's writings.

Reynold Hillenbrand was born at a time when the institutional model of Church was reaching its height. This was the era of strong, authoritarian bishops and priests. In addition, the classicist or neo-Scholastic view dominated Roman Catholic theology until the middle of the twentieth century. Leo XIII's August 4, 1879, encyclical, *Aeterni Patris*, "On Christian Philosophy," insisted on the use of Scholastic theology in order that "it may continue to be 'the invincible bulwark of faith.'"[15] This classical approach permeated Papal teaching until Vatican II and definitely slowed down the acceptance of alternative methods (biblical, historical, cultural, and linguistic) of theological reflection.[16] In Hillenbrand's case, institutionalism and neoscholasticism led him to adopt an authoritarian approach to pastoral leadership and a theological method unduly influenced by papal teachings. Hillenbrand closely interpreted three Papal Encyclicals (*Quadragesimo Anno, Mystici Corporis, Mediator Dei*) and failed to integrate newer insights into his pastoral approach, especially those found in the documents of Vatican II.

In the late nineteenth century many American Protestants embraced an historical, evolutionary model of church with an emphasis on an immanent God who is progressively establishing the Kingdom in our midst. If the classical or neo-Scholastic model saw the church as unchanging and immune to the influences of history, the modernist model saw the church as historically conditioned and open to development.[17]

When on September 8, 1907, Pius X condemned Modernism in his encyclical, *Pascendi domini gregis*, American Catholic theologians adopted a conservative, defensive posture. The insights of biblical and patristic studies, which surfaced more in the European version of Modernism, had little impact on American theology until almost the middle of the twentieth century. As James Hennessey says, American

15. Leo XIII, "Aeterni Patris," no. 24 in *The Church Speaks to the Modern World, The Social Teachings of Leo XIII*, ed. Etienne Gilson (Garden City: Doubleday & Company, 1954), p. 47.

16. See Jay P. Dolan, *The American Catholic Experience*, pp. 303–304. See Bernard Lonergan, "The Transition from a Classicist World-View to Historical Mindedness," in William F. Ryan and Bernard J. Tyrell, eds. (*A Second Collection*, Philadelphia: Westminster Press, 1975), pp. 1–10.

17. See Jay P. Dolan, *The American Catholic Experience*, pp. 304-311 and *The Encyclopedic Dictionary of Religion* (Washington: Corpus Publications, 1979): "Modernism (Protestant)," by N. H. Maring, pp. 2399–2400 and "Modernism (Roman Catholic)," by J.J. Heaney, pp. 2400–2401.

theologians "now slipped more or less peacefully into a half century's theological hibernation."[18] It took the liturgical and social action movements to reawaken American theology to the fact that it had fallen behind Europe in its creativity and pastoral leadership.

The one place where the theological hibernation that characterized American theology was absent was in communities open to the influences of German theology and the German biblical, liturgical, and youth movements. German American Catholics of Hillenbrand's childhood were influenced by the progressive thinking of the Tübingen School of Theology, which addressed the challenges of the Enlightenment to the traditional Scholastic theology and religious practices of the early nineteenth century.[19] As Mark Schoof explains in *A Survey of Catholic Theology, 1800-1970*:

> The whole life of the Church, her customs, worship and moral attitudes, were for these theologians as much a basis for theological reflection as the Church's teaching.[20]

The contemporary theologian's task was to make the life of the Church, her customs, worship, and moral teachings applicable to the problems of daily life. Of course, this is what Hillenbrand saw the popes attempting to accomplish in their encyclicals and official teachings.

Two Tübingen theologians greatly influenced the pioneers of the American liturgical movement—Johann Adam Möhler (1796–1838) and Matthias Joseph Scheeben (1835–1888). Two of Möhler's early works, *Die Einheit in der Kirche* (1825) and *Symbolik* (1832) pioneered a new ecclesiology based on an organic conception of Church and an ecumenical openness to learning from the insights of Protestant theologians.[21] Scheeben's two works, *Nature and Grace* (1861, tran. C. Vollert, 1954) and *Mysteries of Christianity* (1865, tran. C. Vollert,

18. James Hennessey, *American Catholics, A History of the Roman Catholic Community in the United States* (New York/Oxford: Oxford University Press, 1981), p. 203.

19. See Olivier Rousseau, *The Progress of the Liturgy: An Historical Sketch from the Beginning of the Nineteenth Century to the Pontificate of Pius X*, tran. Westminster Priory Benedictines, Westminster: Westminster Priory, 1951, 58–61.

20. Mark Schoof, *A Survey of Catholic Theology, 1800–1970*, trans. N.D. Smith (New York: Paulist Newman Press, 1970), p. 26.

21. See J.R. Geiselmann, *Johann Adam Möhler*, 1940 and R. H. Nienaltowski, *Johann Adam Möhler's Theory of Doctrinal Development*, 1959.

1961) were masterpieces that built upon Möhler's work and moved beyond the limits of late 19th century Scholastic theology, providing a broader framework in which the liturgical pioneers could work.[22]

We see evidence of this new theological framework in the fact that early twentieth century Germany had thriving biblical, liturgical, and social action movements. In fact, Germany's youth movement originates in the desire of young people

> to be independent, inwardly true to themselves and to develop freely as persons and thus to penetrate through the stale patterns of contemporary society and behavior to the real essence beneath and in this way create a new way of life.[23]

Certainly, Hillenbrand's joining the liturgical and social action movements is influenced by his exposure to the ideals of the German youth movement at St. Michael's parish.

CATHOLICS, POVERTY, LIBERALISM, AND PROSPERITY

Hillenbrand's early years were also times of social tension. Catholic immigrants were faced with the challenge of establishing themselves in a country, steeped in Anglo-Saxon Protestantism and often suspicious of Catholic loyalties to their new country. On the whole, Catholic immigrants tended to be poor, unskilled, and at the bottom of the socio-economic ladder.[24] They were often the victims of industrialization and the accompanying problems of materialism, individualism, class consciousness, child labor, wage exploitation, segregation, and slum housing.[25] While Hillenbrand's German middle class background saved him from directly experiencing the worst of these problems, his early formation sensitized him to the social justice issues present at that time in American society.

---

22. Schoof, *A Survey of Catholic Theology*, pp. 36–37.

23. Ibid., pp. 80.

24. John L. Thomas, "Nationalities and American Catholicism," in *The Catholic Church, U.S.A.*, ed. Louis J. Putz (Chicago: Fides, 1956), pp. 163–167.

25. Newman C. Eberhardt, *A Survey of American Church History* (St. Louis & London: B. Herder Book Company, 1964), pp. 102–123.

With the election of Theodore Roosevelt to the Presidency (1901–1909) and his promise of a "Square Deal" for all citizens, including the organization of labor unions and a larger measure of social and industrial justice, the progressive movement in American politics began to address the problems of the working poor, many of whom were Catholic. In 1912 under a banner of "New Freedom," Woodrow Wilson pushed for more reforms to protect small business-men, farmers, and wage earners.[26] These progressive trends were also accompanied by a rise in social activism among American Catholics led by John A. Ryan[27] and Peter E. Dietz,[28] whose leader-ship in the social action movement became a model for Hillenbrand and other socially conscious priests.

After World War I, Chicago experienced an economic transformation. Within a decade nearly three billion dollars was spent on new highways, parks, bridges, rail service, factories, hospitals, hotels, theatres, colleges, etc. The population increased from 2,700,000 in 1920 to 3,376,000 in 1930.[29] Chicago became the city of the Armours, the Insulls, the McCormicks, or the Rosenwalds. Yet, not everyone lived on the North Shore or Chicago's Gold Coast. Along with the growth of commerce and industry, there existed a class of unskilled laborers, who often lived in abject poverty and were frequently the victims of discrimination and injustice.[30]

---

26. Aaron I. Abell, *et. al.*, *A History of the United States of America* (New York: Fordham University Press, 1952), pp. 428–475.

27. See Francis L. Broderick, *Right Reverend New Dealer, John A. Ryan* (New York: Macmillan Company, 1963). After publishing his dissertation on "The Living Wage" in 1906, John Ryan went on to become professor of moral theology at St. Paul's Seminary in St. Paul, Minnesota. In 1916, he published a popular book, "Distributive Justice: The Right and Wrong of Our Present Distribution of Wealth." In this book, he demonstrated his ability to merge the agenda of reform organizations in the U.S. with papal social thought, especially Pope Leo XIII's famous Encyclical Rerum Novarum. In 1917, he became a member of Catholic Committee on Reconstruction and helped draft the "Bishops' Program of Social Reconstruction." Eventually, he became the head of the NCWC's Social Action Department.

28. See Mary Marrita Fox, *Peter E. Dietz, Labor Priest* (Notre Dame: University of Notre Dame Press, 1953).

29. Harold M. Mayer & Richard C. Wade, *Chicago, Growth of a Metropolis* (Chicago: University of Chicago Press, 1969), pp. 283, 290.

30. Charles Shanabruch, *Chicago's Catholics, the Evolution of an American Identity* (Notre Dame: University of Notre Dame Press, 1981), p. 32.

Catholics as a group became more middle class and less socially conscious during the 1920s. In *Chicago's Catholics, The Evolution of an American Identity*, Charles Shanabruch explains:

> As the immigrants and the children gained experience, learned skills, or obtained an education, they moved upward socially and economically, and outward to neighborhoods which bespoke their better conditions.[31]

Businessmen and conservatives frightened the American people into believing that "all (social) reformers were Bolsheviks in disguise or the naive and witless abettors of violent revolution."[32] Consequently, the progressive movement in theology fell into disarray until the onset of the Great Depression in 1929.[33]

CARDINAL MUNDELEIN AND HIS SEMINARIES

After World War I the brick and mortar bishops had their day in the Catholic Church. George Cardinal Mundelein was probably the foremost exemplar of this "triumphalist phase" in American Catholicism.[34] For Mundelein was a builder, an organizer, a strict disciplinarian, a politically shrewd businessman, an Americanizer in the mold of James Cardinal Gibbons, and a priest who understood the potential for greatness in the Archdiocese of Chicago. Under his guidance, a tremendous expansion of the Archdiocese occurred with the founding of new parishes,[35] grammar schools, high schools, colleges, hospitals, orphanages, homes for the aged, seminaries, etc.

Mundelein was a bishop who recognized talent in young priests and frequently appointed them to high places in the administration of the Archdiocese. The key to his identifying new talent was

---

31. Ibid., p. 105.

32. Aaron I. Abell, *American Catholicism and Social Action, a Search for Social Justice, a Comprehensive Study of the Catholic Social Movement in the United States from 1865 to 1950* (Notre Dame: University of Notre Dame Press, 1963), p. 264.

33. Ibid., pp. 199–205.

34. John Cogley & Roger Van Allen, *Catholic America* (New York: Sheed & Ward, 1986), pp. 66–67: "By World War I, American Catholicism had entered a "triumphalist" phase and it continued until the shakeup following the Second Vatican Council. It was a period of tremendous expansion, extraordinary stability, and general optimism."

35. See Edward R. Kantowicz, *Corporation Sole, Cardinal Mundelein and Chicago Catholicism* (Notre Dame: University of Notre Dame Press, 1983), p. 9: By 1936 the Archdiocese of Chicago would have 411 parishes in Cook, Lake, DuPage, Will, Grundy, and Kankakee counties.

(Top) Reynold Hillenbrand shown in his 1923 Quigley Preparatory Seminary yearbook of the debate team photo (seated, far right), was already known by his lifelong nicknames of "Hilly" and "Reiny." He evidently showed leadership potential in his educational life, and his high school activities prefigure the many gifts he would use in his priestly ministry. *Archdiocese of Chicago.*

(Above) Hillenbrand's formation remained deeply intertwined with the educational efforts of Cardinal George Mundelein, who founded both Quigley Preparatory Seminary and Saint Mary of the Lake Seminary, insisting on the highest educational standards and using the system to identify men of particular talent. Young Reynold shown here in his yearbook photo. *Archdiocese of Chicago.*

the seminary system. One of Mundelein's first acts as Archbishop was to announce the plans for a new High School Preparatory Seminary on May 14, 1916, barely three months after his installation.[36] Quigley Preparatory Seminary opened on September 9, 1918, and the following

---

36. Ibid., pp. 15–16.

September 1919, Reynold Hillenbrand transferred from St. Michael's
High School to the Seminary.

Quigley was unique as a Preparatory Seminary in that it was
not a boarding school, but one to which the students would commute
while living at home. Quigley also began as a five year program, the
fifth year being the first year of college. During this time, Hillenbrand
learned to read Greek and Latin, adding to his already fluent ability to
read and speak German. Always an excellent student, Hillenbrand
became a leader and spokesman for his class. In fact, in his senior year
he was elected class president and was appointed editor of the
Seminary year book.[37]

St. Mary of the Lake Seminary opened on October 5, 1921
and Hillenbrand arrived two years later, in 1923, to complete his
college education. The major seminary was approximately 1,000
acres with fourteen major buildings, constructed in Colonial Revival
architecture. Each seminarian had his own room with bath and there
were accommodations for 475. It was the largest Roman Catholic
seminary in the nation. Its academic faculty was provided by the
Missouri Province of the Society of Jesus, who taught philosophy and
theology according to the Scholastic method with lectures in Latin.
Its administrative posts (rector, procurator, prefects of discipline) were
filled by diocesan priests.[38]

Mundelein's vision was to create a thoroughly American clergy
for the Archdiocese and to cease being dependant upon foreign clergy
to staff diocesan parishes. He objected to establishing new national
parishes (for example, parishes that served only Italian, German, or
Polish people), preferring instead territorial parishes that would serve
all the Catholics in a geographical region. In addition, after World
War I, Catholics in large numbers moved to the suburbs, where they
mixed freely with people of various ethnic backgrounds. Mundelein
wanted the Archdiocese to be led by priests who had gone through his
seminary system and understood his vision of an American Church.[39]

---

37. Msgr. Frederick Hillenbrand to the author, St. Mary's Church, Evanston, Illinois,
April 29, 1986 interview.

38. See Harry C. Koenig, ed., *A History of the Offices, Agencies, and Institutions of the
Archdiocese of Chicago, Vol. I* (Chicago: Archdiocese of Chicago, 1981), pp. 315-332 and
Kantowicz, *Corporation Sole*, pp. 116–117.

39. See Charles Shanabruch, *Chicago's Catholics*, p. 214 and Kantowicz, *Corporation Sole*,
p. 61.

Hillenbrand developed his love of literature and poetry during his years at the major seminary. He became the local expert in Gerard Manley Hopkins. He also participated in the Bellarmine Society, the school literary club which produced an annual book of poetry, essays, and debates. By the time he began his second year of theology, Hillenbrand's theological expertise was rewarded with his selection for advanced doctoral studies. During his last two years in the seminary he was elected President of the Bellarmine Society and shared the responsibility for organizing its literary programs. In short, respect for Hillenbrand's talents as a scholar, a polished speaker, and a popular leader grew steadily among the faculty and students throughout his years in the seminary.

THE EUCHARISTIC CONGRESS, FATHERS MICHEL, HELLRIEGEL, AND ELLARD

Two important religious events occurred during Hillenbrand's years in the major seminary, which greatly affected his life. Undoubtedly the most significant religious event that occurred in Chicago during the decade of the 1920s was the 28th International Eucharistic Congress of June 20–24, 1926. In my opinion, the second most important religious event was the emergence of the liturgical movement and its common theological base with the social action movement.

The Archdiocesan Newspaper, the *New World*, defined the Eucharistic Congress as "a gathering of Christians from all over the world for the sole purpose of honoring Jesus Christ in the Most Blessed Sacrament of the altar."[40] This Congress brought to Chicago almost a million visitors and mobilized the entire Archdiocese in implementing its many programs.[41] Bishops and invited guests were assigned to preach at all the parishes of the Archdiocese. Special Masses were held in Soldier Field (Chicago's lakefront stadium), drawing crowds over 250,000. The opening liturgy was in the

---

40. "The Great Congress and What it Stands for Arranged in Catechism Form for Convenience," *New World* 34 (June 20, 1926), p. 4.

41. See Paul R. Martin, *The First Cardinal of the West, the Story of the Church in the Archdiocese of Chicago under the Administration of His Eminence, George Cardinal Mundelein, Third Archbishop of Chicago and First Cardinal of the West* (Chicago: New World Publishing Company, 1943), p. 200.

Cathedral and a choir of 60 seminarians from the major seminary, including Hillenbrand, sang at the ceremony. The closing ceremonies were held at the major seminary and drew almost 350,000 people.[42]

For the Congress, St. Mary of the Lake Seminary became more of a showplace than ever with the addition of a large pier extending into the lake with a bronze cupola for Solemn Benediction on the final day of the Congress, the installation of a bronze statue of Mary on a 52' pillar in the plaza in front of the main chapel, and the erection of a Marian grotto similar to the one at Lourdes. Of course, many of these additions drew attention to the importance of the liturgy in the life of the Church.

Bishop Joseph Schrembs of Cleveland, director of the Priests' Eucharistic League, spoke of the Congress fulfilling the dream of Pius X to see the Christian spirit flourish again through active participation in the most holy mysteries and the public and solemn prayer of the Church. He said a large portion of the discussion of the Priests' Eucharistic League would revolve around "the topic of restoring the liturgy of the Church to its rightful place in the Catholic life of our people."[43] He also spoke of the problem of people praying their private devotional prayers during Mass instead of praying the Mass. He recommended that priests work to increase congregational singing and the chanting of the Kyrie, Gloria, Credo, Sanctus, and other portions of the Ordinary of the Mass. His words made a big impression on Hillenbrand, who followed the proceedings of the Congress with great attention.

Cardinal Mundelein in his opening address to the Congress on June 20, 1926 spoke of the close connection between liturgy and life. The real remedy for the world's ills lies in God and in the liturgy. Regarding the Eucharist, Mundelein said:

> Look at it as you will, the evils of today come from an absence of charity, an abnormal love of self, a lack of consideration for others. But this sacrament is the living monument of the greatest, purest, most divine love, such

---

42. See "The Official Program of the 28th International Eucharistic Congress, 1926," *New World* 34 (June 18, 1926), pp. 2–3.

43. See "Head of the Eucharistic League on Devotional Subject," *New World* 34 (May 28, 1926), p. 12. In addition to the leadership of Bishop Schrembs, Abbot Alcuin Deutsch of St. John's Abbey, Collegeville, Minnesota also spoke at the Congress, calling for the birth of the liturgical movement in the United States. See Paul R. Marx, *Virgil Michel and the Liturgical Movement* (Collegeville: Liturgical Press, 1957), p. 103.

as only God could establish, the very immolation of self for others. Where could our people better acquire this same spirit of charity than at the foot of this altar, in the presence of the Sacred Host.[44]

In this brief passage, you find many of the same themes and ideals that Hillenbrand adopted as his own. In addition, during this period Hillenbrand came under the influence of some first-rate leaders: Fathers Virgil Michel, Martin Hellriegel, and Gerald Ellard.

Virgil Michel, OSB, of St. John's Abbey in Collegeville, Minnesota, was one of great exponents of liberal theology in the United States. Early in 1924, Abbott Alcuin Deutsch sent Michel to study scholastic philosophy and liturgy in Rome. During his time in Europe, Michel travelled extensively, visiting many of the European liturgical centers. At Mont César in Belgium, Michel met the renowned monk, Lambert Beauduin, who in September, 1909 gave fresh impetus to the European liturgical movement by his address at the National Congress of Catholic Action held at Malines.[45]

Beauduin inspired Michel's interest in the liturgy, Mystical Body theology, and social action. In Rome, Michel took Beauduin's liturgy course at the College of St. Anselm.[46] There he became convinced that the liturgy was the indispensable means of instilling the true Christian spirit in society and that the answer to so many of society's problems was to be found in an organic conception of society based on the Mystical Body. He believed that in the early church living membership in the Mystical Body was "the inspirational idea of Catholic life as it should be."[47] To the young Hillenbrand, Virgil Michel's ideas were a welcome continuation of the progressive theology he had learned at St. Michael's parish.

Michel was convinced that there was a necessary connection between liturgy and social action, that the liturgy gave Christ's apostles courage, the grace of perseverance, spiritual strength, and the power

44. "Reply of Cardinal Mundelein (to the Apostolic Legate)," *New World* 34 (June 25, 1926), pp. 5–6.

45. See Sonya A. Quitslund, *Beauduin, A Prophet Vindicated* (New York: Newman Press, 1973), pp. 22–36.

46. See Paul R. Marx, *Virgil Michel and the Liturgical Movement* (Collegeville: Liturgical Press, 1957), pp. 21–28. Michel became good friends with Beauduin. In 1926, Michel translated Beauduin's book, *La Piété de l'Eglise*, whose English title is *Liturgy: the Life of the Church.*

47. Virgil Michel, "The True Christian Spirit," *Ecclesiastical Life* 82 (1930), pp. 131–132. Cf. "Apostolate," *Orate Fratres* 33 (1929), pp. 181–188.

to transform a Christless world. In fact, the whole cause of God
on earth "depends in some degree on the responsible action of each
member of Christ."[48] Consequently, the true significance of the
liturgical movement lies in this:

> that it tries to lead people back to the "primary and indispensable source of
> the true Christian spirit"; it tries to restore that of which Catholic Action
> is the further flowering and fruitage.[49]

For Catholic Action is simply the continuation in the outside
world of the sacrificial dedication to God and God's people that we
celebrate in the liturgy. It was this synthesis, which Michel so con-
vincingly articulated, that Hillenbrand eventually made his own.

On January 18, 1925, Michel wrote his Abbott about his plan
to popularize the ideals of the European liturgical movement in the
United States by creating a Popular Liturgical Library. At this same
time, William Busch, professor of church history at St. Paul Seminary,
was also petitioning Abbott Alcuin Deutsch of St. John's Abbey to
publish some of the European literature on the liturgical movement.[50]
On April 25, 1925 Michel wrote to Abbot Deutsch that he would like
to begin a review to be called *Orate Fratres* in addition to the Popular
Liturgical Library.[51] However, it was the Christmas Eve, 1925
meeting with Martin Hellriegel and Gerald Ellard at Hellriegel's
residence in O'Fallon, Missouri, that solidified Michel's plans for
Liturgical Press and *Orate Fratres*.[52]

---

48. Virgil Michel, *The Christian in the World* (Collegeville: Liturgical Press, 1939), p. 77.

49. Virgil Michel, "The Significance of the Liturgical Movement," *NCWC Bulletin* 10
(1929), p. 26. See Marx, pp. 195–196.

50. Busch is often described as the "proto-evangelist" of the liturgical movement in the
United States. Busch wrote articles in *America* (August 30, 1924) and in *Commonweal*
(November 4, 1925) about the liturgical awakening in Europe and the need for a popular
liturgical movement in this country. Hillenbrand read these magazines and was probably
educated about the liturgical movement through articles such as these. See Marx, pp. 108–109.

51. See Paul Marx, pp. 38–40, 79. In addition to convincing Abbott Deutsch to begin
a major publishing project in support of the liturgical movement, Michel also convinced the
renowned chant expert, Dom Ermin Vitry, a disciple of Abbott Marmion of Maredsous,
Belgium and a former secretary of Beauduin, to teach at St. John's University. Through Michel,
Hillenbrand met Dom Ermin Vitry and invited him to work at his parish after he became
a pastor.

52. See John Leo Kline, *The Role of Gerald Ellard (1894–1963) in the Development of the
Contemporary American Catholic Liturgical Movement*, Ph.D. Dissertation (New York: Fordham,
1951), pp. 71–12, and Noel Hackmann Barrett, *The Contribution of Martin B. Hellriegel to the*

Martin Hellriegel was born in Heppenheim, Germany in 1890 and attended the seminary at Mainz, where he first encountered *L'Annee liturgique*, the 15-volume work on the liturgical year by Abbot Prosper Gueranger of Solesmes. In 1906, he emigrated to the United States and was ordained in 1914 for the Archdiocese of St. Louis. After three and a half years as an associate pastor at St. Charles, Missouri, Hellriegel was appointed chaplain of the Motherhouse of the Precious Blood Sisters in O'Fallon, Missouri where he served from 1918–1940.

Hellriegel had close ties to his native Germany, especially to the work of Abbot Ildefons Herwegen and Odo Casel of the monastery of Maria Laach.[53] It was through Hellriegel's writings that Hillenbrand was encouraged to learn more about Herwegen and Casel. In September, 1925, when Hellriegel first began corresponding with Virgil Michel, he also began his long-term correspondence with Pius Parsch in Klosterneuberg, Austria.[54] Joseph Jungmann called Hellriegel the Pius Parsch of America, because he popularized at the local level the theology that was produced by the great liturgical centers like Maria Laach and Maredsous.[55]

In 1925, Hellriegel co-authored with Anthony Jasper an article, "Der Schluessel zur Loesung der sozial Frage," which appeared in the July-August issued of *Social Blatt*. This article definitely influenced Hillenbrand's ideas about the liturgy and social action. It states

> The liturgy is that divine worship which the mystic Christ, that is, the
> Church as a body joined with Christ as its head renders to the heavenly

---

American Catholic Liturgical Movement, Ph.D. Dissertation (St. Louis: St. Louis University, 1976), pp. 120–125.

53. Ildefons Herwegen was Abbot of Maria Laach from 1913 to 1946. In 1922 he founded the series *Ecclesia Orans*, of which the first issue was Romano Guardini's *Vom Geist der Liturgie*, which later was published by Sheed & Ward in 1935 as *The Spirit of the Liturgy*. Herwegen also founded the scholarly periodical, *Jahrbuch für Liturgiewissenschaft*, which spread the research of the leaders of the liturgical movement. Odo Casel (1886–1948), a monk of Maria Laach, served as editor of the *Jahrbuch* from 1921–1941 and is best known for his *Mysterientheologie*, mystery-theology, which explained the *Mysteriengegwart*, the mystery-presence, of Christ in the liturgy. Casel's emphasis on the connection between liturgy and the ongoing work of redemption became a cornerstone in Hillenbrand's liturgical theology.

54. Pius Parsch was an Austrian Canon Regular of St. Augustine and the founder of the periodical *Bibel und Liturgie*. His most famous work is *Das Jahr des Heiles*, which explained the Mass and Office for the Sundays and feast days of the liturgical year. Many of his ideals (the importance of a daily sermon, the laity's share in offering the sacrifice, the necessity of teaching the laity to sing the Mass, etc.) Hillenbrand embraced as his own.

55. Barrett, p. 86.

Father; it consists in the a) celebration and b) application of the mysteries of redemption, executed in mystery-drama by the particular priesthood made up of those specially endowed by Holy Orders, and by the universal priesthood, made up of those baptized and confirmed.[56]

This definition is one that Hillenbrand adopted as his own and used in numerous lectures and writings.[57]

Martin Hellriegel met Gerald Ellard for the first time on November 1, 1925. However, Ellard had already shown an interest in the liturgy even before meeting Hellriegel. In fact, on April 25, 1925, Ellard had written a letter to *America* Magazine expressing the need for liturgical instruction and more active participation in the liturgy. Since he had heard that good things were happening at O'Fallon, which was not too far from St. Louis University where he was studying, Ellard decided to see for himself. Ellard was so impressed with the All Saints' Day liturgy at O'Fallon that on December 19, 1925, he wrote a letter to *America* Magazine, praising the liturgical spirit and prayer of Hellriegel's community.[58] Since Hillenbrand frequently read *America* magazine, he may have read Ellard's letter and as a result been influenced to learn more about Hellriegel's approach to the liturgy.

In less than two years after meeting Michel and Hellriegel, Ellard left the United States to study for a doctorate in liturgy and medieval history at the University of Munich in Germany. Ellard is generally considered the first American scholar to receive a doctorate in liturgical studies. While in Europe from September, 1927 to May, 1931, Ellard visited the liturgical centers at Maria Laach, Bueron, Mont-César, Maredsous, St. André, Solesmes, and Klosterneuberg. He consulted with some of the great leaders of the liturgical movement: Odo Casel, Ildefons Herwegen, Joseph Jungmann, Joseph Kramp, and Pius Parsch. He also experienced first hand the German Youth Movement (Neudeutschland), celebrating Mass for several groups during his years in Germany.[59] With such a rich background in

---

56. Martin B. Hellriegel and A. J. Jasper, *The True Basis of Christian Solidarity*, trans. William Busch (St. Louis: Central Bureau of the Central Verein, 1947), pp. 14–16, cited in Barrett, p. 110.

57. Further evidence of Hillenbrand's dependence on Hellriegel is seen in Hillenbrand's definition of liturgy and the liturgical year, which is discussed on pages 46, 142–145.

58. See Barrett, pp. 122–125 and Klein, pp. 66–12.

59. See Leo Klein, pp. 63–83. While Hillenbrand never corresponded directly with Casel, Herwegen, Jungmann, or Parsch, he was acquainted with the work of Gerald Ellard, who

At the University of Saint Mary of the Lake, Hillenbrand excelled academically, and was ordained to the priesthood earlier than the rest of his class as a special recognition of his abilities. He later completed his Licentiate in Sacred Theology and Doctorate at the University of Saint Mary of the Lake and would eventually become its rector. His 1929 ordination picture is shown here. *University of St. Mary of the Lake, Mundelein Seminary, Archdiocese of Chicago.*

German theology, Ellard became a strong influence on Hillenbrand's development of an interest in the liturgy.

ORDINATION, DOCTORAL STUDIES, EUROPEAN EDUCATION

As a reward for excelling academically, Cardinal Mundelein had the policy of ordaining some members of the class earlier in their final year. Hillenbrand was chosen for this honor and was ordained by Cardinal Mundelein in the main chapel of the Seminary on September 21, 1929. He chose as the homilist of his First Mass at St. Michael's Parish Robert S. Johnson, SJ, the Seminary professor of sacramental theology. In my opinion, this selection of Johnson as homilist reflected Hillenbrand's positive orientation toward the liturgy. However, the joy of Hillenbrand's ordination was surely tempered by the tragedy that struck the economy in October.

Few people could have predicted the tremendous changes that would sweep the United States after the great stock market crash of 1929. Chicago was especially hard hit.

---

popularized in the United States the insights of these men and the German social action movement. Hillenbrand invited Ellard to speak at the seminary, quoted him in his seminary liturgy course, and promoted the use of Ellard's book, *Christian Life and Worship.*

Every year after 1929 seemed a step down. By 1933 employment in the city's industry had been cut in half; payrolls were down almost seventy-five per cent. Foreclosures jumped from 3,148 in 1929 to 15,201 four years later; over 163 banks, most located in the outlying areas closed their doors. Land values which had reached the five-billion-dollar level in 1928 dropped to two billion dollars at the beginning of 1933.[60]

The hungry, the unemployed, the financially ruined turned to prayer and the sacraments for assistance and hope. Catholics looked to the Church for a solution to the economic and social problems that had beset society. It was in the midst of social turmoil that Hillenbrand began his studies for the doctorate in theology at the University of St. Mary of the Lake.

Hillenbrand's doctoral dissertation, *De Modo quo Deus Justificatos Inhabitat (The Way that God Lives in the Just)*, is written in Latin in the typical Scholastic style of his day. It consists of five parts, each part divided into questions, and each question discussed in terms of the theories of classic and contemporary authors concerning the way God inhabits the just.[61] Hillenbrand's principal conclusion is stated in the form of a rather controversial (for its time) thesis:

> Inhabitatio explicatur per effectum formalem primarium gratiae sanctifican-tis, nempe naturae divinas participationem. Adest Deus propter gratiam donaque, quatenus haec fruitionem essentialiter reddunt possibilem et acutalem connaturaliter inducunt.[62]

In May 1931, he successfully defended this thesis in a Latin oral examination before a board composed of Cardinal Mundelein,

---

60. Harold M. Mayer and Richard C. Wade, *Chicago: Growth of a Metropolis* (Chicago/London: University of Chicago Press, 1969), pp. 358, 360.

61. Hillenbrand discusses the theories of Augustine, Bonaventure, Cajetan, Lombard, Suarez, and Thomas. Among contemporary theologians a prominent place is given to the works of Galtier (*L'habitation en nous des Trois Personnes*), Gardeil (*La structure de l'ame et l'experience mystique*), Pohle (*Grace, Actual and Habitual*), Scheeben (*Handbuch der katholisches Dogmatik* and *Die Mysterien des Christenhums*), and Van der Meersch (*Tractatus de Gratia Christi* and *Tractatus de Deo Uno et Trino*). A copy of Hillenbrand's unpublished dissertation is found in the Feehan Memorial Library at Mundelein Seminary.

62. Reynold Hillenbrand, *De Modo quo Deus Justificatos Inhabitat*, S.T.D. Dissertation (Mundelein: St. Mary of the Lake Seminary, 1931), p. 82. Hillenbrand's thesis, translated into English, is: Inhabitation is primarily explained by the formal effect of sanctifying grace, of course, a participation of (in) the divine nature. God is present on account of grace and gifts, since God essentially restores this possibility and leads to its reality in a natural way.

the Apostolic Delegate, Archbishop Pietro Fumasoni-Biondi, and the entire pontifical faculty. He was awarded his doctorate on June 13, 1931.

Hillenbrand's thesis clearly shows the influence of the Tübingen school with its emphasis on the ongoing process of God's saving action in the present. Drawing on the work of Scheeben, *Die Mysterien des Christenthums*, and Galtier, *L'habitation en nous des trois personnes*, Hillenbrand moves beyond a static conception of grace to a dynamic understanding of the transforming power of the inhabitation of the Trinity in the human soul. In his understanding of grace, one also finds the theological base for Hillenbrand's future concern for social justice. He defines the formal effect of sanctifying grace as twofold: orienting us both to the beatific vision and to a supernatural life on earth, modeled after Christ.[63]

As a reward for successfully defending his thesis, Cardinal Mundelein sent Hillenbrand to study at the Gregorian University in Rome, from June, 1931 until the summer of 1932. He lived at the Canadian College, a graduate residence for priests. He was assigned to study Latin and Church history with eventual assignment at Quigley Preparatory Seminary upon his return to the United States. During this period Hillenbrand travelled extensively, visiting some of the key liturgical centers in Europe: Maria Laach, Mont-César, and Klosterneuberg. He experienced first hand the biblical, liturgical, and youth movements that he had read about in *America, Central Blatt and Social Justice, Commonweal,* and *Orate Fratres*. In addition, he also learned of the work of a Belgian priest, Joseph Cardijn, whose approach to ministry would permanently affect Hillenbrand's entire life.[64]

---

63. Hillenbrand's dissertation addressed a classic debate regarding nature and the supernatural. Thomas taught a natural desire for the beatific vision. Bellarmine said our nature can only reach its true completion through the supernatural, which is gratuitous. Suarez taught the need for grace was twofold: for life in heaven and for life on earth. Thomas popularized Augustine's position on the divinization of the Christian, explaining that by sanctifying grace we enjoy a participation in the divine persons themselves. Scheeben popularized the theory that the Holy Spirit is both the efficient and formal cause of our sanctification. For Scheeben, it is the gift of the Holy Spirit which is primary, uniting us in love to God and one another. See Henri Rondet, *The Grace of Christ, A Brief History of the Theology of Grace,* trans. Tad W. Guzie (New York: Newman Press, 1967), pp. 330–334, 370–377.

64. In 1912 Joseph Cardijn founded near Brussels the Jeunesse Ouvriere Chretienne (JOC), or, in English, the Young Christian Workers (YCW). In 1932 the JOC/YCW was internationally chartered. Its purpose was to prepare young workers to become lay apostles, to minister to their peers in an effort to solve common labor problems.

Hillenbrand arrived in Rome shortly after *Quadragesimo Anno*, "On Reconstructing the Social Order," was issued. He heard Pius XI explain this encyclical, which called all Christians to work for the restoration of society on an organic basis (no. 90), to reform their institutions, and to foster Christian morality (no. 98). *Quadragesimo Anno* adopted the Cardijn principle of "like ministering to like":

> The first and immediate apostle to the workers ought to be workers; the apostles to those who follow industry and trade ought to be from among themselves.[65]

It also challenged bishops and priests "to search diligently for these lay apostles both of workers and of employers, to select them with prudence, and to train and instruct them properly."[66] Hillenbrand took up this challenge and eventually discovered in the liturgy the source and the center for his efforts in training lay apostles.

Reynold Hillenbrand received a broad liturgical and social education during his early years in St. Michael's Parish. He was a product of the Americanization of the immigrants that occurred during the first quarter of the twentieth century. He was influenced by the popular cult of the papacy that developed during his years in the seminary, and by the clerical dominance of the Church. During these years, American Catholics grew wealthier and less concerned about the social Gospel.

Hillenbrand's models among the clergy were strong administrators like Cardinal Mundelein, Scholastic theologians from the faculty of St. Mary of the Lake Seminary, his priest uncles in Milwaukee, his priest brother, and Fathers Michel, Hellriegel, and Ellard. American Catholic theologians feared being accused of Americanism or Modernism. Hence, the boldness of the call to reform the liturgy, to restore active participation to the faithful, and to reconstruct society on an organic model must have stood out in the rather staid theological climate in which Hillenbrand was trained.

Hillenbrand's dissertation on a controversial topic in theology is an indication that the theological climate was starting to change.

---

65. Pius XI, *Quadragesimo Anno, On Reconstructing the Social Order* (Washington: National Catholic Welfare Conference, 1942), pp. 51–52, no. 141.

66. Ibid., p. 52, no. 142.

With the assurance of competence that the conferral of the doctorate gave him and the new ideas he was exposed to during his European education, Hillenbrand was ready to make a major contribution to the liturgical and social action movements in the United States.

Chapter 2

The American Liturgical Movement: 1931–1944

Developing a Synthesis on Liturgy and Life

When Hillenbrand returned to the United States in 1932, he was assigned to teach Latin and English literature at Quigley Preparatory Seminary.[1] He became a very popular teacher, respected by faculty and students alike. He resided at Holy Name Cathedral, where he came under the influence of Joseph Morrison, the Cathedral rector, whose love for the liturgy and social action were well known throughout the Archdiocese. Morrison had been Cardinal Mundelein's master of ceremonies at the 1926 Eucharistic Congress in Chicago. He also attended the July 25, 1929 National Liturgical Day at St. John's Abbey. Perhaps, it was his positive experience at this day and at the many Eucharistic Congresses he attended that led to his interest in sponsoring the first Liturgical Week in Chicago.[2]

Morrison was very concerned about the problems of the poor, the unemployed, and the socially disadvantaged. During his tenure as rector many meetings were held at the Cathedral to raise the social conscience of priests and lay people. He was one of the first leaders in

---

1. *Quigley Preparatory Seminary North, Seventy-Fifth Jubilee: 1905–1980* (Chicago: Archdiocese of Chicago, 1980), p. 9.

2. Even before the 1940 Liturgical Week, Morrison had demonstrated his interest in liturgy by speaking at the 1937 National Eucharistic Congress in Cleveland, Ohio, and attending three others: the 1937 International Eucharistic Congress in Manila, Philippines, the 1938 International Eucharistic Congress in Budapest, Hungary, and the 1938 National Eucharistic Congress in New Orleans. He became the first president of the Liturgical Conference in 1943, the first president of the Vernacular Society in 1946, and a member of the board of directors of the Liturgical Arts Society. See *100 Years, the History of the Church of the Holy Name* (Chicago: Cathedral of the Holy Name, 1949).

the Archdiocese to respond to Pius XI's call to train lay apostles to minister to others.[3] Like many of the early liturgical and social action pioneers, he believed the key to the rechristianization of society was a return to the true Christian spirit, whose source was the liturgy.[4] He was joined in his social activism by Auxiliary Bishop Bernard Sheil, the founder of the Catholic Youth Organization (CYO), and "a tireless public speaker, a friend of labor unions, interracial groups, and other movements that worked for slum clearance, desegregation, and civil rights."[5]

On May 1, 1933, in New York City, Dorothy Day, a leftist journalist of the day and recent convert, and Peter Maurin, a French peasant and philosopher, founded the *Catholic Worker*, the first Catholic labor paper in the United States. Its philosophy was based on an organic conception of society. Its method was to connect Christian piety to the concrete moral challenges of everyday life. Its theology was based on papal encyclicals, providing the solution of the social problem.[6] Maurin and Day saw themselves continuing the tradition of Romano Guardini, criticizing the rich for their indifference to the needy and popularizing in the United States the papal call for a just social order.[7] Catholic Worker Houses provided an early source of support for the liturgical pioneers, whose desire to increase the active participation of the laity was founded upon an organic conception of society.[8]

In 1933, Cardinal Mundelein founded an Archdiocesan Mission Band as part of the preparations for his twenty-fifth anniversary as a bishop. Since Hillenbrand had distinguished himself as a polished

---

3. Pius XI wrote Cardinal Segura of Spain on Nov. 6, 1929 about the shortage of priests and the need for the participation of the laity in the apostolate of the hierarchy. In 1931, in *Quadragesimo Anno* (no.76), 76), he again repeated this call for the clergy to train lay apostles to re-christianize the institutions of society by renewing within them the true Christian spirit.

4. See Eugene S. Geissler, *An Introduction to Catholic Action and an Exposition of the Jocist Technique* (South Bend: Apostolate Press, 1945), pp. 24–25, 30–31.

5. Don Brophy & Edythe Westenhaver, eds., *The Story of Catholics in America* (New York: Paulist Press, 1978), p. 114. Cf. Edward R. Kantowicz, *Corporation Sole*, pp. 174–175.

6. Francis Joseph Sicius, *The Chicago Catholic Worker Movement, 1936 to the Present*, Ph.D. dissertation (Chicago: Loyola University, 1979), p. 14.

7. See Hennessey, *American Catholics*, p. 267 and Leo R. Ward, *Catholic Life, U.S.A.,* *Contemporary Lay Movements* (St. Louis: B. Herder Book Company, 1959), ch. 11: "Dorothy Day and the Catholic Worker," pp. 183–201.

8. Hillenbrand's papers (Collection, Msgr. Reynold Hillenbrand or CMRH) in the University of Notre Dame Archives (UNDA) contain several letters to and from Dorothy Day. Day lectured at St. Mary of the Lake Seminary on February 26, 1938.

speaker, Mundelein relieved him of his duties at Quigley and appointed him full time to the mission band. Hillenbrand's participation in this mission program reflected the growing support of the Archdiocese for the lay retreat movement and gave him an important opportunity to develop his synthesis on liturgy and life.[9]

In February of 1935, Hillenbrand taught a course at Rosary College (now Dominican University in River Forest, Illinois) on Catholic Action, in which he moves beyond the usual scholastic explanation of church and society by offering a fresh synthesis of Mystical Body theology, grace, liturgy, and social action.[10] This course later became the basis of his liturgy course at the seminary.[11] In addition, it showed Hillenbrand's brief involvement with Catholic Evidence Work.[12] Finally, it was typical of the type of involvements entered into by the leaders of the liturgical and social action movements in the United States.

During the 1930s, many liturgists provided leadership to the social action movement and many social activists were concerned about liturgy. Among the liturgists, Virgil Michel was one of the most forceful advocates of liturgical and social change. In 1930, in "Advertising our Wares," an article in *Orate Fratres*, Michel expressed his belief that a fundamental renewal of the whole Christian life in all

---

9. Paul R. Martin, *The First Cardinal of the West*, p. 190. The growth of the lay retreat movement was reflected in the increasing numbers of lay people making use of the Franciscan Retreat Center at Mayslake, the Divine Word Missionary Retreat Center at Techny, and the Convent of the Cenacle in Chicago.

10. In 1933, Gerald Ellard published the first college textbook in religion that reflected the insights of the liturgical movement: *Christian Life and Worship*. While it is impossible to know how much Hillenbrand drew upon the insights of Ellard for his 1935 course at Rosary College (Hillenbrand's 1935 lecture notes have not been preserved, but letters about the course content do exist in UNDA), we can say with certainty that Hillenbrand's seminary course drew upon insights found in Ellard's textbook.

11. See Kantowicz, *Corporation Sole*, p. 199. Kantowicz incorrectly dates the beginning of this course in 1933. Rev. Steven Avella in an unpublished paper, "I've Brought You a Man with Imagination, the Life and Career of Reynold Hillenbrand until 1944," quotes a letter from Hillenbrand to Sister Thomas Aquinas, the Dominican President of Rosary College, referring to his course beginning on Feb. 19, 1935.

12. See Jay P. Dolan, *The American Catholic Experience*, p. 409. The emergence of lay activists was assisted by the resurgence of Catholic thought and belief that accompanied the opening of the New York publishing house of Maisie Ward and Frank Sheed in 1933. It was a special time in the American church when many of the best ideas of the European biblical, liturgical, and youth movements found an eager audience of young Catholic men and women. In 1925, Sheed and Ward compiled the Catholic Evidence Guild textbook, *Catholic Evidence Training Outlines*, which explained how to train small groups for street preaching.

its aspects was the scope and task of the liturgical apostolate.[13] The much-needed social reconstruction will only occur as a result of the renewal of the Christian spirit, whose source and center is the liturgy. If the ultimate purpose of Catholic action is to christianize society, then the renewal of the liturgy must undoubtedly play the decisive role in achieving this goal.[14]

In the fall of 1934 at St. John's University, Michel and Alphonse Matt, in conjunction with the Central Verein, founded the Institute for Social Study to train lay leaders in Catholic social principles.[15] The Institute sponsored conferences on all phases of the social question, Catholic Action, papal encyclicals, and socio-liturgical activities. A special effort was made to encourage the attendance of seminarians and college students. In 1936, the Institute for Social Study published its best lectures in four brochures: I: *Social Concepts and Problems*, II: *Economics and Finance*, III: *Political Theories and Forms*, and IV: *The Mystical Body and Social Justice*.[16]

In 1935, Virgil Michel's book, *Our Life in Christ*, appeared at the same time as the pamphlet, *Organized Social Justice*, was published by John A. Ryan and Francis McGowan of the NCWC Social Action Department. These works complement one another: Michel's synthesis on the principles of social reconstruction provides the theological basis for the concrete actions recommended by Ryan and McGowan. In fact, for many years there had been a happy association between St. John's and the Social Action Department. As early as 1930 John A. Ryan was promoting in his NCWC newsletter the use of the leaflet missal. In 1936 Ryan and McGowan agreed to publish the previously mentioned lectures given at the Social Institute at St. John's.[17] And so, Hillenbrand began his career as a liturgist in Chicago at a time when liturgists and social activists worked closely together.

In 1934, in Chicago, a group known as CISCA (Chicago Inter-student Catholic Action) began to actively promote participation

---

13. Virgil Michel, "Advertising Our Wares," *Orate Fratres* 4 (1930), p. 124.

14. See Virgil Michel, "The Liturgy: the Basis of Social Regeneration," *Orate Fratres* 9 (1935), pp. 536–545 and "The Liturgical Movement and the Future," *America* 54 (1935), pp. 6–1.

15. See Marx, pp. 361–368.

16. See Marx, p. 369. Hillenbrand ordered these materials for his course at the seminary.

17. See Marx, p. 217.

in the liturgy as a basis of genuine apostolic work.[18] This group is important for several reasons. After becoming rector of the major seminary, Hillenbrand encouraged his seminarians to become part of CISCA. CISCA's program for studying the papal encyclicals and engaging in Catholic Action was closely related to the type of work Hillenbrand became involved in when he began to work with the Young Christian Students (YCS) in Chicago. Finally, CISCA served as a bridge between the less intellectual approach of Bishop Sheil's CYO and the specialized ministry of priests trained in the social encyclicals by Hillenbrand.[19]

In addition to the efforts made by CISCA to promote active participation, Hillenbrand was also influenced by the German born pastor of St. Aloysius Church, Bernard Laukemper, who was implementing many of the ideals advocated by the liturgical pioneers. At St. Aloysius Church in Chicago, Laukemper successfully introduced the dialog Mass and an offertory procession. He encouraged congregational singing and the active participation of the laity. In renovating the church, he removed the ornate main altar and replaced it with a simpler altar in a less obstructed sanctuary with cleaner sight line which focused on the action on the altar. He also installed the baptistry just off the sanctuary on the epistle side of the church. From January 19–26, 1936, he sponsored the first Liturgical Week to be held in the United States in a parish. Hence, there were early attempts made by individual members of the Chicago clergy to improve the conditions of parochial liturgy. However, the Archdiocese lacked an officially appointed leader who could capture the attention of the pastors and the bishops and mobilize the people.[20]

---

18. Jane Marie Murray & Paul Marx, "The Liturgical Movement in the United States," in *The Catholic Church, U.S.A.*, ed. Louis J. Putz (Chicago: Fides Publishers Association, 1956), p. 312.

19. Kantowicz, *Corporation Sole*, pp. 280–281.

20. See Harry S. Koenig, ed., *A History of the Parishes of the Archdiocese of Chicago, Vol. I* (Chicago: Archdiocese of Chicago, 1980), pp. 51–52. Bernard Laukemper was a frequent speaker at National Liturgical Weeks, a member of the Advisory Board of the Liturgical Conference in 1943, and Treasurer in 1946. He died March 9, 1949 at the age of 61.

University of Saint Mary of the Lake
Mundelein Seminary Rector,
1936–1944. *University of St. Mary of
the Lake, Mundelein Seminary,
Archdiocese of Chicago.*

RECTOR, SOCIAL ACTIVIST, LITURGIST

In April 1936, Cardinal Mundelein appointed Reynold Hillenbrand rector of St. Mary of the Lake Seminary.[21] Hillenbrand, only 31 years old, was probably the youngest rector of a Pontifical faculty in the world. He inherited a seminary that had been strictly formed on the Roman model and was staffed by the Jesuits of the Missouri Province, under the leadership of John B. Furay, the former president of Loyola University of Chicago.

His first seminary orientation talk in 1936 provides a good insight into his vision of an organic society. He spoke of a certain lethargy in the comfortable lifestyle of many priests, living in large rectories with cooks and housekeepers, and judging their success more often by how quickly they paid off the parish debt than by their concern for the social order. What the priests of the Archdiocese needed was a wider vision that

> Sees beyond their comfortable parishes and beyond their own comfortable lives—to see the suffering in the world, to have a heart for the unem- ployed, not to shy away from misery, but to feel the injustice of inadequate wages...to have some of the vision that Day and Maurin and priests who are coping with social problems have.[22]

21. "Rev. R. Hillenbrand is Rector of Seminary, Mundelein, Brilliant Alumnus, Noted Preacher in New Office," *New World* 44 (April 10, 1936), p. 1.

22. Hillenbrand, "Seminary Social Thoughts, 1936," UNDA, CMRH 3/25.

One of these priests he referred to was Virgil Michel, whom Hillenbrand invited to speak to the seminarians in the spring of 1937.

The former rector, J. Gerald Kealy, taught a course in liturgy to the third-year theologians. This precedent provided Hillenbrand with the opportunity to expose the seminarians to the new ideas that he had been working with in his course at Rosary College and in his missions throughout the Archdiocese. When Hillenbrand became rector, the liturgy course was almost entirely on rites and ceremonies with little emphasis on active participation or communal celebration. In addition, there was a tremendous void in the curriculum regarding papal social teachings and the need for social action. It was in these two areas that Hillenbrand concentrated his attention during his first two years as rector.

Hillenbrand completely reorganized the liturgy course which the rector taught the third-year theologians. Hillenbrand explained:

> While it is true that the students are getting their dogma, yet, they are not likely to relate it to the liturgy as they should. For that reason, I spend a good portion at the beginning of the year on the doctrine of the divine life and the Mystical Body, because without understanding these it is quite useless to talk about the details of the Mass and the historical elements that enter into the Mass.
>
> The course must have in mind that the people need what Pius X advocated, an active participation in the Mass and in the divine office. Only the doctrines of the supernatural life and the Mystical Body will give both priests and laity the proper background for active participation. . . .
>
> The rest of the year is devoted to taking up the Mass itself, step by step, explaining the meaning and some of the history, some of the practical objectives, possibilities of active participation, relationship to the whole structure of the Mass, etc. The text that we use is the best that I have been able to find—Parsch, *The Liturgy of the Mass.* Fortescue does not have the right approach, though a very good book in its field. I have no taste for the other manuals.[23]

In the above description, we find a very clear expression of Hillenbrand's goals in his liturgy course: to expose the seminarians to

---

23. Hillenbrand to Rev. Joseph A. Brunner of the Redemptorist Fathers, Oconomowoc, Wisconsin, Nov. 17, 1942. UNDA, CMRH 35, Correspondence A-D, 1940–1941, Liturgy.

the best insights of the European and American liturgical movements and to implement the papal mandate to foster active participation.[24]

Hillenbrand also conducted classes for the seminarians and interested faculty in the social encyclicals. On January 16, 1938, Hillenbrand wrote to his brother Fred:

> We [Hillenbrand and the deacons] have a bull-session in the shape of a class every Saturday night from eight to nine in the rec hall, where a blackboard has been rigged up. I use McGowan's "Toward Social Justice" as a basis for my notes, amplify it, and explain it. Until Christmas, we had the added feature of a study club on these problems every Wednesday night from eight to nine. There were five clubs, meeting in my room, the guest room across the way, the three reception rooms downstairs. We drew up the outlines, went over the material with the leaders (who changed from week to week), and talked—with great success and stimulation of interest. The summer school at St. Francis was an incalculable help.[25]

This letter definitely understated the positive influence Hillenbrand's informal courses and study clubs had on the seminary. In addition, it also indicated another important influence in Hillenbrand's development as rector: the social activism of Francis J. Haas, rector of St. Francis Seminary in Milwaukee.[26]

Prior to 1938, Hillenbrand's main attention was directed to revising the liturgical program of the seminary and to organizing his liturgy course and study clubs. Hillenbrand was quite concerned that

---

24. The Notre Dame Archives has the handwritten and typed lecture notes from Hillenbrand's liturgy course. In these notes Hillenbrand quotes the works of Adam, Baumstark, Benedict XV, Bishop, Busch, Cabrol, Cagin, Casel, Diekmann, Ellard, Fortescue, Hellriegel, Jurgensmeier, Leo XIII, Mersch, Michel, Parsch, Pius X, Pius XI, Probst, Reinhold and other well known authors. These notes indicate how well read and conversant he was with the scholarship of the 1930s. Hillenbrand's liturgy course notes function as the basic source for all his subsequent lectures and writings. Unless there is some development in his thought, I will usually refer to these notes in order to demonstrate the earliest point at which Hillenbrand began to espouse certain key ideas.

25. Hillenbrand to Fred Hillenbrand, January 16, 1938. UNDA, CMRH 38, Charlton Fortune, Correspondence.

26. Francis A. Haas was rector of St. Francis Seminary from 1935–1937. He had studied under John Ryan at Catholic University in Washington, where he became dean of the School of Social Science in 1937. He served as an arbitrator in numerous labor disputes. He also helped organize the first Summer School of Social Action for Priests which took place in Milwaukee, July 6–30, 1937. Hillenbrand attended this conference and invited many of the same speakers to the Summer School of Social Action that took place at St. Mary of the Lake Seminary in 1938. See Thomas E. Blantz, *A Priest in Public Service, Francis J. Haas and the New Deal*, (Notre Dame: University of Notre Dame, 1982).

the seminary choir had usurped the role of the congregation. On solemn celebrations like Holy Thursday or Pentecost, music filled every available moment and stifled the assembly's participation, making it impossible to follow the prayers of the liturgy.

Often the seminarians attended two daily Masses—one in their house chapel, at which they did not communicate, and one in the main chapel. Hillenbrand introduced the practice of the dialog Mass and preferred to have the entire community attend a single, common Mass in the main chapel.[27] He encouraged priests to celebrate the Mass of the day, rather than the frequent Black Masses (Requiem Masses) that required little or no preparation. Finally, he expected presiders at the Eucharist to preach a daily homily based on the Scriptures, the particular feast, or the liturgical season—a practice that was considered quite novel at the time.[28]

Hillenbrand was influenced by Virgil Michel and William Busch's League of the Divine Office, which provided materials to reintroduce the practice of lay people reciting the Breviary.[29] Hillenbrand was convinced that the seminarians needed to understand the words they were praying. He encouraged them to write into their Breviary the English translation of the Latin words they did not understand. He also published a booklet of Breviary hymns, with English translations of the Latin hymns in the Breviary.[30] He used the materials of the League so that the seminarians would be familiar with the vernacular translations of the Office which were then becoming popular among the laity. In addition, he opposed the practice of

27. See Gerald Ellard, "Progress of the Dialog Mass in Chicago," *Orate Fratres* 14 (1939), pp. 19–25.

28. See Hillenbrand's Seminary Liturgy Course Notes. UNDA, CMRH 4/18. Hillenbrand took seriously the liturgical year and even went so far as to cancel the Tre Ore service from Holy Week, maintaining it detracted from the official liturgical celebrations of the Triduum. He also celebrated the 1938 Easter Mass at sunrise, in an attempt to restore the spirit of the first Easter morning. In these innovations, Hillenbrand closely resembled Martin Hellriegel, who followed these same practices at O'Fallon. See *Chronicle of the Philosophy House, 1931–1938* (Chicago: St. Mary of the Lake Seminary, 1938) and Noel H. Barrett, pp. 210, 213.

29. Hillenbrand, Seminary Notebooks. UNDA, CMRH 5/4. See Marx, *Virgil Michel and the Liturgical Movement*, pp. 157–158, 235: Marx quotes a June 28, 1937 letter from Hillenbrand to Virgil Michel that shows Hillenbrand had acquired a large amount of liturgical materials from Liturgical Press, was familiarizing the seminarians with Michel's Christ-Life Series (whose aim was to build a primary school religion curriculum based on and inspired by the liturgy), and was encouraging them to read *Orate Fratres*.

30. Breviary Hymns, 1942. UNDA, CMRH 4/15.

simply reciting rather than singing the psalms at matins and, especially, vespers. Instead, he required all the seminarians to learn to sing plain chant.

Hillenbrand's liturgical innovations must have appeared quite strange to the Jesuit faculty, which did not share Hillenbrand's understanding of the corporate nature of worship. Instead, Jesuit piety centered around meditation, popular devotions, and the spiritual exercises. As John Leo Klein explains:

> The tradition of piety in which the Jesuit scholastics were formed was rather a-liturgical than anti-liturgical. . . . Mass is the means by which Christ is brought down into the midst of men. Loyalty to the cause of Christ will lead Jesuits to lives of great sacrifice in the apostolate, but with little or no emphasis on the Eucharist as the unifying and motivating bond for their zeal.[31]

Hillenbrand's explanation of the Eucharist as "the effective presentation of the Mystical Body" and the liturgical year as "the reproduction of the life of the Head in the lives of the members of the Mystical Body" must have sounded quite radical to the more traditionally trained Jesuit faculty.[32]

Even more radical were some of the ideas presented by the lecturers Hillenbrand invited to the seminary. During Hillenbrand's tenure as rector (1936–1944), the following persons offered lectures and/or mini-courses at the seminary: Donald Attwater, William Boyd, Paul Bussard, William Busch, Dorothy Day, Godfrey Diekmann, Catherine DeHuech Doherty, Gerald Ellard, John Gilliard, Francis Haas, Martin Hellriegel, Maurice Lavanoux, John LaFarge, Bernard Laukemper, Robert Lucey, Raymond McGowan, Paul McGuire, H. A. Reinhold, and others.

The above list of speakers combines both liturgical and social reformers, thus demonstrating the close relationship that existed between the liturgical and social action movements in the United States. One did not study the liturgy in isolation from one's concerns about society. Hillenbrand explained the reason for this in his liturgy

---

31. John Leo Klein, *The Role of Gerald Ellard (1894–1963) in the Development of the Contemporary American Catholic Liturgical Movement*, Ph.D. dissertation (New York: Fordham University, 1971), pp. 54, 61.

32. Hillenbrand, Liturgy Course Notes. UNDA, CMRH 5/21.

course: both movements were based on the same principles: divine life, the Mystical Body, and papal teachings.[33]

Like Francis Haas in Milwaukee, Hillenbrand became involved in forming study clubs for priests in Chicago and even served as an arbitrator in numerous labor disputes.[34] However, this social activism outside the seminary began only after 1938.[35] Certainly, the move of the socially active rector of St. Francis Seminary in Milwaukee, Francis Haas, to the School of Social Science in Washington and the death of Virgil Michel on November 26, 1938, put increased pressure on Hillenbrand to supply leadership to the numerous social action groups developing in the Archdiocese.[36] In addition, many of these groups were accustomed to looking for leadership from respected liturgists such as Virgil Michel and Gerald Ellard.[37]

Cardinal Mundelein gave Hillenbrand permission to establish at the Seminary the first Summer School of Social Action for priests from July 18–August 12, 1938.[38] Among the speakers at the Summer School of Social Action was a young priest from Ponca City, Oklahoma, Don Kanaly, who had recently returned to his native

---

33. Ibid. These foundational principles will be explained in Part II of this book.

34. Hillenbrand's letters in the UNDA indicate that he arbitrated labor disputes with Artcraft Statuary, Cambell Soup, CBS, Colombia Art Manufacturing, Manganese Steel, and Universal Statuary Co., to name just a few. See UNDA, CMRH 34, Correspondence, Tulsa, 1950; CMRH 40, Union Arbitration, 1943–1944; CMRH 40, Labor Arbitration, Hillenbrand as Arbitrator, 1943–1945.

35. On Jan. 16, 1938, Hillenbrand wrote to his brother Fred that he had "done little outside talking this year." Instead he had concentrated on developing his liturgy course, his seminary study clubs, and his lecture program, e.g., Donald Attwater and Virgil Michel spoke at the seminary in 1937. Shortly after this letter, Hillenbrand agreed to do a Lenten series on economics at Holy Name Cathedral, which led to an invitation to speak on May 2, 1938, at the Milwaukee Social Action Conference. UNDA, CMRH 38, Charlton Fortune, Correspondence.

36. Hillenbrand's personal papers in the UNDA indicate his interest in Summer Schools was awakened by the 1937 Summer School of Social Action in Milwaukee, where he heard Gerald Ellard give a course on "Corporate Worship, the Mystical Body, and Social Relations." Moreover, Hillenbrand corresponded with Francis Haas regarding the organization of his Summer Schools of Social Action at Mundelein Seminary. See UNDA, CMRH 5/20, Summer School of Catholic Action, 1937, Milwaukee.

37. See Francis J. Sicius, *The Chicago Catholic Worker Movement, 1936 to the Present*, Ph.D dissertation (Chicago: Loyola University, 1979), pp. 90–101.

38. See *Summer School of Social Action for Priests, July 18–August 12, 1938, 4 Vols.* (Mundelein: St. Mary of the Lake Seminary, 1938). Hillenbrand personally supervised the publication and distribution of these volumes. See UNDA, CMRH 5/19, Chicago Summer School of Social Action, 1938 and Raymond McGowan, "Clergy Hails Schools of Social Action," *Catholic Action* 19 (1937), pp. 16–17; "Clergy Social Action in Buffalo and Chicago," *Catholic Action* 20 (1938), p. 20; "Social Action Schools for the Clergy," *Catholic Action* 21 (1939), p. 21.

diocese after studying in Louvain, Belgium and being exposed to the work and methodology of Joseph Cardijn and the JOC (Jeunesse Ouvrière Chrétienne)—the Young Christian Workers.[39] Kanaly spoke of the need to establish cells (small groups) of young Christian workers in this country who are trained as apostles to the workingman. He explained the SEE-JUDGE-ACT methodology of Joseph Cardijn and the success Cardijn was having in Europe. However, the war and the newness of the Cardijn method made its initial growth in the United States quite slow.[40]

During the summers of 1939 and 1940, Hillenbrand would organize additional Summer Schools of Social Action at the seminary. Hillenbrand invited bishops from across the nation to send their priests to these schools, thereby giving these schools nationwide publicity and in the process identifying himself as a leader of the liturgical and social action movements. Moreover, Hillenbrand provided in the curriculum of these schools a course on liturgy. Originally, he had considered beginning a Summer School of Liturgy at the same time as the School of Social Action.[41] However, the amount of effort involved in establishing the School of Social Action made it impossible to accomplish this. Nonetheless, these Schools of Social Action became a very important prelude to Hillenbrand's involvement with the National Liturgical Weeks and his Liturgical Summer Schools in the 1940s.

What liturgical principles and issues were discussed at the Summer Schools of Social Action? While each lecturer had his own emphasis, Gerald Ellard's "Public Worship Clinic" at the 1939 Summer School at St. Mary of the Lake Seminary is typical of the principles and issues discussed at these Schools. Ellard defined the liturgy as the corporate worship of the Mystical Body and the doctrine of the common priesthood as the basis for active lay participation in

---

39. YCW members are young men and women between school age and marriage, about 18 to 30.

40. See Jim Cunningham, "Specialized Catholic Action," in *The American Apostolate, American Catholics in the Twentieth Century*, ed. Leo R. Ward (Westminster: Newman Press, 1952), pp. 41–65.

41. Hillenbrand wrote Godfrey Diekmann, May 1, 1941: "The School for Priests on the Liturgy had been scheduled by the Archbishop for a long time. We had it in mind even the first year, when we started the social action schools." Hillenbrand took the occasion of the first National Liturgical Week in Chicago to recruit faculty for the Chicago Summer School of Liturgy for priests in 1941. UNDA, CMRH 35, Correspondence A-D, 1940–1941, Liturgy.

the liturgy. He also called for an official English translation of the Mass, an increase in congregational chant, greater use of the dialog Mass, reception of Communion during Mass, and fewer Black (Requiem) Masses.[42] Consequently, the Summer Schools of Social Action were an important part of the diffusion of the ideals of the liturgical movement in this country.

Many important changes in leadership occurred in 1939 that permanently effected the direction of Hillenbrand's ministry. On February 10, 1939, Pius XI, the "Pope of Catholic Action," died. He was replaced on March 2, 1939, by Eugenio Pacelli, Pope Pius XII. On October 2, 1939, Cardinal Mundelein, the aggressive mentor of Hillenbrand, died. He was replaced on December 27, 1939, by the popular and intellectually gifted Archbishop of Milwaukee, Samuel Stritch.[43]

One of Archbishop Stritch's first actions in Chicago was to call for the revision of the seminary curriculum to bring it into accord with Roman practice (in Mundelein's day the seminary did not have a full four year college program). In 1940, Hillenbrand seized this opportunity to bring about some permanent changes in the curriculum that he had experimented with previously.[44] He added to the faculty some diocesan priests to teach these new courses.[45] In addition, he asked the Archbishop to send some diocesan priests for advanced degrees to insure that the new curriculum would permanently take hold. The Jesuit community may have interpreted these academic changes as unwanted interference in their field of academic responsibility. Certainly, the addition of more diocesan priests to the faculty led to conflicts with the Jesuits.

It is often said that Hillenbrand produced a generation of socially conscious priests whose ministry permanently affected the

---

42. See Hillenbrand's Notes on Ellard's Public Worship Clinic. UNDA, CMRH 5/19.

43. See Marie C. Buehrle, *The Cardinal Stritch Story* (Milwaukee: Bruce Publishing Company, 1959).

44. See Kantowicz, *Corporation Sole*, 200–201. Kantowicz' comment about Hillenbrand being unable to affect directly the curriculum needs to be nuanced. Hillenbrand had a direct affect on the college curriculum but was generally unable to affect the graduate theology curriculum, which was controlled by the Jesuits.

45. Some of the new faculty were William Clark, Daniel Cantwell, John Hayes, James Killgallon, and Gerald Weber. Among those sent for studies were George Higgins, Martin Howard, John Kelly, John McMahon, William McManus, William Rooney, Henry Wachowski. UNDA, CMRH 4/18.

shape of the Chicago Archdiocese.[46] Part of the reason for this claim
may be found in the reforms Hillenbrand initiated in the curriculum,
especially in the college department. The second-year religion course
dealt with the doctrines of supernatural life, the Mystical Body,
and the sacramental system. In addition, one hour a week was devoted
to the current week's liturgy in order to stimulate the student's participation in Mass and the Hours. The second-year education course
dealt with Catholic Action, papal encyclicals, the Cardijn method
for educating lay apostles, and the work of the YCW. The third-year
college religion course again dealt with the liturgy, while the third-year
economics course exposed the seminarians to the same ideas covered
by the Labor Schools that had begun in Chicago after the 1938
Summer School of Social Action.[47]

With his reforms now in place at the Seminary, Hillenbrand
began to foster liturgical missions in the Archdiocese. Their theme
was "the Living Parish—one in worship, charity, and action." The
objective of these missions was to develop "the laity's appreciation of
their parish as a living organism—a local concrete expression of the
Mystical Body of Christ."[48] A further consequence of participation in
these missions was the development of a deeper sense of unity as
members of a parish family and unity with their pastor in the worship
of God and in Catholic Action. These missions were still another way
Hillenbrand brought to Chicago the understanding of liturgy and
social action that was espoused by pioneers like Ellard, Michel,
Hellriegel, and Reinhold.[49]

In 1940, Louis Putz, a Holy Cross priest, returned to the
University of Notre Dame after serving as a parish priest in France,
where he experienced first hand the Cardijn method and the JOC.
Putz was highly instrumental in encouraging Hillenbrand's efforts to

---

46. See Andrew Greeley, *The Catholic Experience, An Interpretation of the History of American Catholicism* (New York: Doubleday & Company, 1967), ch. VIII: The Chicago Experience, esp. pp. 249–253 and Dennis Geaney, "The Chicago Story," *Chicago Studies* 2 (1963), pp. 281–300.

47. See Hillenbrand's Notes on the Curriculum Revision. UNDA, CMRH 4/18, Seminary, Suggestions 1940–1944.

48. Hillenbrand, "Program for a Liturgical Mission." UNDA, CMRH 4/14.

49. H. A. Reinhold emigrated to the United States in 1938 and in February 1939 began to write his famous "Timely Tracts" for *Orate Fratres*. In September 1940, he wrote about his first "Liturgical Mission" in Everett, Washington. Hillenbrand's liturgical missions were not as well known as Reinhold's, but were certainly influential, especially in Chicago.

foster an understanding of the Cardijn Method in the seminary and the establishment of Young Christian Student groups in the Archdiocese. Putz himself was quite successful in establishing the YCS at Notre Dame and with his support Hillenbrand formed a YCS group at Senn High School.[50] Like the YCW on which it is based, part of every YCS meeting is dedicated to the study of the liturgy.[51]

ORGANIZING AND DIFFUSING THE LITURGICAL MOVEMENT

In the late 1920s, Virgil Michel had discussed the possibility of sponsoring a National Liturgical Week similar to the European weeks held so successfully in Belgium since 1910.[52] However, the time was not right for such an event and no episcopal sponsor was found during Michel's lifetime. The credit for keeping Michel's dream alive and initiating the first National Liturgical Week in 1940 goes in great part to the Benedictine monk, Michael Ducey, of St. Anselm's Priory. Ducey believed that

> unless the movement was guided by and centered around contemplative Benedictine houses where considerable time and talent were dedicated to scholarly research in the liturgy and where the liturgical life could be lived in its ideal setting, the movement would be in danger of superficiality and eventual failure.[53]

He also knew that he could count on the support of Joseph Morrison, the rector of Holy Name Cathedral, and Reynold

---

50. Hillenbrand's Senn High School YCS group produced the first national chairman of the YCW, George "Red" Sullivan. See Martin Quigley, Jr., & Edward Connors, *Catholic Action in Practice* (New York: Random House, 1963), ch. 4: Youth Apostolate, pp. 91–99, 149, and UNDA, CMRH 13/5, College YCS.

51. Documentation on the beginnings of YCS can be found in the publication, *Leaders' Bulletin, Catholic Action Students, University of Notre Dame* (Notre Dame: University of Notre Dame, 1940–1950).

52. See Marx, p. 146.

53. Lawrence J. Madden, *The Liturgical Conference of the U.S.A.: Its Origin and Development: 1940–1968*, Ph.D. dissertation (Trier: University of Trier, 1969), p. 16. Unfortunately, Ducey failed to see the contradiction between his conviction that the ideal setting of the liturgy was in the monastery and the definition of liturgy as the corporate worship of the Mystical Body.

Hillenbrand, who by this time was recognized as a leader of the liturgical movement.[54]

In January 1940, the Benedictine Liturgical Conference, a voluntary organization of American Benedictine abbots, was formed at St. Procopius Priory in Chicago and on April 18, the Conference asked Archbishop Stritch to sponsor the first National Liturgical Week in Chicago. Morrison and Hillenbrand were chosen as the local co-chairpersons of the Week, which took place on October 21–25, 1940, on the theme: "The Living Parish: Active and Intelligent Participation of the Laity in the Liturgy of the Catholic Church." Morrison placed the Cathedral and its facilities at the complete disposal of the Conference. Hillenbrand was selected for the delicate task of setting the proper tone in his keynote address on the history and ideals of the liturgical movement.

The results of the Week went well beyond the expectations of the planners. Not only did people interested in liturgy throughout the country have the opportunity to meet each other, but episcopal sponsorship by a bishop from a prominent Archdiocese was also obtained.[55] The planners were encouraged by the closing remarks of Archbishop Stritch who clearly indicated that more was involved in celebrating the liturgy than merely following the rubrics or providing good art and good music. The liturgy was the Mystical Body of Christ at worship. Hence, its proper celebration held "immense promise for strengthening and elevating Catholic life and Catholic action."[56] Hillenbrand must have been pleased with this positive endorsement of his work in the movement by his new Archbishop.

Hillenbrand capitalized on the presence in Chicago at the National Liturgical Week of so many leaders in the liturgical movement to organize his first Summer School of Liturgy at St. Mary of the Lake Seminary from July 14 to August 1, 1941. The 60 classes covered key doctrines (H.A. Reinhold), the sacraments (Godfrey Diekmann), the Mass (Martin Hellriegel), the liturgical movement (Gerald

---

54. See the March 1, 1940, letter from Michael Ducey to Hillenbrand, seeking Hillenbrand's advice on the theme of the Liturgical Week. UNDA, CMRH 4/14.

55. See Madden, p. 23: 1,260 people registered: 320 priests, 549 religious, 391 laypeople.

56. Samuel Stritch, "Closing Sermon, Oct. 25, 1940," in *National Liturgical Week 1940* (Newark: Benedictine Liturgical Conference, 1941), p. 238. See Benedict Ehmann, "The First Liturgical Week," *Liturgical Arts* 9 (1941), p. 28 and Gerald Ellard, "A Liturgical Week Is Held in Chicago," *America* 64 (1940), p. 150.

Ellard), the liturgical year (William Busch), parish participation (Bernard Laukemper *et al*), dialog Mass and High Mass (Gerald Ellard), the office (Bede Scholz), Catholic Action (William Boyd), the liturgy and peace (Paul Bussard). While the emphasis was mainly on the liturgy, the liturgy was always connected with the lives of real people, who are called to spread the kingdom through their participation in the apostolate.[57] This Summer School demonstrated an important characteristic of the American liturgical movement, which from the very beginning was conceived as a popular movement addressing the lives of lay Catholics.[58]

Hillenbrand wrote to Archbishop Stritch that the Summer School of Liturgy "is the first one of its kind" organized on a national basis in the United States.[59] In addition to the classes that were taught, the School also provided well planned liturgies which modeled the active participation in the liturgy that the lecturers spoke of. The priests were taught to sing a chant Mass and compline. Over 25 dioceses were represented and copies of the *Proceedings of the Summer School of Liturgy* were circulated throughout the United States, from New York to San Francisco, from Collegeville to San Antonio.[60]

As we noted previously, Michael Ducey believed that the liturgical movement needed a firm grounding in the contemplative life of the Benedictine Order. However, many of the abbots represented on the Benedictine Liturgical Conference believed that a wider sponsorship of the Liturgical Weeks was needed. On September 8, 1943, the Benedictine Liturgical Conference was dissolved and all its assets were turned over to the American Liturgical Advisory Committee, which eventually became known as the Liturgical

---

57. See Hillenbrand's notes on the Summer School. UNDA, CMRH 28/21, Summer School of Liturgy, 1941. Hillenbrand's work on this Summer School led to an invitation from Maurice Lavanoux to join the Board of Directors of the Liturgical Arts Society, an invitation Hillenbrand accepted on January 5, 1942. UNDA, CMRH 35, Correspondence E-L, 1940–1944.

58. See Madden, p. 57. Madden notes that the liturgical movement in Germany did not directly embrace the mass of the faithful, while the American movement was directly related to efforts by social activists and popularizers.

59. Hillenbrand to Archbishop Stritch, June 9, 1941. UNDA, CMRH 35, Correspondence, M–Z, 1940–1941, Liturgy.

60. Hillenbrand personally supervised the publication and distribution of the *Proceedings of the Summer School of Liturgy* and his papers contain the long list of bishops, priests, and religious who wrote to obtain copies. UNDA, CMRH 28/22, Seminary, Liturgical Summer School, 1941.

Conference, with an Advisory Board of fifteen members. Its first officers were Joseph Morrison, President; Michael Ducey, Secretary; William Huelsman, Treasurer. The advisory committee included William Busch, Benedict Ehmann, Gerald Ellard, Paul Furfey, Reynold Hillenbrand, Bernard Laukemper, Sister Madeleva, H.A. Reinhold, Joseph Stedman, and Max Jordan.[61] At the same time, Reynold Hillenbrand was chosen as chairman of the Program Committee to plan future Liturgical Weeks.

Hillenbrand was heavily involved in the Liturgical Weeks and the work of the Liturgical Conference throughout the rest of this decade. He was a speaker at the 1940, 1941, 1943, 1945, 1946, 1947, and 1948 Weeks. He was elected Treasurer in 1944 and Vice-President in 1949. During this decade Hillenbrand was highly instrumental in obtaining a site and episcopal sponsorship for the Liturgical Weeks. He also influenced the themes and speakers chosen for these weeks. At the same time, in the early part of this decade Hillenbrand was becoming a popular speaker at various liturgical/social action study weeks for seminarians, students, priests, and laity.

Among the groups that Hillenbrand influenced during this time, the Grail is of special significance. Founded originally in Holland in 1921, the Grail was established at Doddridge Farm, Libertyville, Illinois in 1940 under the sponsorship of Bishop Sheil. According to the vision of the Jesuit founder, Jacques van Ginneken, the laity, especially lay women, held the key to a renewed influence of Catholicism in the West and the world. In 1944, the Grail moved to a large farm in Loveland, Ohio, where they established its

> Year's School of the Apostolate, offering training in rural living, community service, and the several aspects of Christian culture (weaving, sculpture, music, dance, and writing), all these in the context of liturgical celebration and other spiritual exercises (especially for those who aspired to lifetime celibate membership in the movement).[62]

Before they moved, they invited Reynold Hillenbrand in July 1943 to speak to them about the liturgy and the laity's role in society.

---

61. See Madden, pp. 39–41. Ducey was the only Benedictine on the Advisory Board and was quite concerned about the loss of Benedictine sponsorship.

62. Alden Vincent Brown, *The Grail Movement in the United States, 1940–1972: The Evolution of an American Catholic Laywoman's Community*, Ph.D. dissertation (New York: Union Theological Seminary, 1982).

His lectures were written down and became an important resource in the formation of the Year's School of the Apostolate in Loveland.[63]

In February 1943, a Catholic Action "cell" was organized in a Chicago law office by seven businessmen interested in finding a way to implement Pius XI's exhortation to "restore all things in Christ."[64] In March, Louis Putz had spoken to them about the Cardijn method used in YCW & YCS and in April Hillenbrand was asked to speak to them on the Mystical Body. At this meeting, Hillenbrand met Pat Crowley who in 1944 helped him organize a men's cell at Sacred Heart Church, Hubbard Woods which eventually led to the founding of the Christian Family Movement.[65]

This group also drew inspiration from Pius XII's June 29, 1943 encyclical, *Mystici Corporis*, "On the Mystical Body of Christ." In it, Pius XII appeals to all the members of the Body of Christ to become involved "in mutual collaboration for the common comfort and for the more perfect building up of the whole body."[66] At the same time, this encyclical gave new prominence to the role of the liturgy in the restoration of the social order. As such, it solidified Hillenbrand's conviction that he was on the right track in bringing the ideals of the liturgical movement to these small "cells" who were open to Catholic Action.[67]

While Hillenbrand was gaining notoriety as a leader in the liturgical and social action movements, he was also suffering from complaints made by pastors, business leaders, and seminary faculty over his "liberal" policies. Some pastors were upset over the criticisms they received from their new socially and liturgically minded associates. Business leaders saw Hillenbrand as biased in favor of labor. The new

---

63. See the October 31, 1955 letter from Ms. Jeanne Plante of Grailville to Hillenbrand: "The lectures which you gave during the first years of the Grail establishment outside of Chicago have been carefully kept and have been a treasure for many of the students who have been trained here since then." UNDA, CMRH 8/13, Grail.

64. See Jeffrey Mark Burns, *American Catholics and the Family Crisis, 1930–1962, The Ideological and Organizational Response*, Ph.D dissertation (Notre Dame: University of Notre Dame, 1982), pp. 283–284.

65. Quigley & Connors, *Catholic Action in Practice*, pp. 149–150.

66. Pius XII, *Mystici Corporis*, no. 15.

67. See Hillenbrand's August 5, 1943 letter to Michael Ducey, where he made it clear that he saw the renewal of the liturgy as his top priority and the ultimate solution to the social problem: "We do not have a solution for any social problem unless we build it upon the altar— the Mystical Body at sacrifice." UNDA, CMRH 35, Correspondence, A–D.

diocesan faculty that Hillenbrand had appointed represented a loss of control on the part of the Jesuit faculty. In addition, Hillenbrand's aloof manner and liturgical innovations troubled the faculty's Jesuit superior, John Clifford, who had many contacts in the diocese due to his post as the moderator of clergy conferences. Moreover, Hillenbrand's lecture series and Summer Schools filled the Seminary with visitors all year long.

Gone were the days of peace and tranquility under the old rector. Gone too was the rector, who had begun to attend more meetings of the Advisory Board of the Liturgical Conference, YCW and YCS cells, numerous clergy weeks, etc. Recently, he had lectured at the Grail, an organization which Archbishop Stritch criticized as unorthodox in its teachings.[68] Stritch may also have received some criticism from the bishops for his sponsorship of the National Liturgical Week.[69] In any case, on July 15, 1944, Archbishop Stritch notified Hillenbrand that he was "promoting him to the pastorate of Sacred Heart Parish in Hubbard Woods, Illinois."[70] The appointment was to take effect August 3, 1944.

Hillenbrand was an intelligent, gifted speaker, whose genius at popularizing the ideals of the liturgical and social action movements made him a very effective leader during his years as rector of St. Mary of the Lake Seminary. Prior to his assignment as rector, he was exposed to the thinking and work of many important liturgical and/or social action leaders: Dorothy Day, Gerald Ellard, Martin Hellriegel, Bernard Laukemper, Peter Maurin, Francis McGowan, Virgil Michel, Joseph Morrison, John Ryan, Sheed & Ward, Bernard Sheil, and the students of CISCA. These leaders and their insights, combined with Hillenbrand's devotion to papal encyclicals, provided the rich soil for his synthesis on liturgy and social action.

Hillenbrand revised the curriculum and the liturgical life of the seminary to conform to the ideals of the liturgical and social

---

68. See Brown, *The Grail Movement in the United States*, pp. 45–47.

69. Stritch warned John Egan in the creation of Cana, in 1945, that Cana was not to become a national movement. Msgr. John Egan to the author, May 10, 1986 interview. See Madden, p. 36: Madden notes that liturgy was an unpopular cause with the bishops at this time.

70. Stritch's letter of appointment to Sacred Heart Church. UNDA, CMRH 27/8, Chancery Office Letters. See Greeley, *The Catholic Experience*, p. 253 for a good summary of what was the commonly accepted explanation for Hillenbrand's removal from his post as rector.

action movements. Francis Haas, Don Kanaly, Louis Putz, and Pat Crowley moved Hillenbrand to become more involved with forming lay apostles using the Cardijn method. Virgil Michel provided a model of an activist intellectual, whose vision linked the renewal of the liturgy with the lay apostolate. The National Liturgical Weeks gave Hillenbrand national prominence but also took him away from the seminary, thus indirectly contributing to his dismissal as rector.

Chapter 3

Pastor, Vice-President, and National Chaplain: 1944–1955

Hillenbrand left his post at the seminary with the thesis that a good theology of the Eucharist would lead to a sense of the Mystical Body, a proper understanding of divine life (grace), and a conviction about the necessity of Catholic Action.[1] He firmly believed that the solutions to social problems were grounded in a return to the altar. He brought this thesis to the five groups that occupied the bulk of his efforts liturgically: Sacred Heart Parish, the Liturgical Conference, the Vernacular Society, the Specialized Lay Apostolate (YCW, YCS, CFM), and the various schools where he lectured. This chapter will treat Hillenbrand's ministry with each of these groups from 1944 to 1955, a peak year and a turning point in his career.

Bringing Liturgical Renewal to Sacred Heart Church

When Archbishop Stritch appointed Hillenbrand pastor of Sacred Heart Church[2] in Hubbard Woods (Winnetka, Illinois) on July 15, 1944, Hillenbrand accepted the appointment as the will of God for his life. When Hillenbrand arrived at Sacred Heart Parish, he judged it to be resting on its laurels—having successfully built its first Church in 1897, a combination school and Church in 1908, and a Gothic Church in 1925. As Hillenbrand said in his history of the parish, "From this time [1925] on, the years were less storied. The spiritual

---

1. Hillenbrand, "The Social Nature of Grace in the Mystical Body of Christ," June 25, 1947 lecture. UNDA, CMRH 8/4.

2. Sacred Heart Church was located about 20 miles North of Chicago, in an affluent suburb, with an active, but traditional congregation.

work carried on quietly, through the years of the depression and another world war."[3] The quiet years came to an end with Hillenbrand's appointment.

While Hillenbrand was rector of the seminary, he described to the seminarians the work of the priest as: giving a daily homily, doing convert instruction, visiting the sick in the hospital, organizing study clubs, instructing the altar boys, working with the sisters in the school, supervising the ushers, and caring for the poor.[4] Basically, this is what Hillenbrand did in his first year at Sacred Heart Church. He got to know his new parishioners, did the work expected of a pastor, and planted the seeds for future changes.

In 1945, Hillenbrand introduced the dialog Mass and formed a boy's choir. He preached at all the Masses, explaining the rationale behind these changes and the importance of the sung Mass.[5] In 1945, he established Study Clubs on the Mass[6] and the first parish Christian Family Action group (later called CFM) with the help of Patrick Crowley.[7] In 1946, he sponsored the first Cana Conference for married couples and in 1947, the first Pre-Cana Conference for engaged couples. In these last two activities, we see the influence of the Catholic Family Action groups, which we will discuss below, and his former student, John Egan, whom Cardinal Stritch had appointed director of the Cana Conference.[8]

In 1948, Hillenbrand began his parish music program, which is described below, established a parish library to assist in explaining his ideas about liturgy, church as Mystical Body, lay apostles, Catholic

---

3. Hillenbrand, "History of Sacred Heart Church," 1957. UNDA, CMRH 38, Charlton Fortune Correspondence.

4. Hillenbrand, "Talks on Priest's Work," 1940, 1941. UNDA, CMRH 41.

5. Hillenbrand's papers in the UNDA document the fact that he regularly preached at all the Masses explaining the focus of a particular season, the origin of a feast, the doctrine of sacrifice as a gift-offering to God, the need for active participation, the importance of receiving Communion, the staples of the spiritual life (daily Mass, Confession, mental prayer), the social teachings of the Church, the latest papal encyclical, etc.

6. Hillenbrand, "Notes on Mass for Parish Study Clubs, Parish House Meetings," May, 1946. UNDA, CMRH 22/29 Parish Notes.

7. Quigley & Connors, *Catholic Action in Practice*, p. 150.

8. These parochial ministries centered around the family and happily coincided with the theme of the 1946, National Liturgical Week on "The Family in Christ," at which Hillenbrand spoke on "The Family and Catholic Action." See Vincent Giese, "The Lay Apostolate in Chicago," in *The Catholic Church, U.S.A.*, ed. Louis J. Putz, p. 363 and Leo R. Ward, *Catholic Life, U.S.A.*, ch. 4: The Cana Movement, pp. 53–14.

Action, the Cardijn method, the spirituality of the layman, and the demands of social justice. Throughout these years, Hillenbrand's study clubs, music groups, Catholic action groups, days of renewal, homilies at Mass, and work with the grammar school children, faculty, and parents literally transformed Sacred Heart Church into a model parish on a par with Holy Cross Parish in St. Louis, where Martin Hellriegel was pastor.

In January 1948, Hillenbrand invited two groups of 50 parishioners to the parish house to listen to a lecture by the renowned chant expert, Dom Ermin Vitry, editor of *Caecilia*, a national monthly review of liturgical music.[9] Sixteen small groups were formed from those who attended these initial lectures. Twelve of these groups were composed of couples and varied in size from 14 to 26 people. There were also groups for college students, high school students, and maids. After hearing Vitry's lecture, the groups were asked to continue preparing for the parish sung Mass by attending practices in their homes. Vitry and the three parish priests conducted these practices. After just three weeks of practice in the homes, the groups were prepared to sing the responses, the *Kyrie, Sanctus*, and *Agnus Dei* on Septuagesima Sunday, February 1948. It took four more weeks to add the Creed to the people's repertoire. Finally, the groups learned the Ambrosian *Gloria* and the following chants for Holy Week: *Gloria, Laus* for Palm Sunday, *Pange lingua* for Holy Thursday, *Venite adoremus* for Good Friday, Litany, *Alleluia*, and a vesper service for Holy Saturday.

In all the chants, a division of parts was arranged between the congregation and the vested boys' choir, which sat in the front pews. The propers were sung either recto-tono or using a psalm tone by a boys' schola from the choir loft and men's schola of eight voices. The *Introit* was divided between the boys and the men. The boys' choir sang the *Gradual, Alleluia* Verse, and Communion song, while the men's choir sang the Offertory song. An English hymn was sung at the conclusion of Mass, while the priest and choir recessed through the body of the church. After Easter, an English hymn was also added to the beginning of Mass, while the priest and the vested boys' choir processed into Church. Ermin Vitry composed a booklet titled, *Our*

---

9. See Ermin Vitry, "Restoration of the Parish High Mass and Vespers," in *National Liturgical Week, 1944* (Chicago: Liturgical Conference, 1945), pp. 145–156, p. 22, note 50.

Chanted Mass, One in Song, One in Christ, which contained the words
and music for various Masses.[10]

    Hillenbrand's music program created a good deal of interest.
On April 24, 1948, Clifford A. Bennett, Editor of the Gregorian
Institute of America, wrote that the music program at Sacred Heart
Church "is most unique and proves that what the Church wants is not
impossible."[11] Shortly thereafter, the parish began to become known
as a center of active participation in the liturgy. On October 31, 1949,
Helen Fleming wrote an article in the *Daily News,* "Parish Flock Joins
in Latin Mass," in which she praises the parish for its active participation in and attention to every part of the Mass.[12] Thus, in a very short
time, Hillenbrand had transformed the "quiet" suburban parish of
Sacred Heart into a model of active participation.

    By 1952, Hillenbrand's music program had become famous
nationally. At the urging of Godfrey Diekmann,[13] Hillenbrand asked
Bob Senser to write an article for the April issue of *Orate Fratres* in
which he describes the continuing progress of the music program at
Sacred Heart.

> Each parish school child from fifth grade on owns and uses a St. Andrew's
> Daily Missal. Adults at Sunday Masses have the choice of using either
> their own missals or leaflet missals provided by the pastor . . . . In all,
> about one-fifth of the parishioners have taken part in the special training.[14]

    Senser remarks that in addition to producing active participa-
tion in the liturgy, the parish's music program has also produced a
greater unity among the parishioners who have gotten to know each
other better as a result of participating in the special musical training.[15]

---

10. See a complete description of the program in the May 4, 1948, letter of Hillenbrand to
Clifford A. Bennett, Editor of the Gregorian Institute of America, responding to Bennett's
invitation to share his program with a letter to the Gregorian Institute of America Newsletter.
UNDA, CMRH 34, Correspondence 1948, Sacred Heart Church, G–L.

11. Clifford A. Bennett to Hillenbrand, April 24, 1948. UNDA, CMRH 34.

12. Helen Fleming, "Parish Flock Joins in Latin of Mass," *Daily News,* October 31, 1949.
UNDA, CMRH 33, Correspondence, Tulsa, 1949.

13. Godfrey Diekmann, editor of *Orate Fratres,* wrote Hillenbrand on March 30, 1951:
"You have done a good job in getting your congregation to implement the sung Mass. And
you use a technique that no one else, so far as I know, has employed." UNDA, CMRH 35,
Correspondence, Liturgy, 1951.

14. Bob Senser, "How a Parish Came to Sing," *Orate Fratres* 26 (1952), pp. 257, 259.

15. See Thomas P. Conley, "I Hear Whole Congregations Singing" in *National Liturgical
Week 1952* (Elsberry, Mo.: Liturgical Conference, 1953), pp. 49–56. Conley was the associate

Hillenbrand always had a strong belief that the formation of children needed to be grounded in the experience of daily worship. As Hillenbrand says:

> Mass is the center of a Catholic School. It is a class, with Christ as the teacher. Mass is part of the curriculum. . . . The Mass is Christ. It is the sacrifice of his death brought to the altar. It is his whole life made present on the altar. It is therefore the center of the universe, the center of the world, the center (the heart) of the Church, the center of our lives. . . . Schools shouldn't be built around a system (that has no time for daily Mass) . . . nor around athletics, nor around social science, but around Christ, who supremely and irreplaceably is the Mass.[16]

Eventually, Hillenbrand achieved daily children's Masses at which the children frequently received Communion, sang the chants, and read the scriptures. Finally, implementing a daily children's Mass reveals the influence of his liturgical theology on his pastoral leadership in the parish.

On February 9, 1951, the Congregation of Rites approved the experimental use of the Easter Vigil at night, with the approval of the ordinary. Prior to this, the Vigil had been celebrated in the morning on Holy Saturday with very few people in attendance, little relationship to Easter Sunday, and no renewal of baptismal promises.[17] Hillenbrand had petitioned Cardinal Stritch to use the experimental rite, but Stritch denied him permission, reasoning that he either should grant permission for the entire Archdiocese or not at all.[18]

Hillenbrand was not a person to give up easily and so he petitioned Cardinal Stritch again in 1952 for permission to celebrate the new vigil. On April 7, 1952, Hillenbrand wrote to his parishioners that he had good news:

---

pastor of Sacred Heart Church from 1941–1962, 1963–1964, and actively involved in the parish music program.

16. Hillenbrand, "Position Paper on Children's Participation in the Mass," November, 1973. UNDA, CMRH 26/21.Hillenbrand enjoyed preaching at the children's Mass and his papers in the Notre Dame Archives contain a complete set of children homilies for the liturgical year.

17. See Gerald Ellard, "The New Easter Light and Its Growing Vision," August 19, 1952, lecture, *National Liturgical Week 1952* (Elsberry, Mo.: Liturgical Conference, 1953), pp. 9–22.

18. Cardinal Stritch to Hillenbrand, March 19, 1951. UNDA, CMRH 35, Correspondence, Liturgy, 1951.

His Eminence, the Cardinal, has granted our parish the privilege of having the Easter Vigil service on Saturday night . . . . This service is the one which was held on Holy Saturday morning, where it really doesn't belong. It has now been modified, abbreviated, and made more lovely by the Holy Father. It concludes with Mass—the first joyous Easter Mass.[19]

In 1952, only two parishes in the Archdiocese requested this permission: Hillenbrand's and Joseph Morrison's, although three religious houses also requested it.[20]

With the permission allowing him to celebrate the new vigil coming only two weeks before Easter, Hillenbrand had to move quickly. He wrote the letter previously mentioned in which he invited his parishioners to the vigil. He briefly mentioned the night Vigil at the Palm Sunday Masses. He obtained five children to baptize, all from one family, ranging from seven to fourteen years of age. Hillenbrand began the Vigil at 10:30 PM and the Mass about 12:00 midnight.

The results of his efforts are documented in a letter he wrote to Cardinal Stritch, in which he confirms the positive reaction of his parishioners to the celebration:

The fact that the congregation sings added to the service, as there are brief responses throughout. The boy's choir did very well . . . . The people gathered—in a way not hitherto possible—three profound impressions: the transition from darkness to light, from death to life; the tremendous meaning of Baptism; the joyful impact of the first Easter Mass.[21]

The response of the congregation was excellent, with attendance at 362 in a church that seats 480, on a rainy night, with very short notice. Hillenbrand noted that for the morning Vigil attendance ranged from a low of 12 to a high of 60 or 70. Thus, his first night Vigil was a great success, undoubtedly due to years of catechesis and to a very real sense of solidarity that had been achieved among his people.[22]

---

19. Hillenbrand to Sacred Heart Parish, April 7, 1952. UNDA, CMRH 35, Liturgy Correspondence, 1952–1954.

20. Hillenbrand to H.A. Reinhold, May 2, 1952. UNDA, CMRH 31.

21. Hillenbrand to Cardinal Stritch, April 18, 1952. UNDA, CMRH 35, Correspondence, Liturgy, 1952.

22. A copy of the Easter Vigil Service, translated and arranged for lay participation appears in a 64 page supplement to *National Liturgical Week 1952*, Elsberry, Mo.: Liturgical Conference, 1953.

VICE-PRESIDENT OF THE LITURGICAL CONFERENCE

In order to appreciate what Hillenbrand and the Liturgical Conference set out to accomplish, one must recall the state of liturgical piety in the United States in the 1940s. Public worship was highly individualistic with little sense of the liturgy being a corporate action of the Mystical Body. The liturgy was dominated by the clergy, who often were more concerned about following the rubrics and finishing Mass quickly rather than preaching the Word and involving the people. Mass was said by the priest and sung by the choir, while the congregation occupied its time trying to follow the action on the altar with missals containing the English translations, saying the Rosary or reading from books of devotional prayers.[23]

Eucharistic piety centered around frequent visits to the Blessed Sacrament, the celebration of Benediction which was often attached to the end of a popular novena, and the reception of Communion before, at any time during, and after Mass. Communion had become a separate entity, detached from association with the Mass from which it came. While there was strong emphasis on the real presence of Christ in the Eucharist, little recognition was given to the presence of Christ in the proclamation of scripture or in the assembly gathered for worship. Mass was seen as the sacrifice of Calvary renewed, but there was little recognition that Mass was also a sacrificial meal set in a context of praise and thanksgiving.

Personal spirituality was excessively vertical (emphasizing God and me), mainly concerned with attaining salvation, the pursuit of perfection, and living a good life. However, the horizontal dimension relating the liturgy to life, to the needs of the poor, or to the demands of social justice was seldom referred to. Catholics knew the answers to the questions in the Baltimore catechism, but were amazingly uneducated when it came to knowledge of the bible. Baptism may have made us children of God, but little was said about sharing in Christ's priesthood and the work of the apostolate was mainly the work of the ordained priest. Pius XI had called people to be involved in Catholic

---

23. On December 20, 1928 Pius XI reaffirmed in his Apostolic Constitution, *Divini Cultus*, the content of Pius X's 1903 *Motu Proprio*, "On Sacred Music," which called for active participation by the faithful. Pius XI plainly said that the faithful should not be "merely detached and silent spectators." However, both Pius X's and Pius XI's injunctions went largely unheeded in the United States.

Action, but how this involvement connected with their "religious life" was largely unknown.[24]

Hillenbrand was on the Board of Directors when the Constitution of the Liturgical Conference was composed. Its preamble summarized well the convictions that Hillenbrand personally advocated in his talks at the Liturgical Weeks. As the Preamble stated:

> We desire to lend our aid to the efforts of the Hierarchy in arousing the Christian people to a deeper consciousness of their dignity as members of the Mystical Body of Christ, and of their privilege in uniting themselves with His redeeming Sacrifice by a more active and fruitful participation in the Sacred Mysteries, the primary and indispensable source of the true Christian spirit.[25]

In short, the purpose of the Liturgical Conference was to move the Catholic bishops to deal with the state of liturgical piety in the United States, to adopt a Mystical Body ecclesiology that took seriously the role of the layman in the Church, and to make the liturgy the source and center of the Christian life.

The Liturgical Conference's principal means to achieve its purpose was the sponsorship of National Liturgical Weeks. These weeks were meant to accomplish in the United States what the Belgian *Semaines Liturgiques*, held annually from 1910 to 1939, accomplished in Europe. The Weeks brought together for consultation and cooperation all those interested in a better understanding of and participation in the liturgy.

> Through discussions of the underlying theology and the historical background of the liturgy, current practices in our public prayer are clarified. During Liturgical Weeks, solemn functions of the Catholic Church are not only talked about but are executed inspiringly.[26]

In addition, these meetings gave the leadership the opportunity to petition the bishops to introduce practices already approved in

---

24. See Madden, pp. 149–159 and Jay P. Dolan, *American Catholic Experience*, pp. 388–389.

25. Madden, Appendix A: The Liturgical Conference Constitution and By-Laws, 1944.

26. Excerpt from a Section of the Program Brochure on the "History and Purpose of Liturgical Weeks," October 14–18, 1946, Liturgical Week, Denver, Colorado. UNDA, CMRH 35, Liturgy Correspondence. For a good example of the type of practices being fostered by the Weeks, see Joseph Cirrincione, "The Possibilities of Liturgical Life in City Parishes," *National Liturgical Week, 1944* (Chicago: Liturgical Conference, 1945), pp. 81–91.

European countries (e.g., evening Mass, bilingual ritual, greater use of the vernacular in the liturgy, etc.). Up to 1947, the Liturgical Weeks were characterized by attempts to summarize developments in theology (Mystical Body, baptismal spirituality, etc.) and pastoral practice (dialog Mass, Catholic Action) that had long been accepted in Europe but which were just beginning to be accepted in the United States. While the European centers of liturgical renewal like Maria Laach felt the sting of some of *Mediator Dei's* criticisms, the U.S. Church basically emphasized the positive aspects of this 1947 Encyclical.[27]

After 1947, the speakers at the Liturgical Weeks began to interpret *Mediator Dei* as the *Magna Carta* of their movement, providing the papal mandate for change. For example, in 1949, Martin Hellriegel broke the tradition of never publicly recommending official changes in pastoral practice by recommending that the Pope move the Holy Saturday morning Vigil to the evening.[28] This was the beginning of a movement toward liturgical activism that would culminate in recommendations for liturgical change being sent to the Holy Father from 1952–1955. Many of the pastoral practices that Hillenbrand eventually recommended in his lectures or implemented in his parish came from the resolutions which the Board of Directors passed during Hillenbrand's years of service with the Conference.[29] However, it was

---

27. See John E. Kelly, "The Encyclical, *Mediator Dei*," in *National Liturgical Week 1948* (Conception: Liturgical Conference, 1949), p. 11: "To those interested in the liturgical apostolate, *Mediator Dei* is a beacon light. It makes liturgical endeavor now not a matter of choice, but a *must*, an apostolate incumbent upon all." It is interesting to note that *Mediator Dei* did highlight some caveats for liturgical reform which looked at retrospectively seem prophetic. For example, Nos. 28–30 criticize new theories of "objective piety" which "belittle or pass over in silence" "subjective" or personal piety. No. 59 lists some rash abuses: "the temerity and daring of those who introduce novel liturgical practices, or call for the revival of obsolete rites out of harmony with prevailing laws and rubrics, deserve severe reproof." It identifies these innovations as transferring certain feasts days from their appointed day in the calendar to another day, deleting prayers from the prayer-books used at the liturgy and passages from scripture considered ill suited to modern times. No. 62 criticizes those who desired to restore the shape of the altar to "its primitive table-form," exclude the use of "black" (requiem) Masses in place of the Mass of the day, forbidding the use of sacred images or statues in Churches, using crosses instead of crucifixes, and rejecting the use of polyphonic music or singing in parts (most likely, in favor of congregational singing). Nos. 63–65 refer to an excessive archaism regarding the desire to return to past liturgical forms or take it upon oneself the right to change the rules and regulations for the celebration of the liturgy.

28. See Madden, p. 84.

29. See the lists of resolutions approved by the Board of Directors. UNDA, CMRH 28/28. A good example of the influence of these resolutions on Hillenbrand is his strong advocacy of the new Easter Vigil.

also this direct appeal to the Congregation of Rites in Rome that made some of the Bishops think that the Liturgical Conference had begun to overstep their bounds as representatives of the American Church.

Hillenbrand served the liturgical conference in a variety of posts: Treasurer (1944), Vice-President (1949–1955), Member of the Board of Directors (1943–1955), Speaker at the Liturgical Weeks (1940,* 1941, 1943, 1945,* 1946, 1947, 1948, 1951, 1955).[30] As a former rector and a recognized leader in both the liturgical and social action movements, Hillenbrand enjoyed the respect of his ordinary, Cardinal Stritch, and many bishops in the country. As Vice President, Hillenbrand wrote letters to these bishops seeking their sponsorship of the weeks.[31] Hillenbrand also assisted in the publication of the proceedings of these weeks. From 1943 to 1955, Hillenbrand served on the Program Committee of the Conference, either as chairman or member. Of course, this gave him a great deal of influence in the selection of themes for the various weeks.[32]

Of the many pastoral leaders who involved themselves with the Conference, probably the two leaders who most embodied the "pastoral" ideals of the movement during this period were Martin Hellriegel and Reynold Hillenbrand. In fact, people often got their names confused, so closely did their work parallel each other. Hellriegel popularized the best insights of the German liturgical movement in his writings, lectures, and parish and Hillenbrand

---

30. The asterisks indicate keynote addresses.

31. See Hillenbrand to the Bishops. UNDA, CMRH 28/27.

32. The themes chosen for the weeks from 1940 to 1955:
    1940–The Living Parish, Active and Intelligent Participation of the Laity in the Liturgy
    1941–The Living Parish, One in Worship, Charity, and Action
    1942–The Praise of God
    1943–Sacrifice
    1944–Liturgy and Catholic Life
    1945–Catholic Liturgy in Peace and Reconstruction
    1946–The Family in Christ
    1941–Christ's Sacrifice and Ours
    1948–The New Man in Christ
    1949–Sanctification of Sunday
    1950–For Pastors and People: The Divine Office and the Mass
    1951–The Priesthood of Christ
    1952–The New Easter Vigil
    1953–Saint Pius X and Social Worship
    1954–Mary in the Liturgy
    1955–The New Ritual, Liturgy and Social Order

Hillenbrand served the liturgical conference in a variety of posts through the 1940s and 1950s: Treasurer (1944), Vice-President (1949–1955), Member of the Board of Directors (1943–1955), and Speaker at the Liturgical Weeks from 1940–1955. As a former rector and a recognized leader in both the liturgical and social action movements, Msgr. Hillenbrand enjoyed the respect of his ordinary, Cardinal Stritch, and many bishops in the country. This photo is from the 1960s. *Archives of the University of Notre Dame.*

emphasized the connection between liturgy and social action which became a hallmark of the American liturgical movement, especially in Chicago. These men worked closely together on the Program Committee of the Liturgical Conference and Hellriegel periodically visited Hillenbrand at his rectory.

During the 1940s Hillenbrand and the Chicago Archdiocese became an inspiration for pastoral leadership throughout the United States. So many movements were either born in Chicago or eventually found their home in the Archdiocese.[33] In the eyes of many people, Hillenbrand exemplified the spirit of these movements and provided the example of someone who was successful in implementing their ideals.

Hillenbrand was elected Vice-President of the Liturgical Conference in 1949. On February 9, 1949, tragedy struck the new Vice-President. Hillenbrand was in a serious car accident near Tulsa, Oklahoma. His right leg was broken in several places. Repeated operations left him with a stiff right leg, shorter than the left and a constant source of annoyance and pain. His hospital stay lasted seventeen months and Hillenbrand did not return to Sacred Heart Parish until July 10, 1950. He would be operated on numerous times

33. A partial list includes: Cana Conference, Catholic Action Federation, Catholic Conference on Industrial Problems, Catholic Interracial Council, Chicago Interstudent Catholic Action (CISCA), Chicago Catholic Worker, Chicago Friendship House, Chicago Labor Alliance, Chicago Labor Schools, Chicago Schools of Liturgy for Priests, Chicago Council against Racial and Religious Discrimination, Christian Family Movement, the Grail, Liturgical Conference, Sheil School of Social Studies, Young Christian Students (High School and College), Young Christian Workers, Vernacular Society, etc. Hillenbrand spoke before all these groups during this period and shared with them his synthesis on liturgy and Catholic Action, which is summarized in Part II of this dissertation.

after his return to Chicago to increase mobility in his injured leg. In addition, chronic, migraine headaches made him irritable and hard to work with.[34] Yet Hillenbrand eventually continued as a leader of the movements. According to Godfrey Diekmann, "No one ever lost their loyalty to Hillenbrand, even though after the accident he wasn't the same Hillenbrand at all."[35]

Hillenbrand's work with the Conference declined with his retirement from the Board of Directors in 1955 and his increased involvement with Catholic Action groups. In addition, the members of the Board were starting to see the limitations of his theological methodology with some skepticism. In their view, he had become a theological conservative, who overemphasized papal encyclicals as a source for theology.[36] Hillenbrand's attitude was: if the pope doesn't say it, don't pay attention to it. Yet encyclicals are only part of the concretization of theological thought, reflecting the position of the official Church to the particular needs of the time. They clarify Church teaching, but do no prohibit future growth in orthodoxy. Hillenbrand never seemed to understand that.[37]

A good example of his theological limitations is his emphasis on the moment of consecration as the moment of self-offering.[38] It makes the rest of the Eucharistic prayer appear unimportant. All

---

34. See UNDA, CMRH 33, Correspondence, Tulsa, 1949; CMRH 33, Correspondence, 1949-1950, Hospital Stay in Tulsa, Oklahoma; CMRH 34, Correspondence, Tulsa Hospital Stay, 1949–1950 for information on Hillenbrand's operations, his two Holy Hours over the phone to his parish in 1949, his 1949 letter to the Liturgical Conference Board exhorting them not to cancel the 1950 week, the long list of distinguished visitors: William Busch, Godfrey Diekmann, Gerald Ellard, Martin Hellriegel, Joseph Morrison, H.A. Reinhold, John Ross-Duggan, etc.

35. Godfrey Diekmann to the author, March 30, 1988 interview, St. John's Abbey, Collegeville.

36. Ibid. Godfrey Diekmann stated to the author that "Hillenbrand was an encyclical man, more than a theologian." At the same time, Hillenbrand had good reason for paying attention to the encyclicals. On August 12, 1950, Pius XII issued *Humani Generis*, which affirmed the teachings of the encyclicals as authoritative and their doctrine on faith and morals requiring the assent of all Catholics.

37. One should not underestimate the effect that Hillenbrand's injuries in his 1949 car accident had on his ability to grow theologically. Time-consuming therapy and repeated operations on his bad leg surely affected his ability to keep up with the latest developments in theology.

38. A classic example of this is his October 14, 1943 lecture, "The Spirit of Sacrifice in Christian Society, Statement of Principle," in *National Liturgical Weeks 1943* (Ferdinand, In.: Liturgical Conference, 1944), p. 103. In fact, this was the position he held throughout the course of his life.

Hillenbrand seems to know is that Trent and the Pope emphasized the words of consecration as the key moment in the sacrifice and that was the end of it. That there could be other "orthodox" teachings never interested him. That the Eucharist could also be defined as a sacrament of a sacrifice set in the context of a prayer of blessing—this development never enters into any of his talks or writings. Consequently, his August 25, 1955, lecture at the Worcester Liturgical Week served as a brilliant synthesis of his theories on liturgy and Catholic Action, but betrayed his absolutization of a few papal encyclicals (*Quadragesimo Anno*, *Mystici Corporis*, and *Mediator Dei*)—a limit that led to his demise with the Conference. Hillenbrand was invited back to address the 1956 Liturgical Week, but his effectiveness with this group had come to an end.

While a great deal of emphasis has been placed on the work of Hillenbrand with the Conference, one must also recognize the contribution of other Chicago priests to the liturgical movement. Chicago provided the Conference with its first Episcopal sponsor, Archbishop Samuel Stritch, and its first President, Joseph P. Morrison.[39] Under Morrison's influence, John P. O'Connell, Morrison's associate at Immaculate Conception Parish, became Secretary and Editor of the Proceedings. Bernard Laukemper, pastor of St. Aloysius Church, was both Treasurer and a frequent speaker at the Weeks. Norbert Randolph of St. Philomena Church served for many years as Conference treasurer.

In addition to the priests who served as officers of the Conference, the following Chicago priests spoke at the Weeks from 1940–1955: Barnabas Mary Ahern, William Boyd, Francis A. Brunner, Daniel Cantwell, Thomas P. Conley, Harry C. Koenig, Joseph T. Kush, John P. O'Connell. These men demonstrate the diversity of background—both theological and pastoral—that the Liturgical Conference was able to draw upon in constructing its programs and implementing its resolutions.

---

39. Morrison became pastor of Immaculate Conception Parish on August 24, 1945. This parish is only a few miles from Sacred Heart Parish where Hillenbrand was pastor.

Supporting the Vernacular Society

At the Liturgical Week in Denver, October 14–17, 1946, H. A.
Reinhold called a meeting consisting of Martin Hellriegel, F. Heyer,
Reynold Hillenbrand, Bernard Laukemper, Joseph Morrison, Leo
Ruggle, Bede Scholz, Gilbert Stack, Shawn Sheehan, Bernard Stanley,
H. Velte, and Alphonse Westhoof. The result of their deliberations
was the founding of the St. Jerome Society

> to study, in accordance with the teachings of the Catholic Church and
> with due regard of ecclesiastical authority, the possibilities of a greater use
> of the vernacular in the liturgical rites of the Church.[40]

After this first meeting in 1946, interested parties met at the
Liturgical Weeks to discuss the possibilities of the use of the vernacular.

In its origin the St. Jerome Society was dependant upon the
English Liturgy Society which basically had three goals: 1) to provide
a vernacular *Rituale* for the rites of baptism, churching, marriage,
visitation of the sick, reception of converts, administration of the last
sacraments, funerals, and blessings; 2) to provide vernacular versions
of vespers, compline, the blessing of candles, ashes, palms, and an
extension of the vernacular prayers and hymns used at Benediction;
and 3) to foster the use of the dialog Mass and vernacular in the
liturgy.[41] Hillenbrand embraced these goals as his own, but never
experimented with the use of the vernacular except where allowed
by legitimate authority.

The St. Jerome Society was encouraged by the statement in
Mediator Dei, no. 60, that

> the use of the mother tongue in conjunction with several of the rites
> may be of much advantage to the people. But the Apostolic See alone
> is empowered to grant this permission.[42]

---

40. Information taken from a membership brochure published by the Vernacular Society,
1949. UNDA, CMRH 85, Correspondence, Liturgy, 1951. The statement of purpose is almost
identical with that of the English Vernacular Society. See *The English Liturgist, A Bulletin
Issued to Members of the English Vernacular Society*, December, 1948, No. 8, p. 8: "The Vernacular
Society in the U.S.A."

41. Information taken from a membership brochure, published by the Vernacular society,
1949. UNDA, CMRH 85, Correspondence, Liturgy, 1951.

42. Pius XII, *Mediator Dei* (Washington: National Catholic Welfare Conference, 1947),
p. 25.

With this "official" encouragement, the St. Jerome Society felt it safe to identify itself more openly with the English Liturgy Society. It did so at a meeting held in Chicago, at the St. Benet Library, on July 25, 1948.

Hillenbrand served as chairman of the July 25 meeting of a representative group of members, including H. A. Reinhold and Godfrey Diekmann. At this meeting, the name of the St. Jerome Society was changed to the Vernacular Society and the group elected Joseph Morrison as President, John K. Ross-Duggan as Secretary, and Rosemary Fitzpatrick as Assistant Secretary.[43] Although the Society met at the same time and place as the Liturgical Weeks and was composed largely of Liturgical Conference members, it did its work quietly, not wanting its pursuit of the vernacular to be confused with the broader goals of the Conference.

This meeting was the beginning of a lifelong association between the Secretary, John Ross-Duggan, and Hillenbrand. Duggan frequently stayed at Sacred Heart rectory and became close friends with Hillenbrand. In fact, by 1953, Hillenbrand was identified as the "assistant secretary" of the Vernacular Society.[44] Whenever Duggan went on a trip to one of the European Liturgical Conferences, he wrote Hillenbrand and summarized the latest developments in Europe.[45] When Hillenbrand was forced to cancel his trip to the International Congress on the Lay Apostolate held in Rome in 1951, it was Duggan that Hillenbrand asked to represent him and the American YCW.[46]

On April 27, 1953, Michael Mathis wrote Hillenbrand to ask him to be a consultant to the Bishop's Commission entrusted with the publication of the *Collectio Rituum Anglicae Linguae*. His feedback was sought "especially in terms of securing a funeral service ritual that will

---

43. The Society published in Chicago the quarterly magazine, *Amen*, from 1951 through 1961, reaching a peak circulation of 5,000 subscriptions in 1955. See William E. Wiethoff, *Popular Rhetorical Strategy in the American Catholic Debate over Vernacular Reform, 1953–1968*, Ph.D. dissertation (Michigan: University of Michigan, 1974), p. 8.

44. UNDA, CMRH 28/29, Liturgy, August 1953, Liturgical Conference, 1953–54.

45. A September 25, 1953, letter of Ross-Duggan to Hillenbrand summarized Duggan's visit with the officers of the English Liturgy Society and his experiences at the Lugano Conference, which recommended that the Epistle and Gospel of all Masses be recited or chanted in the vernacular. The public Masses of this Conference were said facing the people and the Gospel was sung in Italian after the priest first chanted it in Latin. UNDA, CMRH 28/29.

46. Hillenbrand to Ross-Duggan, September 30, 1951. UNDA, CMRH 31, Correspondence, CA (1950-1952).

be faithful to the Catholic tradition and the practical situation in the United States."[47] Mathis and Ellard had based their revision on the German *Rituale* which had been approved for use on March 21, 1950.

When Mathis received the feedback that the bilingual Ritual might be opposed because it was identified as a project of the Vernacular Society, he became concerned about his role with the Society and the Liturgical Conference. His concern increased when the August 11–23, 1953, Liturgical Week endorsed the Epistle and Gospel being read in the vernacular. He felt that many bishops would interpret this as the influence of the Vernacular Society on the Liturgical Conference. And so, on August 28, 1953 Mathis asked that his name be removed as one of the sponsors of the 1953 Liturgical Conference resolutions.[48] However, the *Rituale* was approved by the Congregation of Rites on June 2, 1954.[49]

This incident reveals the great suspicion and hostility under which the Vernacular Society worked in the early 1950s. On October 4, 1954 Bishop Vincent S. Waters wrote the President of the Vernacular Society, Joseph Morrison, about the Bishops' opposition to the Vernacular Society:

> To be entirely candid . . . the only real opposition to the new ritual in English came from those who confused the work done by the Liturgical Conference with the avowed aims of the Vernacular Society and this opposition is still prevalent among the hierarchy. If the Liturgical Conference is looking for guidance, this is the guidance I would give: keep the two (Vernacular Society and Liturgical Conference) entirely distinct.[50]

Unfortunately, the Vernacular Society had developed among the bishops the image of being "ultra-liberal"[51] in its views on the vernacular in the Mass. Thus, the Liturgical Conference decided it

---

47. Michael Mathis to Hillenbrand, April 27, 1953. UNDA, CMRH 28/25, Liturgical Conference Correspondence, 1945-1962. In 1968, Hillenbrand volunteered his parish to participate in the experiment on the new funeral ritual.

48. Michael Mathis to the Liturgical Conference Board of Directors, August 28, 1953. UNDA, CMRH 28/29.

49. See Robert J. Kennedy, *Michael Mathis: American Liturgical Pioneer* (Washington: Pastoral Press, 1987), pp. 18–20.

50. Bishop Waters to Joseph Morrison, October 4, 1954. UNDA, CMRH 28/25, Liturgical Conference Correspondence, 1945–1962.

51. Bishop Waters to Joseph Morrison, October 22, 1954. UNDA, CMRH 28/25.

would be in its best interests to remain independent from the Vernacular Society.

The Specialized Lay Apostolate: CFM, YCW, YCS

On April 6, 1945, Hillenbrand received a letter from Cardinal Stritch on the need to intensify Catholic Action, especially by working among young Catholics. Stritch writes:

> I have followed the work of Catholic Action cells, and I approve wholly and hope from it ever increasing good. It is my wish that it continue and expand and that the Directors, under your guidance, meet often to study programs of action and exchange experiences. I appreciate deeply your giving time and talent to this work and I ask you to keep me fully informed on it.[52]

Hillenbrand must have felt this was God's way of directing him toward a new apostolate. With this mandate, he expanded his work with Catholic Action cells both in his parish, the Archdiocese, and outside the Archdiocese as well.

All three groups making up the specialized lay apostolate (Christian Family Movement, Young Christian Workers, and Young Christian Students) share the Cardijn methodology of Catholic Action Cells (or small groups of 12 to 14 people). Their weekly meeting follows the same format: short Gospel discussion, liturgy discussion (on the Mass, Sunday, the liturgical year, Mystical Body ecclesiology, baptismal spirituality, Confirmation as the sacrament of Catholic Action, the connection between the liturgy and social justice, etc.), the social inquiry into some social problem, a report on actions taken, the help of a chaplain to prepare the discussion leaders and to speak twice at the meetings—after the gospel and liturgy discussions and at the conclusion of the meeting.[53]

A four-year training program was developed which covered these aspects of the lay apostolate: marriage and family, economic life, political life, international life, parochial life, leisure time, and the

---

52. Cardinal Stritch to Hillenbrand, April 6, 1945. UNDA, CMRH 7: Cardinal's Letters re: Movements and Catholic Action.

53. The Cardijn method is really an adaptation of Thomas' writings on the virtue of prudence in the Summa Theologica. Thomas talks about counsel, judgment, and command and Cardijn speaks of See, Judge, Act.

racial problem.[54] The spirituality of the program was based on the liturgy. Only by drawing close to the liturgy can the lay apostle make the priorities of Christ his or her own personal priorities. Consequently, liturgical life was the center and core of a deep Christian formation, which took seriously the layman's participation in the priesthood by virtue of their baptism and confirmation. To think that all the leadership, initiative, and responsibility for the apostolate could be clerical was "to have a deficient sense of the Church as a living, organic oneness of all its members."[55]

As we noted previously, Hillenbrand became convinced of the value of the Cardijn method through the influence of Donald Kanaly and Louis Putz. However, it was Hillenbrand's June 25, 1947 lecture at the YCW International Study Week in Montreal, Canada, that led to the establishment of the National Council of the YCW, the location of the national offices in Chicago, and his selection as National Chaplain of the Specialized Lay Apostolate.

After 1947, Hillenbrand travelled across the United States speaking at Study Weeks, Chaplain Training Programs, and Days of Renewal—all of which fostered his basic synthesis on liturgy and Catholic Action. In addition, Hillenbrand modeled at the liturgies of these conferences the type of active participation advocated by the Liturgical Conference. Since Stritch appointed him *Censor Liborum* (doctrinal editor) of all the publications of the Specialized Lay Apostolate, Hillenbrand proceeded to embody his synthesis in all their written materials.[56]

Hillenbrand's goal for his work with the Specialized Lay Apostolate was to create lifelong apostles who would restore all things in Christ. This vision was nothing unique but had been taught quite consistently by social and liturgical activists of the 1930s and 1940s. Among these activists, Hillenbrand saw most clearly the full implications of the encyclicals he studied so thoroughly. However, times change and the issues that produced *Quadragesimo Anno*, *Mystici*

---

54. Due to this specialized training in a contemporary apostolic method, the Catholic action cells became known as the specialized lay apostolate. See Hillenbrand's history of the YCW. UNDA, CMRH 10/16.

55. Hillenbrand, "Prayer and Sacrifice," April 1, 1948 lecture. UNDA, CMRH 18/26, YCW Priests' Study Weeks, 1948–1956.

56. Hillenbrand had outlines composed of the liturgical subjects covered in the national program booklets, which he edited and helped write. See UNDA, CMRH 17/11.

Corporis, and *Mediator Dei* eventually appeared outdated to many despite Hillenbrand's best efforts to keep them alive.[57]

Hillenbrand articulated the initial vision of the Christian Family Movement and helped write the liturgical sections of their first publication in 1949, *For Happier Families: How to Start a C.F.A. Section*, which became the basic training booklet for all CFM groups.[58] Hillenbrand attended most of the Coordinating Committee meetings of the Specialized Lay Apostolate, influencing them in much the same way as he had influenced the Program Committee of the Liturgical Conference. A high point in his involvement with CFM came with his widely acclaimed lecture, "Five-Point Social Plan," of August 21, 1955, at the CFM National Convention. This lecture, which basically revived the old liberal synthesis of the 1930s and 1940s, raised his stature and further solidified his conviction that the Cardijn methodology and his liturgical theology, based as it was on papal teachings, would last forever. However, resistance to Hillenbrand's leadership began to grow, when he stubbornly refused to accept new interpretations of Cardijn methodology or the new Eucharistic theology, which was emerging in the middle of that century.[59]

Lecturing at Schools and Study Weeks

In 1916, Justine Ward and Georgia Stephens founded the Pius X School of Liturgical Music at Manhattanville College of the Sacred Heart in New York. Virgil Michel asked Justine Ward to serve on the

---

57. See Andrew Greeley, *The Catholic Experience* (Garden City: Doubleday, 1967), Ch. 5: the Chicago Experience, p. 261, where he makes the point that Hillenbrand's vision, ideology, and theoretical thrust grew stale in the 1950s and by 1955 was highly questionable in the minds of many people. See Dennis Michael Robb, *Specialized Catholic Action in the United States, 1936-1949: Ideology, Leadership, and Organization*, Ph.D. dissertation (Minnesota: University of Minnesota, 1972), pp. 50–55 where Robb describes Hillenbrand's influence.

58. See John N. Kotre, *Simple Gifts: the Lives of Pat and Patty Crowley* (New York: Andrews and McMeel, 1979), p. 62: *For Happier Families* was a great success and sold 2,300 copies in over one hundred cities in the first year alone. See Martin Quigley & Edward Connors, *Catholic Action in Practice* (New York: Random House, 1963), pp. 111–168 for a short history of the development of CFM.

59. See Jeffrey Mark Burns, *American Catholics and the Family Crisis: 1930–1962, The Ideological and Organizational Response*, Ph.D. dissertation (Notre Dame: University of Notre Dame, 1982), pp. 281–299, where Burns describes the ideology of CFM, including its weaknesses. A less critical history of CFM is found in Rose M. Lucey, *Roots and Wings, Dreamers and Doers of the Christian Family Movement* (San Jose: Resource Publications, 1987). See pages 123–125, 250–253 for a discussion of the weaknesses of Hillenbrand's theology.

first board of associate editors of *Orate Fratres*.[60] Perhaps, it was through Virgil Michel that Hillenbrand first became acquainted with the Pius X School. Moreover, Hillenbrand was a musician himself—he could play the piano and he loved to sing.

As a well known liturgist, who strongly advocated the teaching of chant, Hillenbrand was invited back many times to teach at the Pius X School. In 1946, he presented his latest synthesis on the liturgy. In his course, he recommended greater participation in daily Mass, more frequent Communion, the use of the missal, the dialog Mass, the chanted Mass for all, more intelligent participation in the sacraments, wider use of the sacramentals, greater knowledge of the ritual, and singing the divine office.[61] While there was nothing unique about his ideas, his recommendations reflected the type of pastoral concerns that were being raised by liturgical leaders throughout the nation.

Hillenbrand was the first in the nation to organize a national summer school of liturgy in 1941. However, by 1947 it became apparent to Michael Mathis at the University of Notre Dame that more was required than simply the National Liturgical Weeks or attempts like Hillenbrand's summer school of Liturgy. As Mathis says:

> The chief difference between the Notre Dame program and that of preceding schools was to abandon the idea of offering courses to special groups of interested students—priests, brothers, sisters, and lay people, who could attend only for a limited period of the summer session—and to put it on an academic basis similar to all the other courses offered by the university.[62]

Lauds, a daily *Missa Cantata* with homily, Terce, None, and Compline were considered an integral part of the Notre Dame program. A liturgical forum was held each day on "Some Aspects of the Liturgy." It was at this forum that Reynold Hillenbrand was asked to speak.

The first Summer School at Notre Dame took place from June 17 to August 13, with a distinguished faculty that included Gerald Ellard, Godfrey Diekmann, Bernard Laukemper, Willis

---

60. See Madden, *The Liturgical Conference*, p. 8.

61. Hillenbrand, 1946 Course Notes. UNDA, CMRH 29/18.

62. Michael Mathis, 1947 Paper on the Notre Dame Liturgy Program. UNDA, CMRH 28/27.

Nutting, H. A. Reinhold, Bede Scholz, Damasus Winzen, and Reynold Hillenbrand, who lectured on "The Place of Liturgy in Catholic Action." In his lectures, he presented himself as a spokesman both for the liturgical and the social action movements in the country. He showed how

> both movements emphasize the re-emergence of the layman to the dignity of his proper place in the life of the Church. Both movements have for their object a fuller participation in divine life through grace.[63]

His talks at the first Notre Dame Summer School are a fine example of how much Hillenbrand had begun to embody the spirit of both the liturgical and the Catholic Action movements.

From 1944 to 1955, Hillenbrand's freedom from seminary responsibilities gave him the opportunity to lecture before Seminarian Study Weeks on Catholic Action across the nation. Of course, Hillenbrand was very popular. Here was a priest who not only had proven himself capable of working with seminarians, but also had a synthesis on liturgy and Catholic Action that was considered quite orthodox due to its basis in papal teaching. His success at the 1946 Seminarians Study Week at Notre Dame possibly influenced Mathis' decision to include him among the speakers at the 1947 Summer School.

SUMMARY

The period from 1944 to 1955 were filled with both triumphs and tragedy. Hillenbrand's programs at Sacred Heart Church were a tremendous example to the Archdiocese and the nation. His leadership and support of the goals of the Liturgical Conference played a major role in winning acceptance and official recognition of the theology and pastoral practices advocated in the National Liturgical Weeks. His work with the Vernacular Society, while less prominent than with the Conference, added credibility to this organization's goals. Unfortunately, his car accident in 1949 created physical problems that interfered with his ministry and caused him much pain.

Hillenbrand's work with the Specialized Lay Apostolate dominated the rest of his life. During this period, we see most plainly

---

63. Hillenbrand, "The Place of Liturgy in Catholic Action," July 7, 1947, lecture. UNDA, CMRH 28/27.

his inability to deal with the limitations of his theology and method: papal encyclicals are not the only source of orthodox teaching; the Cardijn method is not the only way to train lay apostles. Throughout this period, Hillenbrand enjoyed great popularity and widespread influence due to his lectures at Study Weeks, Chaplain Training Programs, Summer Schools, etc. and his editing of YCW, YCS, CFM publications. However, the first signs of his synthesis on liturgy and Catholic Action loosing its appeal become evident by 1955.

Chapter 4

Preparing for and Implementing Vatican II: 1956–1979

Reynold Hillenbrand's contributions to the American liturgical movement from 1955 to 1979 were made in his parish, in the specialized lay apostolate, in the Archdiocese of Chicago, in the Vernacular Society, and in the Liturgical Conference. Unfortunately, he was in and out of the hospital quite often during this period, undergoing operations or hospitalization in 1956, 1958, 1959, 1966, 1967, 1974–1979.[1] As mentioned before, Hillenbrand's illness and constant pain at times made him irritable, increased the pressures upon him, and interfered with the consistency of his ministry. Nonetheless, he seldom complained about his health, and maintained a very hectic schedule until his retirement on May 7, 1974.[2] He died on May 22, 1979, and his death was mourned by thousands of people in and outside the United States.[3]

LITURGICAL LEADERSHIP AT SACRED HEART CHURCH

In renovating Sacred Heart Church in 1957, Hillenbrand was influenced especially by H. A. Reinhold's book, *Speaking of Liturgical*

---

1. Hillenbrand's papers in the UNDA contain letters with information on the dates of his operations or hospitalizations. See UNDA, CMRH 32, Lay Apostolate, Correspondence, A-B; CMRH 33, Movement, Correspondence, 1951–1976; CMRH 32, Lay Apostolate, Correspondence, M; CMRH 32, Lay Apostolate Correspondence, Q–R–S; CMRH 32, Lay Apostolate Correspondence, J–K; CMRH 38, Correspondence, 1965; CMRH 38, Correspondence, 1975–1976.

2. John Cardinal Cody to Hillenbrand, May 7, 1974, accepting his resignation as pastor and appointing him pastor emeritus of Sacred Heart Church. UNDA, CMRH 38, Correspondence, 1961–1977.

3. See Robert McClory, "Hillenbrand: U.S. Moses," *National Catholic Reporter* 15 (Sept. 7, 1979), pp. 3, 38–39.

Architecture, Peter F. Anson's book, *Churches, Their Plan and Furnishing*, which Reinhold also edited, and Martin Hellriegel's theology of the Mass. Like Reinhold and Hellriegel, Hillenbrand believed that the parish church is primarily designed for the Eucharist and Baptism.[4] Consequently, he installed a new, free-standing, main altar more closely related to the nave, improved the lighting in the nave, and put a new baptismal font in the place where one of the old side altars formerly stood. In addition, Hillenbrand believed in eliminating shrines, stations, and other items that appeal to private devotion from the main worship space. And so, the Stations of the Cross were removed from the nave and placed along a side aisle of the church.[5]

Hillenbrand wanted a symbol for the sanctuary that complimented his liturgical theology and ecclesiology, which were based on the doctrine of the Mystical Body. And so, on February 25, 1957, he wrote his architect, Albert Harkness, the following:

> I do not favor any of the conventional symbols that are used in Catholic Churches. If we have to use a symbol anywhere, I should prefer "the Vine and the Branches," which Christ used as a symbol for the Church, the Mystical Body.[6]

Of course, such a request followed logically from Hillenbrand's definition of the liturgy as "the Mystical Body at worship."[7]

---

4. In 1957, Hillenbrand received the Cardinal's permission to celebrate Mass facing the people. He had a low, moveable tabernacle designed so that it could be removed from the main altar and used during the Triduum at the one side altar which he retained. Moreover, it was a simple task to remove the tabernacle permanently from the main altar to the side altar when this was allowed after Vatican II. Matching holy water fonts of the same stone and design as the new baptistry were placed at the doors of the church.

5. Hillenbrand called this side aisle "the cloisters" and to this day (1-20-89) the stations remain in this area. See H.A. Reinhold, *Speaking of Liturgical Architecture* (Notre Dame: University of Notre Dame, 1952), pp. 3, 5, 17. Reinhold was influenced by the designs of the German Architect, Rudolph Schwarz, and the 1947 German Liturgical Commission document, *Guiding Principles for Designing and Building a Church in the Spirit of the Roman Liturgy*, reprinted in Theodor Klauser, *A Short History of the Western Liturgy* (Oxford: Oxford University Press, 1979), Appendix II. See July 21, 1941 lecture of Martin Hellriegel, "The Holy Sacrifice of the Mass," Chicago School of Liturgy, 1941, Mundelein Seminary. UNDA, CMRH 28/23, Lectures of Martin Hellriegel.

6. Hillenbrand to Albert Harkness of Providence, Rhode Island, Feb. 25, 1957. UNDA, CMRH 38, Charlton Fortune, Correspondence.

7. Hillenbrand, "The Meaning of Liturgy," in *National Liturgical Weeks, 1941* (Newark: Benedictine Liturgical Conference, 1942), pp. 25–26.

Hillenbrand asked Professor Joseph O'Connell, who at that time was teaching art at St. John's University, to create a vine and the branches design in marble for the back wall of the sanctuary, a stone baptismal font with a crucifixion and resurrection design, matching holy water fonts, and a metal sculpture of Christ the teacher on the pulpit.[8] In addition, he hired the world-celebrated artist, Ivan Mestrovic, to design a crucifix which would be suspended over the main altar and new statues of St. Joseph and Mary, which were of higher quality, but less prominence than the old statues.[9]

Hillenbrand also obtained the advice of an artist, Charlton Fortune of the Monterey Guild (Newport, Rhode Island), in putting together a list of items that needed attention in the plans for the renovation.[10] However, he did not agree with Charlton in every recommendation. Nonetheless, her input enabled him to finalize his plan which he sent to his architect, covering all dimensions of the building: from ventilation to lighting fixtures (Rambusch Studios), from lessening the recesses in the area of the old side altars to a new screen (designed by Frank Kacmarcik) for the baptismal font, from a new ambry for oil stocks to new sanctuary furniture.[11] In addition to the above changes, in 1958 Hillenbrand installed a Wicks Pipe Organ and 14 bronze relief stations of the cross, created by the Quaker artist, Sylvia Shaw Judson.[12]

---

8. Joseph O'Connell related in an interview with the author, April 1, 1988, at the College of St. Benedict, that Hillenbrand was quite opinionated and stubborn. He wanted the vine and branches designed a certain way. When he first saw O'Connell's design, he was displeased. O'Connell told him: "I didn't have anything to do with it. God designed it and that's the way he wanted it." Hillenbrand laughed and agreed to accept the design. "He understood the creative process."

9. Hillenbrand's retention of the statues of Mary and Joseph in the sanctuary area was a compromise and possibly reflected the influence of the artist, Ivan Mestrovic. Joseph O'Connell in an interview with the author, April 1, 1988, at the College of St. Benedict, related that when Hillenbrand was not sure of what to do, he usually trusted the judgment of experts, allowing them to influence him.

10. See Letters from Charlton Fortune, 1956–1957. UNDA, CMRH 38, Charlton Fortune, Correspondence.

11. See Hillenbrand's 1957 notes to his architect concerning the details of the renovation. UNDA, CMRH 22/2, Church, Harkness and Geddes Architects, 1951–1958.

12. Hillenbrand's notes on Church renovation. UNDA, CMRH 22/2, Church, Harkness and Geddes Architects, 1957–1959. The organ was installed on October 6, 1958. On April 14, 1963, the *Chicago Tribune* had an article on the high quality of the Stations of the Cross. See CMRH 37, Correspondence, 1963, and CMRH 22/5, Parish, Stations of the Cross, Sylvia

Hillenbrand is shown in Sacred Heart Church after the 1957 parish renovation. As a pioneer of liturgical reform, Hillenbrand sought permission to say Mass "facing the people" in the late 1950s, shown here in the short interim period when tabernacles were still placed on altars. *Archives of the University of Notre Dame.*

One of the results of Hillenbrand's research for the renovation of Sacred Heart Church was an increase in visitors to see what a Church designed for active participation looked like. In addition, the renovation also produced a number of requests for Hillenbrand to share his insights on architecture, building and renovation in Catholic worship. For example, early in 1958 he lectured at the opening of the new headquarters of St. Benet's Library and Book Store on "Art and the Liturgy," in which he maintained that the liturgy is the most complete embodiment of the beauty of the Mystical Body.[13] On May 8, 1958 he lectured at the Fine Arts Festival at Clarke College in Dubuque, Iowa, on "Contemporary Church Art," spreading his synthesis to the Church outside Chicago.

In addition to his lectures on environment and art, Hillenbrand began to receive requests to critique the renovation plans of churches and cathedrals. He often used these requests as opportunities to teach a lesson on how to preside at the sacraments. For example, on August 20, 1964, Bishop Tracey of Baton Rouge sought Hillenbrand's guidance regarding the renovation of St. Joseph Cathedral.[14] In November,

Shaw Judson. So successful was Hillenbrand's renovation, that Sacred Heart Church today (12-1-88) is basically the way Hillenbrand renovated it.

13. Hillenbrand, "Art and the Liturgy," 1958 lecture. UNDA, CMRH 21/13.

14. Bishop Tracey to Hillenbrand, August 20, 1964, and Hillenbrand to Bishop Tracey, November, 1964. UNDA, CMRH 37, Correspondence, 1964.

(Left) Before the 1957 renovation of Sacred Heart Church. This renovation of was Hillenbrand's most significant intervention in the parish's physical plant. Hillenbrand knew well the artistic leaders of the Liturgical Movement. Hillenbrand was greatly influenced by the architectural standards of the day, which saw the altar, freestanding tabernacle, crucifix, and rear wall hanging to constitute the "liturgical altar." His renovation reveals the somewhat radical influence of the dominant architectural establishment, which preferred singularity of image to multiplicity. *Archives of the University of Notre Dame.*

(Right) Hillenbrand's signature intervention was the "Vine and Branches" sculpture by Joseph O'Connell on the rear wall of the sanctuary, a reminder to the people of their status as Mystical Body of Christ. The baptistery was moved to the front of the church to reinforce the connection between baptism and Eucharist. While Hillenbrand's renovation was certainly foreign to the architectural lines of the existing church, it nonetheless preserved the use of high quality marble for the altar and sanctuary and the highest level of craft, reiterating the importance of the sacred building and sacral action. This photo shows Sacred heart Church after the renovation in 1957. *Archives of the University of Notre Dame.*

1964 Hillenbrand recommended moving the font to the front of the Cathedral "to show the relationship of baptism and Eucharist." He also took this occasion to teach the bishop a lesson on how to baptize: greeting the baptismal party at the door of the church, walking down the center aisle while slowly saying the initiate prayers (the Lord's Prayer and Apostle's Creed), anointing the child with the oil of the catechumens at the end of the center aisle, processing to the font for the pouring of waters, asking all the baptized to light small candles from a large paschal candle and renew their own baptismal promises.[15]

---

15. The old rite provided for questions & prayers at the entrance of the church, the saying of the creed and Our Father in procession to the font, anointing before entering the baptistry, baptism in the baptistry. Hillenbrand's innovations involved the use of the paschal candle and the renewal of baptismal promises by all the baptized. Hillenbrand saw the rite of baptism at the Easter Vigil as the prototype for all baptism ceremonies. He also believed in using various stations (door, center aisle, baptistry), much like the revised rite of May 15, 1969. Many priests had abandoned the use of these stations.

He also recommended moving the organ console to the sanctuary and having the choir sit in the front pews of church, near the console.

The renovation of Sacred Heart Church provided Hillenbrand with the occasion to further the education of his people regarding art and environment. From March 3 to 17, 1957, he sponsored a contemporary art exhibit in Sacred Heart School with works from Marc Chagall, Margaret Dagenais, Eric Gill, Elaine Isaac, Henri Matisse, Ivan Mestrovic, Abbott Pattison, Georges Rouault, Raymond Toloczko, and others. Recognizing the fact that some people might find some of the religious art disturbing, Hillenbrand wrote in the brochure describing the exhibit:

> Many of us were reared in a misunderstanding of art as a conformity to nature. But art is a creative expression of an idea of the artist in terms of a new beauty in a form of his own devising. In this very poetic expression is to be found the talent and genius of the artist. He is not a copyist. Nature is not an end but a tool, a source, a point of departure.[16]

Not only does this brochure reveal Hillenbrand's openness to new artistic developments, but it also indicates that some of his parishioners may not have been happy with some of the art works that were on display.[17]

On September 3, 1958, the Sacred Congregation of Rites issued the *Instruction on Sacred Music and Sacred Liturgy.* While clearly supporting the Latin liturgy, it permitted a greater use of the vernacular, allowing lectors to read the Gospel and Epistle in the vernacular on Sundays and feast days. Hillenbrand had long prepared his parish for this day and immediately began the training of lay readers in the parish. From 1958 forward, Hillenbrand published a small booklet describing the ministry of reader and providing guidelines for the reader's participation in the liturgy. In his 1958 booklet, he wrote:

> It is a great privilege to break the bread, which is God's word, with your fellow parishioners . . . . By reading and helping the congregation with

---

16. Brochure, Sacred Heart School, Contemporary Religious Art Exhibit, March 3–17, 1957. UNDA, CMRH 25/1.

17. On March 3, 1957, Hillenbrand arranged for a panel discussion on religious art with Maurice Lavanoux, editor of *Liturgical Arts* magazine, George Culler, Director of the Dept. of Education at the Chicago Art Institute, and Sydney Harris, syndicated columnist and critic. On March 7, Alfred Caldwell, Associate Professor of Architecture at the Illinois Institute of Technology, spoke on "Faith and Form."

their prayer, you, a layman, are furthering the historic restoration of the laity's participation in the Mass.[18]

These booklets summarize the evolution of the reader's role in the liturgy at Sacred Heart Parish during Hillenbrand's tenure as pastor.

Hillenbrand also took the occasion of the 1958 Instruction to further educate his ushers on their role in the liturgy. In 1958 he wrote:

> As an usher, you are helping in a special way with the Mass to give it dignity and beauty, to create an atmosphere that makes it easier for people to worship, to love God. The setting of the Church is not enough; the people who help with the liturgy, as you do, can add much more.[19]

In addition to creating a suitable atmosphere for worship, Hillenbrand reminded the ushers to offer Mass themselves, to listen to the sermon, to make the responses, sing the hymns, use the leaflet Missal as much as they can, and receive Holy Communion every Sunday. Like his reader booklets, the usher booklets record the evolution of Sacred Heart's liturgy during Hillenbrand's pastorate.

Hillenbrand provided many other programs to keep his parish abreast of the latest developments in the liturgical movement. He had a six-year Study Club program on the liturgy, a parish library with over 800 volumes, a lecture series that included scholars such as Martin Marty, and regular evenings of renewal for the liturgical ministers. However, the chief source of input was always his homilies. Whenever a major document was issued by the Vatican Council or the *Concilium* or the Congregation of Divine Worship, Hillenbrand summarized its main points in his homilies and/or formed a small group to study it. With years of catechesis on the need for active participation, Sacred Heart Parish was among the very first parishes in the Archdiocese to implement the new rites as they appeared, always with an explanation from the pulpit by the pastor. Finally, Hillenbrand used his parish bulletin to print excerpts and short articles on the various documents that came out during and after the Council. Consequently, Sacred Heart Parish was well equipped to deal with the Vatican II mandated changes in the liturgy.

---

18. Hillenbrand, *Readers, Sacred Heart Church* (Winnetka: Sacred Heart Church, 1958), p. 1.
19. Hillenbrand, *Ushers, Sacred Heart Church* (Winnetka: Sacred Heart Church, 1958), p. 1.

Hillenbrand began to loose his influence in his parish with the onset of serious illness in 1973. Thomas Raftery was appointed administrator of the parish on August 31, 1973—a clear indication of Hillenbrand's declining health.[20] In the fall 1973, the parish School Board voted against Hillenbrand's policy of having a daily children's Mass, something he had worked long and hard for throughout the 1940s and early 1950s.[21] These troubles weighed heavy on his mind, almost overwhelming the obvious success his efforts at renewal had in the parish.

Liturgical Leadership in the Specialized Lay Apostolate

Hillenbrand kept a liturgical focus in the programs published by the Specialized Lay Apostolate, despite a growing desire to drop or modify the liturgy section of the meeting.[22] Repeatedly, Hillenbrand had to explain that the basic theology of these movements was centered in a correct understanding of Mass as a corporate act, church as the Mystical Body, the transforming power of divine life, and baptism/confirmation as a deputation for ministry.[23] In numerous talks on lay spirituality, Hillenbrand insisted on the necessity of Catholic action, on a return to the staples (daily Mass and Communion, mental prayer, penance, devotion to Mary, spiritual reading, spiritual direction) of the spiritual life, and on an appreciation of the basic theology of the movements.[24]

---

20. Raftery letter of Appointment as administrator. UNDA, CMRH 27/8, Chancery Office, Letters, 1938–1973.

21. See a complete description of the debate regarding the policy on a daily children's Mass in UNDA, CMRH 26/11, CMRH 26/21, CMRH 26/25, CMRH 26/28.

22. Criticisms were made that the liturgy sections were becoming repetitive. Part of the reason for this was that Hillenbrand refused to adopt the liturgical theology of the late 1950s and chose to repeat his 1940s synthesis. His notes from Coordinating Committee Meetings show his repeated defense of the old synthesis.

23. A good example of how Hillenbrand kept his 1940s synthesis as the rationale behind the movements is found in the "Fundamentals of the Christian Family Movement" section of the 1965 revision of *For Happier Families*. UNDA, CMRH 9/4, CMRH 10/12 *For Happier Families*, 1965.

24. Hillenbrand's August 29, 1958, lecture, "Review of the Essential Work of the Chaplain," at the CFM Chaplain's Meeting, Notre Dame is a good example of the theology that Hillenbrand fostered as national chaplain of the YCW, YCS, CFM. UNDA, CMRH 11/28.

Hillenbrand conveyed his conviction about the necessity of keeping a liturgical focus for the movements in his meetings with the chaplains of the Specialized Lay Apostolate. On August 29, 1958, he told the chaplains that they had to foster a better appreciation of the liturgy:

> One of the bloody struggles is to get the layman to understand what the liturgy is and through this understanding to lead to some participation which is the necessary object of our efforts in the parish.[25]

As we have seen, Hillenbrand believed the apostolate was rooted in the Mass. If one obtained the people's participation in the Mass, then one could get them interested in spreading Christ's redemption throughout the world by becoming lay apostles.[26]

Hillenbrand saw liturgical renewal and parish renewal as inseparable. At the Coordinating Committee Meeting of the Specialized Lay Apostolate, February 7, 1957, he said:

> The job for CFM is to allow Catholics to restore the parish to doing what it ought to be doing. And that means the restoration of the Mass. What impedes Christ in the world more than anything else? It's the fact that there is no participation of lay people, to speak of, in the Mass.[27]

He then spoke of the need for greater use of the Leaflet Missal, the dialog Mass, participation in the sung Mass, a song leader who would lead the singing from the front pew, receiving Communion at Mass, promoting family Communion, the importance of the Easter Vigil as a time for baptism, making baptism more of a ceremony by providing a small booklet so that people can participate and using baptismal robes at every baptism, catechesis at Mass on the liturgy, the implications of sharing in the common priesthood, the necessity of welcoming newcomers and improving hospitality.

A good example of how much emphasis was placed on liturgy in the yearly program of the Specialized Lay Apostolate is the 1956–1957 YCW program, "Working Together." Hillenbrand's papers listed the liturgical subjects covered that year:

---

25. Hillenbrand, "Review of the Essential Work of the Chaplain," August 29, 1958, lecture. UNDA, CMRH 11/28.

26. Hillenbrand, "Lay Spirituality," April 13, 1961, lecture. UNDA, CMRH 11/28.

27. Hillenbrand, "The Parish is Christ," February 7, 1957, lecture. UNDA, CMRH 11/28.

Mass is Calvary,

The difference between Calvary and Mass,

Mass is a sacrifice: gift-offering,

Mass is a great act of love,

Mass is something we do together,

Mass is the corporate worship of the Mystical Body,

Mass is the great teacher,

Taking an active part in Mass,

Using a missal,

The dialog Mass and sung Mass,

Receiving communion at Mass,

Communion and consecration,

Mass is a privilege more than an obligation,

Mass brings redemption to our own time,

Weekday Mass,

All Saints and All Souls Day,

Advent, Christmas, Lent, Palm Sunday, Holy Thursday, Good Friday,

Easter Vigil, Easter Week, Pentecost, Sacred Heart, St. Joseph the Worker,

Immaculate Heart of Mary,

The rosary, mental prayer, daily prayer, compline, etc.[28]

Hillenbrand noted that 25 meetings of the 1956–57 program were devoted to the Mass, 17 meetings covered feasts and seasons, and 9 meetings covered prayer. By adamantly refusing to drop the liturgy sections from the national programs of the Specialized Lay Apostolate, Hillenbrand undoubtedly contributed a great deal to the success of the liturgical movement in this country. For the people in these movements were given the type of education needed to appreciate the changes that were mandated by the popes in this century and especially at Vatican II.[29] In addition, many of these "lay apostles" went on to take leadership roles in their parish by helping to establish the new liturgy.[30]

28. Hillenbrand, "List of Liturgy Subjects, Working Together, 1956–1957." UNDA, CMRH 17/11. This program serves as a reference point for all future programs. It represents a faithful summary of Hillenbrand's liturgical synthesis from his seminary liturgy course and his talks at National Liturgical Weeks.

29. On August 10, 1960, at the YCW Convention, St. Joseph College, Rensselear, Indiana, Hillenbrand spoke on "Why Mass Participation," giving his usual rationale for active participation and then predicting changes (greater use of vernacular, offertory processions, etc.) coming in the liturgy, explaining what the Liturgical Conference is, how we can promote participation in parochial liturgy, etc. UNDA, CMRH 15/1.

30. In 1965, YCW changed its name to the Young Christian Movement. Hillenbrand's papers show the YCM had 200 groups in 43 dioceses with a membership in excess of 2500 in

Hillenbrand organized numerous study weeks, evenings of recollection, and conventions for the specialized lay apostolate. These events provided opportunities to expose the participants to good liturgy. He always used the dialog Mass or the sung Mass. He encouraged the use of English songs before and after Mass, a homily which was frequently on the Mass, a Latin Offertory hymn often sung by the people, an offertory procession (whenever the ordinary of the place would allow it), congregational singing at Communion time, lay readers, and lay song leaders.[31]

So important was the celebration of the liturgy, that it came to be viewed as the center of the entire study week, renewal day, or convention.[32] Moreover, Hillenbrand frequently used these occasions to explain his hopes for future changes in the liturgy or, after Vatican II, the changes that were occurring in the liturgy. Finally, during the interim period after the promulgation of the *Liturgy Constitution* and before the publication of the new Roman Missal, Hillenbrand was often asked to be the presider at the Study Week or Convention Masses so that he could demonstrate the correct way to celebrate the new liturgy.

On February 17, 1965, Albert Cardinal Meyer wrote the priests of the Archdiocese that he was opposed to experimental celebrations of the Eucharist that did not follow the rubrics then in force.[33] However, CFM began to engage in such experiments regardless of the Cardinal's and Rome's admonitions. At the February 11–13,

---

1964. UNDA, CMRH 20/7. In 1966 there were over 200 college YCS groups on 150 campuses and parishes. High School YCS had grown to 35,000 from 25,000 in 1960. UNDA, CMRH 12/20 and CMRH 13/2. In 1965, there were 7,000 CFM groups in the U.S., 40,000 couples, only 7 dioceses were without CFM. UNDA, CMRH 7: Cardinal's letters regarding movements & Catholic Action. See Jeffrey Mark Burns, *American Catholics and the Family Crisis 1930–1962*, p. 285: "By 1952, 5000 couples from 200 cities and 7 foreign countries belonged to CFM, increasing to 20,000 couples in 1956, 30,000 in 1958, and peaking in 1963 with close to 40,000 couples."

31. Hillenbrand, "Participation in View of Pius XII's Decree," August 26, 1959, lecture. UNDA, CMRH 11/16 and CMRH 11/28.

32. The brochure from the August, 1958, YCS Study Week in Memphis, Tennessee, clearly states: "The Study Week centers around the Mass, which is offered in the center of each day; it provides four days of intensive Christian living, plus motivation for an apostolic life in YCS upon one's return to school or parish." UNDA, CMRH 12/25.

33. Albert Cardinal Meyer to the priests of the Archdiocese of Chicago, Feb. 17, 1965. UNDA, CMRH 37, Mixture of letters from Diocese, Hillenbrand's Retirement, Parish Correspondence.

1966, Coordinating Committee meeting a proposal was discussed "to celebrate the Eucharistic banquet in a more meaningful manner" by fostering home Masses around dining room tables, on the pattern of a "dinner party," totally in English, without vestments, with general absolution, with intercommunion between Catholics and Protestants, with Catholic and Protestant clergy concelebrating together, and omitting the "irrelevant parts of the liturgy" (e.g., the names of saints no longer familiar to us, parts of the canon—seraphim and cherubim were deemed hard to believe—and prayers at the foot of the altar). In addition, the proposal was also made to abandon the parish as a base for CFM and the Cardijn methodology used to construct its program.[34] As one might expect, Hillenbrand was greatly shaken by this direct challenge of the areas he had invested so much of his energy into: an understanding of liturgy consistent with papal/conciliar teaching, the importance of a parish base for the small groups, and the necessity of staying with the SEE-JUDGE-ACT methodology.

From 1966 on, Hillenbrand's work with the CFM began to turn sour. Hillenbrand's abrasive, inconsistent leadership was openly opposed. CFM members were caught up in the euphoria that followed the council. The minutes of the Executive Committee meetings demonstrated the increasing resistance of its membership to Hillenbrand's insistence that they stick to the old "fundamentals," which we have already explained. CFM leadership was interested in pushing for more reforms than were allowed at the time. When the Executive Committee voted to have an Episcopal priest celebrate the closing Mass of the 1968 convention, Hillenbrand rightly became completely disillusioned. At the same time, CFM also ceased submitting its annual program to Hillenbrand for censorship.[35]

Hillenbrand's disillusionment with CFM is evident in a 1972 letter he wrote to Bishop Floyd Begin of Oakland, California, discouraging his sponsorship of CFM in his diocese. Hillenbrand blamed the difficulties he was having with CFM on what he called "extreme ecumenism."

---

34. UNDA, CMRH 10/8, CFM Executive Committee, 1963–1966.

35. Burns, *American Catholics and the Family Crisis*, p. 330. CFM was largely a Catholic organization. This decision to have a Protestant clergyman preside at the closing Eucharist indicates CFM's willingness to abandon church policy on intercommunion.

I was at their executive committee meeting in March . . . . I had the
impression that the Protestants want to make the movement unidentifiable
as a Catholic movement, and they want to be more prominent in it. But it
is a Catholic movement and the office is answerable to the local ordinary,
Cardinal Cody.[36]

Notice how Hillenbrand speaks of "their" meeting, clearly
indicating his disaffection from the group. By 1976, Hillenbrand had
decided that CFM "is no longer (Catholic) apostle forming . . . no
longer Jocist training."[37]

The separation from CFM must have been extremely difficult
for Hillenbrand. He had become so identified with the Specialized
Lay Apostolate, that Bishop Ernest Primeau, who was on the Conciliar
commission preparing the *Schema Decreti, De Apostolatu Laicorum*,
sent Hillenbrand a copy of the Schema and sought his critique of the
document. On August 7, 1964, Hillenbrand wrote Bishop Primeau,
suggesting that the commission strengthen the sections of the document that deal with the training of lay apostles. He also gave a list of
the type of church-activities he believed lay people should be involved
in: teaching convert classes, instructing individual converts, reconciling
fallen-away Catholics, directing the CCD program, giving instruc-
tions for mixed marriage, doing Pre-Cana conferences, managing the
parish finances, serving on Parish School Boards, representing the
pastor at board and sodality meetings, serving in the liturgical ministries (readers, commentators, song leaders, musicians, choir members,
ushers, servers), serving on diocesan liturgical commissions, etc. In
addition, he summarized his 1955 "Five-Point Social Plan" in describing the layman's responsibilities in the world and the topics he included
in his chaplain's training course.[38] Finally, he made it clear that the
liturgy is not just another form of prayer, but "the most important of
all the things we do."[39]

---

36. Hillenbrand to Bishop Floyd Begin, July 24, 1972. UNDA, CMRH 11/30, Movements,
CFM, 1972.

37. Hillenbrand to the Board of Directors, March 15, 1976. UNDA, CMRH 12/2.

38. Hillenbrand to Bishop Ernest Primeau, August 7, 1964. UNDA, CMRH 9/4, Movement,
Vatican II, Hillenbrand, Consultant on Lay Apostolate, 1964. Hillenbrand's letter is noteworthy
for breaking out of the old clergy/laity distinction (clergy are responsible for church, laity are
responsible for the world) and for recognizing the laity's role in the liturgical ministries.

39. Ibid. On October 16, 1964, Bishop Primeau wrote to Hillenbrand: "The bishops looked
over your modi, signed them, and that afternoon, Monday, George Higgins, who is on the

LITURGICAL LEADERSHIP IN
THE ARCHDIOCESE OF CHICAGO

On March 6, 1964, Cardinal Meyer appointed Hillenbrand to the Archdiocesan Liturgical Commission.[40] The Commission worked with the Liturgy Training Program (hereafter referred to as LTP) under the direction of Theodore Stone, the Archdiocesan Director of CCD, and Thomas and Mae Dore. In the fall of 1964, 51 parish centers were established throughout the Archdiocese to train lay people to serve as lectors, commentators, leaders of song, and presiders. Over 11,000 people participated in these fall training sessions. After its success in getting people ready for the first changes of the Second Vatican Council that took place on the First Sunday of Advent, 1964, LTP went on to become the liturgical publication and training arm of the Liturgical Commission.[41] Of course, Hillenbrand's long experience training liturgical ministers was drawn upon in the early days of the Commission and LTP.

The Commission was involved in sponsoring demonstration Masses that would be "complete and perfect examples of the liturgical celebration according to the revised liturgy."[42] The Liturgical Commission provided pastoral, spiritual, technical, rubrical, and ceremonial preparation for these Masses. Hillenbrand was heavily involved in these early programs. He was one of four priests selected by the Commission on May 14, 1964, to say a demonstration Mass according to the interim guidelines then in effect. This Mass took place on May 22, 1964.[43]

Hillenbrand's 1964 report to the Commission gives a good synthesis of the type of issues that were being addressed by the Commission in these early meetings: why a priest no longer needs

---

Commission, brought them to the Commission and made sure they will be considered in the redrafting of the text." UNDA, CMRH 9/3, Movement, Council, Vatican II, Hillenbrand Consultant.

40. Cardinal Meyer to Hillenbrand, March 6, 1964. UNDA, CMRH 28/10.

41. See Harry C. Koenig, *Caritas Christi Urget Nos, A History of the Offices, Agencies, and Institutions of the Archdiocese of Chicago, Vol. I* (Chicago: Archdiocese of Chicago, 1981), "Liturgy Training Program," pp. 118–122.

42. Cardinal Meyer to the priests of the Archdiocese, Feb. 17, 1965. UNDA, CMRH 37, Mixture of letters from Diocese, Hillenbrand's Retirement, Parish Correspondence.

43. Liturgical Commission Minutes, May 14, 1964. UNDA, CMRH 28/7, Liturgical Commission Works, 1959–1965.

to keep his fingers held together after the consecration; the Mass is a sacrifice when speaking of the consecration, but a meal when speaking of communion; food and drink are symbols of life; the offertory is a preparation for the giving of oneself at the consecration; the important symbolism of the Mystical Body in one bread of many grains of wheat; hopefully, a Mass totally in the vernacular; possibly, a Mass with everything in the vernacular except the Canon; learning English chants for the Collects, *Gloria*, Creed, Preface, *Sanctus*, Lord's Prayer, Embolism, *Agnus Dei*; use of a presider's chair, new style vestments, processional cross; care in the use of English words rather than words lifted from Latin (e.g., reader instead of lector, leader of song instead of cantor, celebrant instead of president); use of good translations.[44] Most of Hillenbrand's recommendations were adopted by the Commission for its early study days.

Hillenbrand was very much involved in the debate that surrounded the publication of an Archdiocesan Directory on the Liturgy. It's here that Hillenbrand's perceived theological limitations (adherence to earlier papal documents) began to surface once again. Edmund Siedlecki, a member of the Commission with an STD and eventually the chairman of the Liturgy Advisory Board, warned Hillenbrand that his attempt to read into the Constitution on the Sacred Liturgy *(Sacrosanctum Concilium)* the same theology as was expressed in *Mediator Dei* was a serious error.[45] He explained that the Constitution on the Sacred Liturgy represented new developments in scholarship and new insights that supersede those of *Mediator Dei*. However, Hillenbrand remained convinced that *Mediator Dei* "is not superseded in the doctrine it teaches."[46] He even went so far as to oppose the Commission by writing Cardinal Meyer to protest the wording of the Directory, stating that it does not adequately emphasize the element of sacrifice in its description of the Mass, but overemphasized the element of the meal.[47] Hillenbrand's protest to the Cardinal succeeded and the Commission was asked to revise the Directory.

44. Hillenbrand's 1964 Suggestions to the Liturgical Commission. UNDA, CMRH 28/14, Liturgical Commission.

45. Edmund Siedlecki to the author, August 5, 1987.

46. Hillenbrand's 1964 Suggestions to the Liturgical Commission. UNDA, CMRH 28/14, Liturgical Commission.

47. Hillenbrand to Cardinal Meyer, November 4, 1964. UNDA, CMRH 35, Correspond. with Stritch, Meyer, 1953 -1971.

Cardinal Meyer, having heard of the great success Hillenbrand had with his music program at Sacred Heart Church, sought Hillenbrand's counsel regarding the approval of English chants in the Mass. On November 5, 1964, Hillenbrand wrote to Cardinal Meyer in Rome that

> Some parishes, I am sure, would be ready to have their people sing the English High Mass. We have adapted our simple Gregorian chant melodies to the exact English text—with fine effect. It puts to rest the idea that Gregorian Chant is not suitable to our language. I enclose the pages of the Sung Mass Booklet which we have been using and the new adaptations for the English."[48]

Hillenbrand cautioned against accepting the suggestion that the low Mass be in English and the High Mass in Latin, because this would penalize the popularity of the High Mass when the changes were to begin on the first Sunday of Advent.

In addition to his work on the original study days to prepare the people of the Archdiocese for the changes in the liturgy, Hillenbrand also helped compose the 1966 Archdiocesan survey on the progress of liturgical renewal.[49] He received permission on March 28, 1968 to have Sacred Heart Church participate in the Funeral Mass experiment that was sponsored by the Liturgical Commission in conjunction with the Bishop's Committee on the Liturgy.[50] However, Hillenbrand's influence and involvement with the Liturgical Commission began to diminish as soon as Gerard Broccolo, the new professor of liturgy at Mundelein Seminary, returned from Rome with his doctorate in liturgy from the College of Sant' Anselmo.

On September 3, 1968, Cardinal Cody appointed Gerard Broccolo as Secretary of the Liturgical Commission. One of the first things Broccolo did was share with the Commission a short synopsis

---

48. Hillenbrand to Cardinal Meyer, November 5, 1964. UNDA, CMRH 37 Correspondence, 1963–1965. In addition to Bishop Primeau and Cardinal Meyer seeking Hillenbrand's counsel, Bishop S. Young wrote Hillenbrand on September 24, 1963: "With deep interest I read the notes you kindly sent me. I thank you for the insights thus given me and am making use of them." UNDA, CMRH 9/3, Movement, Council, Vatican II, Hillenbrand Consultant.

49. Liturgy Questionnaire. UNDA, CMRH 22/16, Liturgy of the Saints, Liturgy Questionnaire.

50. See UNDA, CMRH 28/2, Archdiocese, Liturgy, 1966–1971 and *BCL Newsletter*, January, 1967, Vol. 3, No. 1 which contains the "General Principles for the Experiment with the Rite of Funerals."

of the fruit of his research for his doctoral dissertation on the relationship between liturgy and Church.[51] He knew of the conflict over the
1965 Directory and so he provided the Commission with an article on
"The Eucharist as Sacrifice," addressing "the fear some priests express
of destroying the sacrificial aspect of the Mass by emphasizing its
"banquet" aspect."[52]

Shortly after Broccolo returned from his studies in Rome,
the Commission was reorganized and Bishop Thomas Grady was
appointed chairman on November 27, 1968.[53] For a time Hillenbrand
served as chairman of the Liturgical Commission's Subcommission on
the Laity, but this chairmanship was more honorary than real. The
real work of the Commission increasingly passed into the hands of
liturgists like Broccolo, Siedlecki, and the Commission's newest member, Daniel Coughlin, an associate pastor at Holy Name Cathedral.

On October 16, 1970, Cardinal Cody appointed Daniel
Coughlin the Director of the Office for Divine Worship, which was to
work "in conjunction with the Archdiocesan Liturgical Commission,
under the chairmanship of Bishop Thomas T. Grady, with Rev. Gerard
T. Broccolo as consultant."[54] The establishment of the Office for
Divine Worship effectively ended the work of the Commission. The
Office basically took over the responsibilities for coordinating LTP,
supervising the implementation of the new rites, setting up parish

---

51. See Gerard Broccolo, *Prophetic Fellowship, The Ecclesial Dynamic of Christian Liturgy*,
S.T.D. dissertation, (Rome: Pontificium Anthenaeum Anselmianum, 1970). Broccolo's
dissertation director was Salvatore Marsili, the director of and professor of theology at the
Pontifical Liturgical Institute of Sant' Anselmo in Rome. Marsili was an expert on Eucharist
and a good summary of Marsili's theology is found in "The Mass, Paschal Mystery and
Mystery of the Church," in *The Liturgy of Vatican II, Vol. II*, ed. William Barauna, trans. Jovian
Lang (Chicago: Franciscan Herald Press, 1966), pp. 3-25. Basically, Marsili advocates the
theory of the Eucharist being a sacrament of a sacrifice, a Communion memorial, a celebration
of the Paschal Mystery.

52. Gerard Broccolo, "The Eucharist as Sacrifice." UNDA, CMRH 28/11, Liturgical
Commission, 1961–1968.

53. UNDA, CMRH 28/11, Liturgical Commission, 1961–1968.

54. Francis W. Byrne, Vicar General, to the clergy, religious, superiors of institutions, and
laity of the Archdiocese, October 16, 1970. UNDA, CMRH 27/8, Chancery Office, Letters,
1938–1973. On September 20, 1988, Dan Coughlin related to this author that Hillenbrand's
involvement with the Commission basically ended with the reorganization of the Commission
under Bishop Grady. Grady wanted to address some of the issues that Broccolo had begun
to raise and get beyond the norms found in the old Archdiocesan Directory. Hillenbrand
became increasingly uncomfortable at these meetings. And so, he lessened his Archdiocesan
work in liturgy and became more involved with Catholic Action work, e.g. the Catholic
Interracial Council.

liturgy committees, and training liturgical ministers.[55] With the founding of the Office, liturgy had begun a new era in Chicago without Hillenbrand's leadership.

SHARING THE VICTORY OF
THE VERNACULAR SOCIETY

Hillenbrand maintained a close relationship with John Ross-Duggan, the Secretary of the Vernacular Society. Ross-Duggan was a frequent visitor at Sacred Heart Rectory, staying several months at a time if he had business in Chicago. Often, Ross-Duggan was in Europe attending the various Liturgical Weeks, the Lugano and Assisi Conferences, the 1951 and 1957 World Congress on the Lay Apostolate, and finally the Second Vatican Council. Through Ross-Duggan and the Vernacular Society Bulletin, Hillenbrand kept abreast of the European developments in the liturgical movement.[56] So much of Hillenbrand's efforts were directed at increasing active participation in the liturgy that he was a natural audience for Ross-Duggan's stories about liturgies he attended while on his many trips abroad.[57]

On September 1, 1965, Hillenbrand supported the decision of the Board of Directors of the Vernacular Society to incorporate their group into the National Liturgical Conference. The resolution that the Board approved reads:

> Whereas the mind of the Church on the use of the vernacular in worship is so happily evidenced by the Council fathers in the Constitution on the Sacred Liturgy, the major objectives of the Vernacular Society have been attained, and in as much as future developments in regard to the use of the mother tongue in worship could be achieved through a united effort, be it resolved: that the members of the Vernacular Society should continue their efforts within the framework of the Liturgical Conference.[58]

---

55. Ibid. See Koenig, *A History of the Institutions of the Archdiocese of Chicago, Vol. I*, "Office for Divine Worship," pp. 86–91.

56. See *The Vernacular Society Bulletin*, July 14, 1950, p. 2 where Ross-Duggan says Cardinal Suhard authorized new altars facing the people and that this was the custom in at least 25% of the city churches.

57. Ross-Duggan to Hillenbrand, July 10, 1965: "May I reiterate the gratitude of all our members to you for your attachment to the vernacular cause down through the years." UNDA, CMRH 29/9 Liturgy, Vernacular Society Correspondence, 1950–1964.

58. "Vernacular Society to Merge with the Liturgical Conference," *Liturgy* 10 (1965), p. 4.

Hillenbrand had long supported an all-vernacular liturgy or at least a greater use of the vernacular in the liturgy.[59] This vote signified the triumph of one of his great dreams. At the time the Vernacular Society joined the Liturgical Conference it had over 10,000 members.[60]

The New Theology of the Liturgical Conference

While Hillenbrand attended and spoke at the August 20–23, 1965, Liturgical Week in London, Ontario, Canada, he failed to appreciate the full implications of the Resolutions passed by the Board of Directors at this Week. While giving credit to Pius XII for laying the foundations of liturgical renewal in the Encyclicals *Mystici Corporis* and *Mediator Dei*, the Board indicated that contemporary efforts at reform were making "a use of history which respects the past without being held by its dead hand," and advocating "a simplification and stressing of those elements which are most important theologically and most conducive to divine worship."[61] In other words, there was fresh research beginning to make its impact on liturgical renewal, research with which Hillenbrand did not agree. Most likely, his attention was focused more on the practical recommendations: petitioning for the Mass of the Catechumens to be in the vernacular, limitations on the use of the Requiem (Black) Mass, reinstating the prayer of the faithful, making the Last Gospel a private prayer of the priest, etc.

Hillenbrand was certainly a great ambassador of the practical recommendations of the Liturgical Conference. He supported these recommendations in countless talks before the many groups he was associated with. However, his preoccupation with papal encyclicals as the determining factor of his liturgical theology brought serious limitations to his theological growth. A major breakthrough in theology

---

59. On June 15, 1962, Hillenbrand circulated a Vernacular Society petition in his parish "that in the USA and English-speaking Canada permission be granted to celebrate the liturgy in the English language so that all may understand what is being said and done, to the greater glory and honor of God and the good of souls." This petition was sent to the Fathers of the Vatican Council through Archbishop Pericle Felici, Secretary-General of the Central Preparatory Commission, Rome. UNDA, CMRH 28/2.

60. "Lt. Col. John Ross-Duggan, Liturgical-Reform Leader, Dies. Well Known Catholic Layman Sought Use of Vernacular -Served British Army," *New York Times*, Feb. 4, 1967.

61. UNDA, CMRH 28/28, Liturgical Conference Resolutions.

occurred in December, 1963 with the publication of Francis X. Durrwell's, *La Résurrection de Jésus mystère de salut*. This book was translated in 1964 by Rosemary Sheed, and published as *The Resurrection*.

The significance of *The Resurrection* for liturgical research was that it signaled the movement away from viewing the death of Christ as the redemptive moment and the resurrection only being a proof of Christ's divinity. It began the movement toward seeing the death and resurrection as one unitive act in the mystery of redemption. Hillenbrand's theological scope never went beyond *Mystici Corporis* and *Mediator Dei*. As we have seen, illness and his heavy workload with the lay apostolate resulted in his liturgical theology becoming outdated during the 1960s and led to his demise with the Liturgical Conference and his own Archdiocesan Liturgical Commission.[62] One of the reasons he abandoned his work with the Liturgical Conference and Archdiocesan Liturgical Commission in the late 1960s may have been his recognition of his theological limitations.[63]

THE FINAL YEARS: 1974–1979

Hillenbrand's last six years (1974–1979) were marked by several operations and lengthy periods of hospitalization. These were distressing times in Hillenbrand's life. His influence in the parish had begun to wane with the appointment of an administrator, Thomas

---

62. As early as the 1961 Liturgical Week, we find emphasis on the passion, death, and resurrection of Christ as part of one redemptive unit in a lecture by A. Boberek, "Liturgy and Spiritual Growth," *National Liturgical Week, 1961* (Washington: Liturgical Conference, 1962), p. 100. On August 20, 1962, Godfrey Diekmann explained the theology of the resurrection in "First Born from the Dead," *National Liturgical Week, 1962* (Washington: Liturgical Conference, 1963), pp. 16–28. At the August 24–27, 1964 Liturgical Week Godfrey Diekmann made explicit reference to the theology of Paschal Mystery in the *Liturgy Constitution* in "The Full-Sign of the Eucharist," *National Liturgical Week, 1964* (Washington: Liturgical Conference, 1964), p. 87. In his talk, Diekmann also mentioned the need to reunite the sacrificial and meal aspects of the Eucharist. In this, he reflected the same theology, fostered by Siedlecki and Broccolo in Chicago. In 1964, Robert Hovda spoke on "The Paschal Mystery and the Liturgical Year," *National Liturgical Week, 1964*, pp. 51–66. Hillenbrand attended this 1964 Liturgical Week, but never seemed to grasp the full significance of Diekmann's and Hovda's talks. See Hillenbrand's notes from the 1964 Liturgical Week. UNDA, CMRH 29/3.

63. While recognizing Hillenbrand's theological limitations, Godfrey Diekmann also praised Hillenbrand's work as an associate editor of *Orate Fratres*. On June 17, 1966, Diekmann wrote that "there can be few spiritual leaders in the history of the Church in our country who have inspired more people profoundly, and with life-long effect." UNDA, CMRH 9/8, Movement, Reunion to Honor Msgr. Hillenbrand, 1976.

Raftery. The Specialized Lay Apostolate had drastically declined in membership and much of his synthesis had been abandoned.[64] However, he was consoled by the fact that many of his ideals had been adopted by the Second Vatican Council. He lived to see the transition to an all-vernacular liturgy. His lifelong commitment to raise the consciousness of the laity as to their rightful place in the Church was not in vain. People at Sacred Heart Parish, in the Archdiocese, in the Specialized Lay Apostolate, and at Liturgical Weeks better understood their identity as a baptized Christians due to his efforts. In addition, a whole generation of clerical and lay leaders was inspired to follow him in the work of the liturgical and social action movements.

When he was near death, his old student and longtime protege, John Egan, comforted Hillenbrand when Hillenbrand suggested that he may have wasted his life working with the specialized lay apostolate. Egan reminded Hillenbrand of what he had taught him many years ago: that liturgy must be connected with daily life.

To the extent that liturgy is unconnected with daily life, it leads us either to a premature withdrawal from this world as beyond hope or to passive accommodation which confines love, peace, and justice to church gatherings, but allows them no role in public life, in work, in economics, politics, or culture.[65]

Hillenbrand's life had inspired many individuals to dedicate their lives to continuing Christ's ministry in the world, and to making the liturgy the source and center of the apostolate, to making those connections between liturgy and social justice, which were the hallmark of his ministry.[66]

---

64. See Rory V. Ellinger, "Decline and Fall of a Student Movement," *Commonweal* 89 (Jan. 30, 1969), p. 346 and Jeffrey M. Burns, *American Catholics and the Family Crisis, 1930-1962*, pp. 317-334. See Harry C. Koenig, *History of the Offices, Agencies, and Institutions of the Archdiocese of Chicago, Vol. I*, "Catholic Action Federations," p. 215: "by the early 1970s, the movements had experienced a great decline in membership. In fact, YCW and YCS had practically ceased to exist and CFM had a membership of about 600 couples."

65. John J. Egan, *Liturgy and Justice: An Unfinished Agenda*, Collegeville: Liturgical Press, 1983, 20. A reprint of a lecture delivered at a Liturgical Consultation at Boston College, June 21, 1983. At that time, John J. Egan was Director of the Office of Human Relations and Ecumenism of the Archdiocese of Chicago.

66. See Daniel M. Cantwell, "Homily Preached at the Eucharist Celebrating the Life and Passing of Msgr. Reynold Hillenbrand," *Liturgy 70* 10 (1979), pp. 2-4.

During this final period of Hillenbrand's life he was involved in many important projects which fostered the spread of the ideals of the liturgical movement in this country. From his influential work at Sacred Heart Church to the many Study Weeks, Days of Renewal, and Conventions that he conducted for the Specialized Lay Apostolate, from his work with the Archdiocesan Liturgical Commission to his involvement with the Vernacular Society and the Liturgical Conference, Hillenbrand demonstrated the tenacity of a fighter whose quest was rooted in achieving a vision, which he learned from his study of the liturgy. While his physical problems brought him much pain and discomfort and limited his effectiveness with people, he nonetheless won their respect and admiration. For Hillenbrand was a genuine apostle, a man who believed the Gospel, preached what he believed, and practiced what he preached.

Part II

Reynold Hillenbrand's Liturgical Theology: Influences and Development

Chapter 5

Hillenbrand's Principle of Liturgical Theology

Hillenbrand based his liturgical theology upon certain fundamental principles: anthropology, grace, Christology, ecclesiology, and liturgiology. He embodied these principles in his numerous lectures and writings as well as the many publications of the Specialized Lay Apostolate which he edited. His use of these principles represented the movement away from the narrow confines of the inductive method, which was typical of Neo-scholastic theologians, to a deductive method, which drew upon the data of culture and history. In this chapter, we shall examine the sources of these principles and Hillenbrand's application of them.

ANTHROPOLOGY AND DIVINE LIFE

Like Virgil Michel, Gerald Ellard, and other Neo-scholastic theologians, Hillenbrand defined human beings as creatures created by God to share His divine life.[1] Yet, human beings can frustrate God's plan of salvation by living merely on a natural level, unaware of a higher level of existence. The Church must teach people that "the most fundamental truth about our race, excepting only the truth of God . . . is the new life, the divine life."[2] Consequently, natural human life is a foundation for participation in divine (supernatural) life.

---

1. See Thomas Aquinas, *Summa Contra Gentiles*, 1. ii. 56; Virgil Michel, The Christian in the World (Collegeville: Liturgical Press, 1939), pp.1 7; Gerald Ellard, *Christian Life and Worship* (Milwaukee: Bruce Publishing Company, 1933), pp.28–30; and Hillenbrand, Liturgy Course Notes. UNDA, CMRH 4/12. Hillenbrand never speaks of human beings without referring to the doctrine of divine life.

2. Hillenbrand, "The New Life," in *National Liturgical Week 1948* (Conception: Liturgical Conference, 1949), p. 28.

At the beginning of creation, God gave the first human a new life, a sharing in the very nature of God (cf. 2 Peter 1:4).[3] As a result of this union, humans partook of the prerogatives of God, prerogatives which are above all created nature.[4] Adam's sin cost humankind its share in the divine life and its destiny to participate in the oneness of God for all eternity. Christ's mission was to restore to humankind a share in divine life and reestablish their oneness with God and God's children.[5]

The result of participating in the divine nature is a form of deification or divinization that transforms humans and empowers them to act as God acts.[6] As Hillenbrand said:

> Divine life, sanctifying grace, makes us divine. It is not enough to *be*; we must also *act*. The most perfect life, God's, is "pure act," is all act. Therefore, in the new existence God has given us not only divine life, but new powers to act divinely, to live divinely.[7]

Divine life empowers humans to share in the mission of the divine persons of the Trinity.[8]

The result of this sharing in the mission is the creation of a oneness in creatures which is a reflection of the oneness of the Trinity itself.[9] Hence, divine life is not a static concept, effecting only the inner sanctification of an individual, but a dynamic sharing in the communitarian life of the Trinity itself, a sharing that moves one to action. In this position, Hillenbrand reflected the theology of Joseph

---

3. See Thomas Aquinas, *Summa Theologica*, I–II, q. 110,3, 4; q. 113, 9; q. 114, 3; II–II, q. 19, 7; III, q. 2, 10 ad 1, q. 3, 4 ad 5.

4. See Joseph Scheeben, *The Glories of Divine Grace*, trans. Monk of St. Meinrad's Abbey (New York: Benziger Brothers, 1898), p. 41.

5. See Hillenbrand, "The Social Nature of Grace in the Mystical Body of Christ," June 25, 1947, lecture. UNDA, CMRH 8/4. In his theology of grace, Hillenbrand finds a rationale for the necessity of Catholic Action to re-christianize the world.

6. See Thomas Aquinas, *Summa Theologica*, I–II, q. 112, a. 1; I–II, q. 3, a. 1, ad 1; III P., q. 1, a. 2; Scheeben, *The Glories of Divine Grace*, pp. 48–49, Columba Marmion, *Christ the Life of the Soul* (St. Louis: B. Herder, 1922), pp. 15–16; and Hillenbrand, "De Modo quo Deus Justificatos Inhabitat," 1931 S.T.D. dissertation, p. 1: "Modus inhabita¬tionis explicatur per effectum formalem primarium gratiae sanctificantis, nempe naturae divinae participationem."

7. Hillenbrand, "The New Life," in *National Liturgical Week 1948*, p. 30.

8. See Edmund J. Fortman, The Theology of Man and Grace: Commentary (Milwaukee: Bruce Publishing Co., 1966), pp. 191–201.

9. See Matthias Joseph Scheeben, *The Mysteries of Christianity*, trans. Cyril Vollert (St. Louis/London: B.Herder Book Company, 1946), p. 179.

Scheeben, who, following the Tübingen School, integrated a profound knowledge of the Greek Fathers into his major works.

The created nature of humankind became a source for the teachings of the liturgical pioneers.[10] Human activity is designed by God to complement our nature. Human beings, created in God's image and likeness, are capable of finding the likeness of God's creative activity in their human activities. And so, the life of the Trinity, in which each Person is a "being for others," is the fundamental pattern for all human existence and activity. "Under the action of Christ, we fulfill our being as Christian persons through 'being for another.'"[11] Thus, the liturgical pioneers saw human beings as fundamentally social in nature and in activity.[12]

The old definition of humans as rational animals failed to bring out the fundamentally social nature of humankind. As Hillenbrand says, "humans by nature live in society and grace never changes nature; it presupposes it or is added to it, built on it."[13] And so, in order to have an adequate definition of human nature one must also address the sexual, economic, political, international, cultural, and religious aspects of human life. This expanded definition of human nature was the result of the use of the deductive method used by Hillenbrand and the liturgical pioneers. It enabled them to forge a link between Neo-scholastic theology and the social encyclicals which called for social reconstruction, for making all things new in Christ (cf. 2 Corinthians 5:17).[14]

---

10. See Karl Rahner, "Theology and Anthropology," in *The Word in History: the St. Xavier Symposium*, ed. T. Patrick Burke (New York: Sheed & Ward, 1966), pp. 1–23. American liturgists were in good company in making anthropology a source for their theology. For scholars like Karl Rahner also maintained that the doctrines of God, Christ, & grace were ultimately one truth, that of God's self-expression.

11. Hillenbrand, "The Theology of Work," July, 1964 lecture. UNDA, CMRH 9/5.

12. The old inductive approach can be seen in the definition of humankind contained in the Baltimore Catechism: "God made us to know him, to love him, and to serve him in this life, and to be happy with him forever in heaven." The new deductive approach used by the liturgical pioneers saw such a definition as inadequately expressing the concrete experience of the Christian life. Thus, the pioneers used human experience as a *locus theologicus* in a truly innovative way.

13. Hillenbrand, "The Spirituality of YCW Leaders," July 1952 lecture. UNDA, CMRH 8/38. Hillenbrand repeated this thesis in every talk on lay spirituality. Cf. Virgil Michel, *The Christian in the World*, pp. 62–65.

14. See Jeremy Hall, *The Full Stature of Christ, the Ecclesiology of Virgil Michel* (Collegeville: Liturgical Press, 1976), pp. 36–54.

As discussed in Part I, Hillenbrand lived at a time when there was a resurgence of interest in "Christian social reconstruction," due to the efforts of popes like Leo XIII, Pius X, Pius XI, and Pius XII.[15] These popes frequently spoke out against individualism and secularism as undermining the very mission of the Church in the world. They called the laity to a more active role in the work of restoring the oneness of society and its corporate sense. They challenged the laity to take on more responsibility for creating a just social order. They saw Christ empowering the baptized member to continue his redemptive work in the world. They saw the loss of participation in the liturgy as a symptom of a deeper problem in society: the loss of its sense of unity.

CHRISTOLOGY AND ECCLESIOLOGY

At the moment of the restoration of unity, at the time of his death on the cross, Christ brought into the world "his great self, his complete self, his Mystical Body, drawing all into living oneness with himself, so that he might through them bring the restored life to the corners of the world."[16] The work of the redemption is continued by all the baptized who have received a share in divine life, spiritual gifts, divine powers (faith, hope, and love), and the inhabitation of the Trinity. God's indwelling reminds us of the organic character of society. Christians are called to share divine life with others and use their spiritual gifts and powers to restore the lost oneness of mankind, thereby manifesting the very life of the Trinity.[17]

Like Beaudin, Ellard, Hellriegel, Marmion,[18] Michel, or Scheeben, Hillenbrand believed that the mystery of the Church is best described as an organically formed and animated body with Christ as its head. The members of the Mystical Body possess a real, inner configuration to and sharing in the life of its head, are hierarchically

---

15. See Aaron I. Abell, *American Catholicism and Social Action: A Search for Social Justice, 1865–1950* (Notre Dame: University of Notre Dame Press, 1963).

16. Hillenbrand, "The New Life," in *National Liturgical Week 1948*, pp. 31–32.

17. Hillenbrand tied his theology of grace to an organic conception of church as the Mystical Body of Christ. See his 1936 notes for a retreat at the Cenacle. UNDA, CMRH 4/7.

18. Columba Marmion was Abbot of Maredsous, Belgium from 1909–1923. His works emphasize the doctrines of Christ, grace, the Mystical Body, and the liturgy. He influenced Lambert Beaudin, who strongly advocated the doctrine of the Mystical Body and passed this doctrine on to Virgil Michel.

arranged as in the case of a physical body, and are raised to a conformity with Christ's divine nature. Hillenbrand's writings frequently emphasized this unity in Christ, much like Joseph Scheeben, who maintained that

> the Church is not merely a society founded and approved by God or a divine legate; but it is built upon the God-man; and all who enter it become members of the God-man so that, linked together in him and through him, they may share in the divine life and the divine glory of their head.[19]

While Hillenbrand claims the Mystical Body means we and Christ are one, living, growing thing, there is no mention of the Church as the Bride of Christ.[20]

In order to appreciate the importance Hillenbrand attached to the work of the Mystical Body in our world, we must examine the role Hillenbrand gave to Christ. Like other liturgical leaders, Hillenbrand saw the Incarnation as the central event in all creation. "The Incarnation is the necessary means for divine adoption, for likeness to God, for regeneration by the Spirit, for 'deification.'"[21] In part, this is due to the rediscovery of the writings of the Fathers of the Church, especially Irenaeus of Lyons and his theology of the recapitulation of all things in Christ. This theology harmonized well with the motto of Pius X: "to restore all things in Christ."

Christ sums up (recapitulates) all being. For he is not only divine, but his human soul sums up the angels and our humans souls. His human body sums up our human bodies and all material creation. Hence, Christ sums up all history: all the time prior to Christ looked forward to him and all the time since Christ, including the future, is an unfolding of him. As Hillenbrand says, "this universe was created with one human in mind—who is the center of it, the peak of its perfection, upon whom everything converges . . . . That human is Christ."[22] Thus, we see that Hillenbrand clearly reflects the influence of patristic studies on his Christology.

---

19. Scheeben, *The Mysteries of Christianity*, pp. 541–542.
20. See Hillenbrand, "The Mystical Body," *Chaplain's Notes* (Jan.–Feb. 1957), p. 1.
21. Fortman, *The Theology of Man and Grace*, p. 102.
22. Hillenbrand, "The Lay Apostolate," January 1951 lecture. UNDA, CMRH 9/5.

Christ acted in the world directly through his Mystical Body, and especially through the sacraments. Hillenbrand agreed with Odo Casel that

> The incarnation of God's Son, and his death on the cross, together with his passage into glory and exaltation which flow from it have fashioned the Church, the body of Christ; it has but one life with that Son of God; he is the real life of the church through Christ. And all of this is made ours through the Lord's Word and the mysteries the sacraments in which the God-Man continuously conveys to us his theandric life.[23]

Like Michel and Hellriegel, Hillenbrand saw the mysteries of Christ's life having a divinizing, transforming power on Christians enabling them to continue the redemptive work of Christ in the world today.[24] Thus, the sacramental sphere of influence was not restricted to the church building but reached out to the whole world.[25]

The Church is permeated by Christ and of necessity organically linked with him. In his lectures, Hillenbrand recommended the works of Karl Adam, who maintained that

> Christ the Lord is the real self of the Church. The Church is the body permeated through and through by the redemptive might of Jesus . . . . For Christ and the Church can no more be regarded separately than can a head and its body (Col.1:18; 2:19; Eph. 4:15).[26]

Not only is the Christian united to Christ, but Hillenbrand eventually says that the Christian is Christ. For you cannot think of Christ today apart from his members.[27]

---

23. Odo Casel, *The Mystery of Christian Worship, and other Writings*, ed. Burkhard Neunheuser (Westminster: Newman Press, 1962), pp. 99–100.

24. See Virgil Michel, *The Liturgy of the Church*, p. 21:"The Church was founded by Christ for the express purpose of continuing his divine mission among us, for completing his work throughout time." See Martin Hellriegel & A. J. Jasper, *The True Basis of Christian Solidarity*, trans. William Busch, p. 14: "The liturgy is the reenactment of the life of Christ; it is the representation (making present) of the work of redemption.

25. Hillenbrand, "Spirituality of the Young Worker," July 1952. UNDA, CMRH 8/38. Cf. Karl Adam, *The Spirit of Catholicism* (New York: Macmillan Company, 1935), p. 19: "That is the deepest purpose of the liturgy, namely, to make the redeeming grace of Christ present, visible, and fruitful as a sacred and potent reality that fills the whole life of the Christian."

26. See Karl Adam, *The Spirit of Catholicism*, p. 16.

27. Hillenbrand, "The Mystical Body in Relation to Spiritual Charity," May 27, 1955, lecture. UNDA, CMRH 8/38.

In numerous lectures, traveling from one end of the country to the other, Hillenbrand spoke about this identity between Christ and the Christian.

> You must have a great sense that Christ is working through us! You, the members of the Mystical Body, are joined to him. Christ is present not only in heaven, but through us teaching, sanctifying, penetrating every corner of earth and school. You are his lips, hands, and feet. Christ is working, conquering, victorious through you."[28]

Usually, Hillenbrand would conclude his remarks by reminding people that the liturgy is the principal place where we discover this organic sense of oneness in Christ.[29]

As we discussed in the earlier chapters, like the other liturgical pioneers, Hillenbrand saw a relationship between the liturgy and the missionary nature of the Church.

> Because the Church is the prolongation of Christ in the world, through the history of humanity, the Church is essentially missionary. The Church must contribute to the renewal in Christ in all aspects of our lives (work, love, culture, customs, diverse human communities) and of all the peoples of the world.[30]

He warned against Christians walling up and isolating the Mystical Body, giving in to provincialism and isolating themselves from other Christian churches.[31] The oneness we celebrate in the liturgy must spread throughout the world.

While calling the laity to greater responsibility in the world, prior to Vatican II, Hillenbrand basically affirmed the traditional clergy/laity distinction that was typical of his day. Christ gave both groups, in different degrees, a share in his kingly work (directing or leading humans), in his prophetic work (proclaiming his truth to the

28. Hillenbrand, May 16, 1947 lecture to a YCS group. UNDA, CMRH 8/6. See Scheeben, *The Glories of Divine Grace*, pp. 380–381.

29. Hillenbrand, "Liturgy as Corporate Worship," December 29, 1945, lecture. UNDA, CMRH 37.

30. Hillenbrand, "Basic Principles of International YCS," August 1957 lecture. UNDA, CMRH 9/6.

31. Hillenbrand, "Double Conscience," July 6, 1954, lecture. UNDA, CMRH 8/38. He supported ecumenical groups in this talk at a YCW convention. He saw Christians working together as a logical corollary of the doctrine of the Mystical Body. See Michel, *Christians in the World*, p. 77 and Leen, *The True Vine and Its Branches*, p. 49.

world), and in his priestly work (offering the sacrifice and giving divine life). To the clergy, he gave a more restricted role: to rule over the Church (King), to teach authoritatively in the Church (Prophet), to nourish his people with his sacraments (Priest). To the laity, he gave a wider task: to minister through ordinary relationships and the communities that stem from these relationships: marriage, economic, political, international.[32]

Christology and Liturgiology

Hillenbrand, following his scholastic training, understood that Christ came to worship God and to restore divine life. In fact, you could say his entire life was an act of worship, an act of redemption and restoration, the climax of which was his sacrifice on the cross.[33] Yet it was unique in that Christ's death was the first time that the human race could give God a sacrifice adequate to him.[34] Consequently, Christ's death must be understood as the central moment in history not only for God but for humankind—it restored human destiny and gave us the possibility of possessing Divine Life.

The two principal activities of Christ in the Mystical Body are liturgical actions. First, he offers the sacrifice of his death, the Mass (that is, he does the essential thing his death was: an act of mind and will by which he accepted death and offered himself to the Father).[35] Second, he brings divine life to humans, principally through the sacraments, when he steps into human life with his divine power to give humans a share in the life of God.[36]

Christ could have done the work of redemption singlehandedly. However, he chose to do it through humans. He did this for two

32. Hillenbrand, "Lay Spirituality," August 17, 1956 lecture. UNDA, CMRH 8/38. When Vatican II spoke of giving greater responsibilities to the laity for the internal life of the Church, Hillenbrand amended his old clergy/laity distinction to reflect this.

33. Hillenbrand, "The Central Position of the Mass," July 9, 1947, lecture. UNDA, CMRH 29/13.

34. See Thomas Aquinas, *Summa Theologica*, II, 85, a. 1; Council of Trent, Session 22, chapter 1 (The nature of humans requires sacrificial worship); and Gerald Ellard, *Christian Life and Worship*, p. 61.

35. See Pius Parsch, *The Liturgy of the Mass*, trans. Frederic Eckhoff (St. Louis: B. Herder, 1937), pp. 44, 233–237.

36. This approach to the Eucharist and the sacraments was quite common. See Virgil Michel, *The Liturgy of the Church*, pp. 50–51.

reasons: first, he is God, the Creator, and he respects the freedom of humans, appealing to them to help, but not forcing them. Second, he is human and has the same instincts of humans, only more perfectly. He has the instinct to share a project and respects this instinct in others by inviting them to help him in his redemptive work. Consequently, the lay apostolate derives from Christ's redemptive death on the cross and requires the free cooperation of Christians in bringing the redemption into the world.[37]

Christ does the work of redemption especially through the sacraments, the privileged means of his grace sanctifying and transforming our lives. Hillenbrand's writings make the same connection between sacramental activity and Christ's death that appears in Thomas Aquinas:

> Although Christ, by his death, atoned sufficiently for the sins of mankind . . . each one must seek the means of his own salvation. Christ's death is by way of being a universal cause of salvation, just as the sin of the first man was like a universal cause of damnation. Now a universal cause needs to be applied to each individual, that the latter may have his share in the effect of the universal cause.[38]

Consequently, the sacraments can rightly be understood as the means whereby the benefits of the redemption, acquired once and for all on Calvary, are transmitted to us.[39]

While Hillenbrand's understanding of the liturgy was heavily based on Thomas Aquinas, it moved beyond the typical neo-scholastic understanding which he received as a student at St. Mary of the Lake Seminary. In 1926, Hillenbrand was taught that liturgy was

---

37. Hillenbrand, "Mystical Body," January, 1954 lecture. UNDA, CMRH 9/5. Notice the way human experience functions as a *locus theologicus* in this theory. Also see Thomas Aquinas, *Summa Theologica*, III, 3, a. 3 and III, 8, a. 6; Scheeben, *Dogmatik*, III, p. 352; and Jurgensmeier, *The Mystical Body of Christ*, pp. 71–12.

38. Thomas Aquinas, *Summa Contra Gentiles*, Bk. IV, ch. 55, trans. the Fathers of the English Dominican Province, in M. M. Philipon, *The Sacraments in the Christian Life*, trans. John A. Otto (Westminster: Newman Press, 1954), p. xvi. Cf. Hillenbrand, Liturgy Course Notes. UNDA, CMRH 5/21.

39. This position was quite common in the 1950s. A good example of this is found in the writings of A. M. Roguet, who is often quoted in the publications of the Specialized Lay Apostolate, which Hillenbrand edited. See A. M. Roguet, *Christ Acts Through the Sacraments*, trans. Carisbrooke Dominicans (Collegeville: Liturgical Press, 1954), p. 23: "The sacraments signify the origin of grace, which is the Passion of Christ: every sacrament in fact put us in touch with the cross, applies to us the power of the cross."

"the words and actions (excepting the matter and form of the Sacraments) instituted or ordered by ecclesiastical authority and called ceremonies or rites." While the etymology of the word "liturgy" was defined as "public service," the "real definition" of liturgy was "the social exercise of the virtue of religion or the public worship of the Church." The primary aim of worship was "to honor God and acknowledge His sovereignty." The secondary aim of worship was "the inculcation of faith and the stimulus to practice the virtues."[40] As seen in Part I, when Hillenbrand became rector of the seminary in 1936 and began to teach the required course in liturgy, he abandoned this excessively vertical presentation of liturgy in favor of a Christ-centered understanding of liturgy as the worship of the Mystical Body.

Hillenbrand interpreted the growing body of social doctrine articulated by the popes as the Church's attempt to present itself and its mission in a fresh, yet traditional way. The popes had warned that the social order was decaying and needed reconstruction in justice and charity.

> A doctrine very capable of supplying a framework (synthesis) of the Church's basic social implications is the *Mystical Body* which teaches: 1) the enormous individual worth of each human, and 2) the organic relation of one to another.[41]

The key to attaining this social reconstruction was participation in the liturgy, the Mystical Body at prayer, and the great teacher of the Church's social doctrine.

How is the liturgy an effective presentation of the Mystical Body?

> Through the liturgy people become conscious of the Mystical Body, become accustomed to communal action, are impregnated with justice and charity, are fired to better things or to set things right because they are members one of another.[42]

And so, the doctrine of the Mystical Body was understood as a religious solution and motive power, driving us to institutional reform and social reconstruction. The liturgy was the preeminent

---

40. Hillenbrand, Seminary Notebooks, Liturgy Course Notes, 1926. UNDA, CMRH 1/9.
41. Hillenbrand, Liturgy Course Notes. UNDA, CMRH 5/21.
42. Ibid.

means by which the Church applied this solution and received divine power to act.

The liturgy is a "great weapon in our hands."[43] The days of fighting the intellectual attacks (e.g., rationalism, higher criticism, etc.) of the nineteenth century were over. The problems of Hillenbrand's day were moral (e.g., birth control, divorce) and social (e.g., individualism, economic injustice, communism, Nazism, etc.). The Church's mission is not so much to mount a defense as it is to educate people as to the right solution of the moral and social evils and particularly on the inner nature (Mystical Body) and living power (divine life) of the Church. "One of the cures for the moral evils and one of the means for overcoming social evils is the liturgy."[44]

The liturgy is not just a question of beauty (gothic vestments, stained glass windows), perfect actions, exquisite singing, or rubrics. Mere obligation and external observance will not hold the people and will certainly not attract them. The people must be told about the two doctrines that underlie the liturgy. "There is no understanding and certainly no love of liturgy possible without seeing that its basic meaning is found in supernatural life."[45] Moreover, the liturgy helps us recognize the true nature of the Church as one unity, one organism, one whole Body. "Therefore, if we are cells in the Body of Christ, then we may be said to live in Christ and he to live in us . . . . The realization of the Mystical Body is a great spur behind the liturgical movement."[46]

Like Odo Casel or Martin Hellriegel, Hillenbrand believed the liturgy is a "reproduction of the life of the head (Christ's physical life) in the life of the members of his Mystical Body."[47] As Christ's Mystical Body, the Church lives over again the one life of Christ

---

43. Ibid.

44. Ibid. See Virgil Michel, "Liturgy and Catholic Life," *Catholic Action* 14 (1934), p. 66: "The whole status of the Christian as a living member of Christ can be expressed functionally, as active participation in the life of Christ, both in her inner worship of God through the liturgy and in her external mission of fostering the growth and spread of the Christ-life in the world."

45. Ibid.

46. Ibid. See Virgil Michel, "The True Christian Spirit," *Ecclesiastical Review* 82 (1930), p. 132: the Mystical Body is *the* inspirational idea of Catholic life as it should be."

47. Ibid. For Hillenbrand the result of celebrating the liturgy, of Christ living in us and us in him, was a growth in holiness. This growth is presented as a greater consciousness of union with Christ and others.

In numerous lectures, traveling from one end of the country to the other, Hillenbrand spoke about this identity between Christ and the Christian. He is shown here at the podium of one of his many lectures during the 1950s.
Archives of the University of Notre Dame.

during the course of the liturgical year. The annual celebration of the events of Christ's life is not just an exercise in the use of our memory (mere commemoration), but it is a manifestation of Christ living in his Church.

> The Mystical Body makes Christ's life my own and makes my interior life a reproduction of Christ's. The more I participate in the liturgy, the more I live in Christ and Christ lives in me.[48]

Consequently, liturgy is an expression and formation of the Church's self-identity in Christ, an effective presentation of the Mystical Body.

Like all the liturgical pioneers, Hillenbrand often quoted Pius X's 1903 Motu Proprio, *Tra la Sollecitudini*: "The foremost and indispensable font of the true Christian Spirit is active participation in the most Holy Mysteries and in the public and solemn prayer of the Church."[49] While Pius X was mainly encouraging the laity to learn to sing Gregorian chant, the reformers frequently used this quotation to connect their efforts to foster active participation in the liturgy with active participation in the apostolate.

---

48. Ibid.

49. Pius X, *Tra Le Sollecitudini*, in James Megivern, Ed., Official Catholic Teachings, Worship & Liturgy (Wilmington: McGrath Publishing Company, 1978), pp. 11–18. See Hillenbrand, "Introductory," October 21, 1940 lecture, in *National Liturgical Week*, 1940 (Newark: Benedictine Liturgical Conference, 1941), p. 6.

In this, the pioneers were helped by Pius XI who called for the participation of the laity in the work of the hierarchy[50] and for a return to an organic conception of society.[51] On December 12, 1938, Pius XI also strengthened the public position of liturgists by declaring: "The liturgy is the most important organ of the ordinary magisterium of the Church."[52] On December 25, 1936, in his encyclical on Christ the King, *Quas Primas*, Pius XI said participation in the liturgy had a stronger educative and teaching power than "even the weightiest pronouncements of the teachings of the church."[53] Thus, during the mid-1930s, the papacy was publicly promoting active participation in both the apostolate and the liturgy, while at the same time moving in the direction of a Mystical Body ecclesiology.

Michel, Ellard, Hellriegel, and Hillenbrand equated the official statements of Pius X and Pius XI in a way they were never intended to be used. They connected their Mystical Body ecclesiology/ liturgiology with a neo-scholastic Christology, which emphasized the liturgy as a privileged means of Christ continuing his work of redemption in our world. For example, Hillenbrand frequently claimed:

> Pius X saw that to restore Christ to the lives of men and penetrating them with the Spirit of Christ required one indispensable means: active participation in the liturgy.[54]

However, it's an equivocation to equate Pius X's use of "restoring all things in Christ" based on a hierarchical model with the liturgical pioneers' interpretation of this phrase based on an organic model. While Pius XI had moved toward an organic conception of society, his understanding of the liturgy is closer to "rites and ceremonies" than to Hillenbrand's "corporate worship of the Mystical Body."[55]

50. See Jeremiah Newman, *What is Catholic Action? An Introduction to the Lay Apostolate* (Westminster: Newman Press, 1958), p. 38: In a July 30, 1928, letter to the Catholic's Women's Leagues, Pius XI states: "Catholic Action is the participation of the Catholic laity in the hierarchic apostolate."

51. Pius XI, *Quadragesimo Anno*, nos. 90, 137.

52. John Fitzsimons & Paul McGuire, eds., *Restoring All Things, a Guide to Catholic Action* (New York: Sheed & Ward, 1938), p. 45.

53. Ibid., p. 44.

54. Hillenbrand, Liturgy Course Notes. UNDA, CMRH 5/21.

55. Undoubtedly, there is a major theological shift when one emphasizes the role of the community as co-offerers of the sacrifice (liturgy is the corporate worship of the Mystical Body) and a more hierarchically oriented theology, which may ask people to sing the chant but

In the 1930s, the sacrifice of the Mass dominated all the other expressions of worship in the Roman Church. In fact, the liturgy was usually presented as sacrificial in nature, the offering of a gift to God: our lives united with Christ.

This gift offering recognizes God's supremacy and our subjection to God. It is primarily an act of satisfaction for the sins of mankind, a priestly act of Christ in and through the Church.[56] However, this explanation is excessively concerned about the forgiveness of sins, thus obscuring other legitimate motivations for prayer.[57] This focus on forgiveness was largely overcome in the late 1950s and early 1960s with the definition of liturgy as a celebration of the Paschal Mystery.[58]

The highest form of sacrifice, the source and center of our spiritual lives, is the Eucharist: Christ's death renewed.[59] At the heart of this analysis (Mass is Christ's death renewed) lies a generic definition of sacrifice, which inadequately describes the sacramental nature of the Eucharist. Nonetheless, this analysis was quite common in the 1930s and 1940s[60] As Hillenbrand said:

> The Mass is the sacrifice of the Mystical Body, and is one with the sacrifice of Calvary . . . . Through the Mass Christ wants us to give ourselves to him that he in our human nature might offer us again in an unending act of priestly sacrifice. Calvary purchased our redemption. Mass applies that redemption. Just as the Mystical Body is the fullness of Christ, Mass is the fullness of Calvary.[61]

---

still accepts the neo-scholastic model which defined people's participation largely in terms of "receiving grace" or "being present" at the sacrifice. See Pius X, *Tra le Sollecitudini*, 1.

56. Hillenbrand, "Meaning of the Liturgy," in *National Liturgical Week*, 1941 (Newark: Benedictine Liturgical Conference, 1941), pp. 21–25.

57. The emphasis on the forgiveness of sins is apparent in many talks. A good example of this is found in his Summer, 1943 lecture on "The Mass": "You must make reparation for other people. . . . You must try through the Mass and through your other efforts to make satisfaction for souls." UNDA, CMRH 4/9.

58. See David N. Power, *The Sacrifice We Offer*, The Tridentine Dogma and Its Reinterpretation (New York: Crossroad, 1987), pp. 171–188.

59. Hillenbrand frequently quoted Pius XII's *Mediator Dei*,66: the Eucharist is "the culmination and center . . . of the Christian life."

60. See Virgil Michel, *The Liturgy of the Church*, pp. 152–154; Gerald Ellard, *Christian Life and Worship*, pp. 74–15; and Thomas Aquinas, *Summa Theologica*, I-II, 102, a.3, Sup. Q.13, a. 2, and Q. 44, a. 3, ad 3.

61. Hillenbrand, "The Mass," Summer, 1943 lecture. UNDA, CMRH 4/9.

While the Mass may be one with the sacrifice of Calvary, it is in the order of signs, a fact nowhere alluded to in the above. And so, while Hillenbrand's Eucharistic theology has some serious weaknesses in terms of contemporary scholarship, it was quite acceptable in the early 1950s.

One corollary of the liturgical pioneers' emphasis on the sacrificial nature of the liturgy was a return to the doctrine of the laity's participation in the liturgy as an exercise of their share in the priesthood of Christ. In fact, the Liturgical Conference identified the spread of this doctrine as one of the goals of the liturgical movement.

> The purpose of the Liturgical Movement is . . . to give all the faithful an awareness of their priestly dignity and privileges . . . to give them the opportunity consciously to exercise their priestly power by taking active part together in the Holy Sacrifice of the Mass through the ministry of their priests; to give them the knowledge that their whole lives may share, through the Mass, in Christ's priestly work of glorifying God and saving man.[62]

And so, if people are aware of sharing in the priestly sacrifice of Christ at the altar, they will hopefully also be aware of sharing in the priestly ministry of Christ in the world.[63]

One must remember that in the 1940s, the doctrine of the common priesthood was seen as dangerous to or a demeaning of the dignity of the ordained priesthood. In order to avoid the charge of not being orthodox in their teachings, the liturgical pioneers often sought protection in quoting Thomas Aquinas. Of course, Thomas taught the doctrine of the priesthood of the faithful in reference to the character imprinted at baptism and confirmation:

> Now the whole rite of the Christian religion is derived from Christ's Priesthood. Consequently, it is clear that the sacramental character is especially the seal of Christ, to whose figure the faithful are likened by reason of their sacramental characters (of baptism and confirmation), which are nothing else than a certain participation in Christ's priesthood, flowing from Christ Himself.[64]

---

62. Liturgical Conference, *What is the Liturgical Movement?* (Boston: Liturgical Conference, 1948), p. 14.

63. See Hillenbrand, "The Spirit of Sacrifice in Christian Society," in *National Liturgical Week* (Ferdinand, In.: Liturgical Conference, 1944), p. 103.

64. Thomas Aquinas, *Summa Theologica,* III, Q. 63, a. 3. See Gerald Ellard, *Christian Life and Worship,* pp. 50–54; Virgil Michel, "The Layman in the Church," *Commonweal* 12 (1930),

Consequently, for Thomas the character imprinted at baptism and confirmation was the distinctive mark through which humankind became configured to Christ and shared in the ministry of his Body, the Church.[65]

Protestant theologians during the Reformation gave strong emphasis to the priesthood of the laity. Catholic theologians countered by emphasizing the role of the "ordained priest." Unfortunately, the result of the Catholic counter-reformation was to lose what Thomas (and Patristic authors before him) taught regarding the sharing in the common priesthood. The liturgical pioneers saw the disappearance of the concept of the common priesthood as at least partly responsible for the state of affairs both within the Church and in the world.

Ordained priests offered Mass for the faithful, who passively watched what was going on, said the Rosary, or read devotional prayers that had little to do with the liturgy. Liturgy was something done for the faithful, not something they did. And so, along with the concept of the common priesthood, the liturgical pioneers also introduced the concept of the liturgy being a corporate action of the faithful with the ordained priest. This concept flowed quite readily from the definition of the liturgy as the Mystical Body at worship.[66]

The liturgy is something we do together, an action of the entire Mystical Body. The liturgy restores our lost sense of oneness, enabling us to act together to restore all things in Christ. "The task, therefore, is to learn our oneness at the altar and to bring that oneness to the other relations of our life."[67] Virgil Michel preceded Hillenbrand in maintaining this same opinion about the Christian who

> must always be a soldier of the cause of Christ and an apostle working for the good of the whole body. This is, indeed, the highest privilege of the Christian, for it includes all the others, and it is this that makes him more than anything else "another Christ" in the world.[68]

---

pp. 123–125; and Ernest Benjamin Koenker, *The Liturgical Renaissance in the Roman Catholic Church* (Chicago: University of Chicago Press, 1954), pp. 71–19.

65. See Friedrich Jurgensmeier, *The Mystical Body of Christ as the Basic Principle of Spiritual Life*, trans. Harriet G. Strauss (New York: Sheed & Ward, 1954), p. 105.

66. Hillenbrand, "The Meaning of Liturgy," in National Liturgical Week 1941, p. 26.

67. Hillenbrand, "With One Another at Mass," in *National Liturgical Week, 1947* (Boston: Liturgical Conference, 1948), p. 64.

68. Virgil Michel, *The Christian in the World*, p. 11.

Notice how daring Michel was in calling the lay Christian to be "another Christ"—a title usually reserved for the clergy. Yet if you believed that Christians were called to be lay apostles, then such an assertion was quite appropriate. Hillenbrand frequently said the same thing.[69]

The liturgical pioneers saw a connection between the great action (the Mass) and Catholic Action.[70] As Hillenbrand said:

> The fact that the Mass is an action should drive us to apostolic action. Otherwise we leave our religion, and the greatest thing it has, Mass, in the realm of the "purely spiritual," with no resulting action.[71]

While all this sounds convincing, the task of changing the thinking of the average Catholic about the nature of their participation in the liturgy was a monumental undertaking in the 1930s and 1940s.

Among the liturgical pioneers, Hillenbrand was one of the strongest advocates of the lay apostolate. He saw active participation in the apostolate and the liturgy as a joint responsibility of all the members of Christ's Body who share in his priesthood. As Hillenbrand said:

> The lay apostolate . . . is part of the whole apostolate of the Church. There aren't two apostolates—a priestly apostolate and a lay apostolate. It's one, total apostolate . . . in which priests play a role and lay people play a role.[72]

Hence, if liturgy is a corporate action of the whole church, then the apostolate must also be one corporate act. Hillenbrand constantly sought to relate the liturgy to life and to make it a source of hope, especially for the victims of social injustice.

> To the Negro who cannot find employment, whose housing is cruelly overcrowded, who cannot enter a Catholic school. To the sharecropper who, in the phrase of Pius XI, had no hope of ever obtaining a share in the land. To the workers who earn too little to rise from their proletarian conditions to the security of owning property . . . . We must bring the effects

69. Hillenbrand, "The Mystical Body in Relation to Spiritual Charity," May 27, 1955 lecture. UNDA, CMRH 8/38.

70. See Marx, p. 54.

71. Hillenbrand, "The Mass as the Source and Center of the Lay Apostolate," in *National Liturgical Week 1955* (Elsberry, Mo.: Liturgical Conference, 1956), p. 179.

72. Hillenbrand, "The Five Essential Qualities of a Chaplain," April 28, 1958 lecture. UNDA, CMRH 10/19.

of the altar to them. Christ died for all; all are the beneficiaries of His justice and charity.[73]

The solution to an unjust social order was to convince lay apostles to act upon the logic of their participation in the Mass and bring Christ and his redemption with them into all their environments: home, classroom, business, farm, neighborhood, etc.

In 1930s and 1940s, the liturgy was frequently a very cerebral experience, with heavy emphasis on the listening and seeing. Yet this is not entirely the fault of neo-scholastic theology. In 1926, at St. Mary of the Lake Seminary, Hillenbrand was taught that

> Through the appeal to the senses, frequent symbolism, and the beauty of art the liturgy in a concrete manner and by the intuitive process incites the mind to reflection, the heart to affection, and the will to action. The liturgy appeals to the senses in a multitude of ways, e.g. the prostrations, the striking of the breast, the crib at Christmas time, the color of the vestments, etc. The liturgy makes use of symbolism . . . [whereby] a sensible thing is used to inculcate an idea of a religious or moral nature . . . because of some similarity in relation between the sign and the thing signified.[74]

While the emphasis here is largely on the mind ("inculcate an idea"), there is also an appeal to the senses and the intuitive process.

From the time he began to teach liturgy at the Seminary, Hillenbrand described the liturgy as an act of the whole person: mind, will, body, senses, and emotions.

> This is why we need participation; the liturgy must be an experience . . . of the whole human. This gives liturgy an additional affinity to art. It will invoke the visual and audible, the dramatic and the poetic; the beauty of line, proportion, and perspective; of color, of light and shadow; of fabric and texture; of wood and stone, and other, good, honest materials; of speech and song; of gesture and posture. The liturgy must be human as well as divine. It should have participation, and it should have art.[75]

---

73. Hillenbrand, "The Spirit of Sacrifice in Christian Society," *National Liturgical Week 1943* (Ferdinand, IN: Liturgical Conference, 1944), p. 106.

74. Hillenbrand, Seminary Notebooks. UNDA, CMRH 1/9.

75. Hillenbrand, "Art and the Liturgy." UNDA, CMRH 21/13 and *Catholic Mind* 60 (1962), p. 43.

It should engage the whole person, thereby giving glory to God and divinizing God's people. For "humans do not worship like angels."[76]

When Hillenbrand or the other pioneers encouraged congregational singing, walking in procession, the use of liturgical symbols such as candles or palms, or attention to the liturgical seasons, they were popularizing a line of thought that had long been advocated in Europe. Like Abbot Ildefons Herwegen, they believed

> The action proceeds through outward forms which are symbolic, thus speaking in a high poetic language, awakening a mystic sense, and producing a spiritual elevation. It employs . . . gestures which are venerable with age, the bended knee, the folded hands, the outstretched arms . . . the use of incense, gestures of reverence, and liturgical vestments.[77]

From its inception, this crucial awareness of the symbolic nature of the liturgy and the multiple dimensions of the liturgical event has been maintained by the leaders of the American liturgical movement.[78]

In summary, Hillenbrand's liturgical theology is based on a neo-scholastic anthropology which has been supplemented by cultural-historical data drawn mainly from papal teachings. His anthropology is heavily influenced by his theology of grace, which draws upon the work of Joseph Scheeben and Tübingen School. He explained the social nature of grace in terms of sharing in the communitarian life of the Trinity. This dynamic definition of grace complemented the Mystical Body theology that served as the basis of his ecclesiology and liturgiology. In addition, it blended well with a renewed emphasis on the Christ-centered nature of liturgy. In all these fundamentals, Hillenbrand, as did other American liturgists of the 1930s and 1940s, popularized ideas and approaches that European leaders like Marmion, Beauduin, Herwegen, and Casel had long been espousing.

---

76. Hillenbrand, Liturgy Course Notes. UNDA, CMRH 4/12.

77. Ildefons Herwegen, *The Art-Principle of the Liturgy*, trans. William Busch (Collegeville: Liturgical Press, 1931), pp. 14–15.

78. See Marx, p. 60; Martin Hellriegel, "A Pastor's Description of Liturgical Participation in His Parish," in *National Liturgical Week 1941* (Newark: Benedictine Liturgical Conference, 1942), pp. 82–90; and H. A. Reinhold, *Speaking of Liturgical Architecture* (Notre Dame: Notre Dame Liturgy Program, 1952).

Along with defining the liturgy as the corporate worship of the Mystical Body, American liturgical reformers also advocated the doctrine of the common priesthood. By virtue of the character we receive at baptism and confirmation, Christians are called to exercise Christ's priestly ministry in the world. The goal of the priestly ministry is the restoration of oneness, the renewal of life, and the reestablishment of the organic structure necessary to establish a just social order. The liturgy is the prayer of the Mystical Body, empowering its members to become Christ in the world, carrying on his redemptive work. Liturgy is a human experience, appealing through the senses to the whole person by means of sights and sounds, symbols and actions. What Hillenbrand's theology represents is a movement away from the Neo-scholastic preoccupation with causality and a recapturing of the symbolic/sacramental dimensions of the liturgical event.

Chapter 6

Liturgy and Social Justice

THE DEPRESSION, THE PAPACY, AND ORGANIC SOCIETY

As was discovered in Part I, while Hillenbrand was working on his doctoral dissertation, *De Modo quo Deus Justificatos Inhabitat*, at St. Mary of the Lake Seminary from 1930–1931, the United States was experiencing the beginning of the Great Depression. The number of unemployed rose from 492,000 in October, 1929 to 4,065,000 in January, 1930. By October 15, 1931, Chicago had 624,000 people out of work. The effects of the depression were uneven and big cities like Chicago, which had large numbers of unskilled workers, suffered more than smaller cities.[1] The depression magnified the divisions in society between rich and poor, skilled and unskilled, black and white, management and labor, etc. Surely, there was a better way to organize society and overcome the sufferings and divisions that were so apparent in and outside of Chicago.

Hillenbrand's lectures on *Quadragesimo Anno* indicate that he heard Pius XI explain this encyclical during his year studying in Rome from 1931–1932.[2] *Quadragesimo Anno* was issued on the fortieth anniversary of Leo XIII's encyclical, *Rerum Novarum*, and like its predecessor called for a return to an organic conception of society. It stimulated Hillenbrand's interest in the social action movement, which was being revived in American Catholic circles due to the

---

1. Irving Bernstein, *A History of the American Worker, 1920–1933: The Lean Years* (Boston: Houghton Mifflin Company, 1960), pp. 254–257, 298.

2. Hillenbrand, "Notes for Talks on Labor and Social Justice." UNDA, CMRH 6/26.

sufferings of so many people during the depression years.[3] In addition, Hillenbrand's investigation of *Rerum Novarum* and *Quadragesimo Anno* led to his forming a new synthesis on the relation of liturgy to life and the relation of liturgy to the apostolate.

Hillenbrand believed that the renewal of society needed in the 1930s and 1940s went back to a renewal begun at the turn of the century by Leo XIII and Pius X.[4] He believed that the problems of society were due to false philosophies (secularism and individualism), which had created an unjust economic order. The solution was to restore the organic basis of society and the true Christian spirit of self-sacrificial love. What the world needed was a fresh diffusion of the true Christian spirit by means of active participation in the liturgy and the creation of lay apostles who would share in the apostolate of the hierarchy.[5]

While the Schema, *De Ecclesia*, which defined the very essence of the Church as a Mystical Body, was never approved by Vatican I, the organic concept of church was kept alive by the Tübingen School of theology and various papal statements. On June 25, 1896, in his encyclical, *Satis Cognitum*, Leo XIII made use of an organic conception of church:

> Because it is a body, it is visible to the eyes of all; because it is the body of Christ, it is a living body, active and growing, for it is sustained and animated by the power (super natural life) which Jesus Christ communicates to it, almost as the vine nourishes and renders fruitful the branches that are united with it.[6]

Leo XIII then spoke of the sanctifying effect of this union, which ultimately leads us to eternal salvation. Like Michel, Ellard, and

---

3. See Vincent J. Giese, "The Lay Apostolate in Chicago," in *The Catholic Church, U.S.A.*, ed. Louis J. Putz, p. 363:"Out of this agitation and unrest on the part of the population in the 1930s came the tremendous efforts of the 1940s—when various lay movements in Chicago, and nationally, had their structural beginnings."

4. Hillenbrand, Notes from a 1941 lecture to the philosophy (college) students at St. Mary of the Lake Seminary. UNDA, CMRH 6/26.

5. See Pius XI, *Quadragesimo Anno*, nos. 76, 90, 96, 110,137.

6. Leo XIII, *Satis Cognitum*, in Emile Meersch, *The Whole Christ, the Historical Development of the Doctrine of the Mystical Body in Scripture and Tradition*, trans. John R. Kelly (Milwaukee: Bruce Publishing Company, 1938), pp. 565–66.

other liturgical reformers, Hillenbrand combed the papal encyclicals looking for quotations to support his Mystical Body ecclesiology.[7]

On May 28, 1902, in his encyclical, *Mirae Caritatis*, "On the Most Holy Eucharist," Leo the XIII deplored the "frequent quarrels and contentions among the various classes of citizens; the arrogance, harshness, dishonesty among the more powerful; the misery, envy and spirit of revolt among the weaker."[8] The remedy for such evils was to live the Eucharist, which Christ left us as a symbol of unity and charity, a symbol of that body of which he is head.

> Yes, truly, here is a most beautiful example of Christian brotherhood and of social equality, that all should approach the same altars without distinction; the nobility and the people, the rich and the poor, the learned and the unlearned, are equally sharers in the same heavenly banquet.[9]

Thus, the social encyclicals of Leo XIII contained the beginnings of the necessary connection between liturgy and social justice which Hillenbrand later developed.

On February 2, 1904, in his encyclical, *Ad diem illum*, Pius X spoke of the gifts all members of the Mystical Body receive from Christ for the increase or "up building of itself in charity."[10] On June 11, 1905, in his encyclical, *Il fermo proposito*, Pius X affirmed the doctrine of Catholic Action, whereby all members of Christ's body cooperate by putting the teachings of the Church

> into execution first in themselves, and then to co-operate effectively in making others put them into practice, each one according to the grace he has received from God, according to his state and office, and according to the zeal that burns in his heart. Here we wish simply to mention the many works of zeal that are being carried out for the good of the Church, of society, and of individuals, and which are commonly referred to as "Catholic Action."[11]

---

7. See Marx, pp. 82–83 and Gerald Ellard, *The Mystical Body and the American Bishops* (St. Louis: Queen's Work, 1939), pp. 22–23.

8. Leo XIII, *Mirae Caritatis*, in James J. Megivern, *Official Catholic Teachings, Worship & Liturgy*, p. 8 and in Gerald Ellard, *Christian Life and Worship*, p. 149.

9. Leo XIII, *Mirae Caritatis*, in Megivern, p. 10.

10. Pius X, *Ad diem illum*, in Mersch, p. 568.

11. Pius X, *Ad Diem Illum*, in Meersch, pp. 568–569.

And so, at the beginning of this century, Pius X's call to participate in Catholic Action was viewed by Hillenbrand and other liturgical pioneers in the light of the more fundamental theology of the Mystical Body.[12]

If the liturgical pioneers connected Pius X with a call to participate in Catholic Action as members of the Mystical Body, they identified him even more with the call to active participation in the liturgy. On November 22, 1903, in his Motu Proprio, *Tra le sollecitudini*, "On the Reform of Church Music," Pius X made a statement that became the most frequently quoted papal text on the liturgy:

> It being our ardent desire to see the true Christian spirit restored in every respect and be preserved by all the faithful, we deem it necessary to provide before everything else for the sanctity and dignity of the temple, in which the faithful assemble for the object of acquiring this spirit from its foremost and indispensable fount, which is the active participation in the most holy Mysteries and in the public and solemn prayer of the Church.[13]

Hillenbrand connected this call to active participation in the liturgy with the goal of "restoring all things in Christ," which Pius X made his motto and first spoke of on October 4, 1903, in the encyclical, E *Supremi Apostolatus*.[14]

Pius XI further developed the connection between active participation in the liturgy and the necessity of Catholic Action. On December 20, 1928, in his Apostolic Constitution, *Divini Cultus*, "On Divine Worship", Pius XI affirmed

> a kind of intimate relationship [existing] between Christian worship and the sanctification of souls. . . . It is most important that when the faithful

---

12. See Hillenbrand, "Doctrine of the Church on the Formation of Lay Apostles," August 21, 1961, lecture. UNDA, CMRH 9/2. The term "Catholic Action" was originally a phrase used by Pius IX to invite the laity to assist in the work of the Church. It received great impetus from Leo XIII's encyclical, *Rerum Novarum*, which called the laity to action in the field of economic life. Its great proponent was Pius X, who, as Patriarch of Venice, in 1890, called for obedience to the pope in Catholic Action. This phrase was tirelessly repeated and expounded by Pius XI. Eventually, the phrase "Catholic Action" took on a more restricted meaning, and the phrase lay apostolate came to refer to many aspects of work done by the laity. Pius XII's address to the Second World Congress of the Lay Apostolate in October of 1957 led to the triumph of the phrase "lay apostolate" over the old "Catholic Action" terminology of Pius XI. This is the terminology that was used at Vatican II.

13. Pius X, *Tra le sollecitudini*, in Megivern, pp. 11–18.

14. See Raphael M. Huber, "Biographical Sketch of Pope Pius X" in *A Symposium on the Life and Work of Pope Pius X* (Washington: Confraternity of Christian Doctrine, 1946), p. 16.

assist at the Sacred Ceremonies . . . they should not be merely detached and silent spectators, but . . . they should mingle their voices with the clergy or the choir, as it is prescribed.[15]

This quote about "detached and silent spectators" would become almost as famous as Pius X's 1903 statement on the true Christian spirit.

In 1931, in *Quadragesimo Anno*, Pius XI called for the return to an organic conception of society as a solution to "the problems besetting the world."[16] In addition, he adopted the Cardijn principle of "like to like" ministry: "The first and immediate apostle to the workers ought to be workers; the apostles to those who follow industry and trade ought to be from among themselves."[17] Thus, Pius XI clearly approved of and desired the selection and training of lay apostles who would assist in the work of the hierarchy, in the work of restoring an organic base for society. In many ways, Pius XI set the agenda for Hillenbrand's future ministry.

In 1934, Pius XI further explicated the sacramental basis of his call for active participation in the apostolate. He says:

The very sacraments of Baptism and Confirmation impose . . . this apostolate of Catholic Action . . . since through [them] we become members of the Church, or of the Mystical Body of Christ, and among the members of this body . . . there must be solidarity of interests and reciprocal communication of life.[18]

Of course, the privileged place for such solidarity and reciprocal communication is the liturgy, the source and center of our spiritual lives.[19] Thus, in the statements of Leo XIII, Pius X, and Pius XI, Hillenbrand found the basis for a necessary connection between

---

15. Pius XI, "On Divine Worship," cited in Ellard, *Christian Life and Worship*, p. 215 and Ellard, *Men at Work at Worship*, p. 10.

16. Pius XI, *Quadragesimo Anno*, no. 137 (Washington: National Catholic Welfare Conference, 1942), p. 49: "And so, then only will true cooperation be possible for a single common good when the constituent parts of society deeply feel themselves members of one great family and children of the same heavenly Father; nay, that they are one body in Christ, 'but severally members one of another,' (Rom. 12:5) so that 'if one member suffers anything, all the members suffer with it' (1 Cor. 12:26)."

17. Ibid., no. 141, pp. 51–52.

18. Pius XI, in Ellard, *Christian Life and Worship*, p. 382.

19. See Hillenbrand, "The Meaning of Liturgy," in *National Liturgical Week 1942*, p. 26: "All the rest of the liturgy revolves around the Mass. It is the great source, the great center."

liturgy (the Mystical Body at prayer) and social justice (the Mystical Body bringing redemption to the world).[20]

When Pius XII issued the encyclical, *Mystici Corporis*, "On the Mystical Body of Christ," in 1943, and the encyclical, *Mediator Dei*, "On the Sacred Liturgy," in 1947, Hillenbrand rejoiced that the above synthesis had been officially sanctioned. For many years American liturgical reformers lived under a cloud of suspicion regarding their loyalty and orthodoxy. Even as late as 1951, Hillenbrand would bemoan

> the lack of acquaintance with papal doctrine. . . . A priest might say, as one did this summer in preaching a retreat, that we are hearing too much about the mystical body and not enough about the Church.[21]

Consequently, it must have been a great consolation to read the definition of liturgy in *Mediator Dei*.[22]

LITURGY, LIFE, AND THE APOSTOLATE

While the organic conception of liturgy and church triumphed in the teachings of Pius XII, it emerged out of a neo-scholastic definition of liturgy, which was based on a static view of doctrine and unchanging essences. However, papal social teachings were based on a more progressive, evolutionary approach to dealing with social problems. That there was a shift in methodology when one applied papal doctrine to social questions from that found in *Mediator Dei* never occurred to Hillenbrand or to the other pioneers, for that matter. Instead, they focused on explaining the connection between liturgy and life, liturgy and the apostolate.

As we stated previously, Hillenbrand was taught that the liturgy was "the social exercise of the virtue of religion or the public

---

20. Hillenbrand was also influenced by the insights of the European biblical, liturgical, and social action movements, which made ever increasing use of Mystical Body ecclesiology, especially in the decade prior to *Mystici Corporis*.

21. Hillenbrand, "The Priesthood and the World," National Liturgical Week 1951 (Conception, Mo.: Liturgical Conference, 1952), p. 163. See Marx, p. 83.

22. Pius XII, *Mediator Dei*, no. 20: "Liturgy is the public worship which our redeemer as head of the Church renders to the Father as well as the worship which the community of the faithful renders to its founder, and through him to the Heavenly Father. It is, in short, the worship rendered by the Mystical Body of Christ in the entirety of its head and members."

worship of the church."[23] The part of this definition that he emphasized was the "social" and "public" aspect.[24] In the past, an individualistic understanding of worship had led some to regard the liturgy to rubrics and ceremony. Like Joseph Jungmann, Hillenbrand believed that

> liturgy must become pastoral. . . . The type of Christian who merely assists at Mass in a bored fashion must disappear. . . . Worship must become both an invitation and a real adoration "in Spirit and in truth": it must become the support of a joyful awareness of faith and of a Christian life in a harsh world.[25]

In countless lectures, Hillenbrand spoke of the need to recapture the social (pastoral) nature of the liturgy by fostering active participation and a correct understanding of the liturgy.[26]

If people had a correct understanding of the liturgy as "the corporate worship of the Mystical Body,"[27] then they would also have a correct understanding of what the church is: "the complete Christ, the extension of Christ into space and time."[28] If people are united with Christ in the corporate worship of the church, then they will be united with Christ in continuing his mission in the world.[29] Like other liturgical pioneers, Hillenbrand had tremendous confidence in the formative effect of active, intelligent participation in the Eucharist.

What Hillenbrand, Michel, Ellard, Hellriegel, and others wanted to bring to the United States was the type of pastoral liturgical movement that Lambert Beauduin had brought to Belgium. This pastoral concept of the liturgy was a way to activate on the parochial

---

23. Hillenbrand, Seminary Notebooks, Liturgy CourseNotes, 1926. UNDA, CMRH 1/9.

24. See Emmanuele Caronti, *The Spirit of the Liturgy*, trans. Virgil Michel (Collegeville: Liturgical Press, 1926), p. 9: Liturgy is "the social form in which religion is practiced by the church."

25. Joseph Jungmann, *Pastoral Liturgy*, trans. Challoner Publications (New York: Herder & Herder, 1962), pp. 98–99.

26. See Hillenbrand, 1946 Liturgy Course Notes, Pius X School. UNDA, CMRH 29/8.

27. Ibid.

28. Ibid.

29. Contemporary theologians maintain this same point of view. See Kevin W. Irwin, *Liturgy, Prayer, and Spirituality* (New York: Paulist Press, 1984), pp. 304–305: "The real issue is to see that both the doing of liturgy and the living of life are interrelated, whether in Rahner's view or any other's approach. . . . The mission and action parts of life are intrinsically connected with the celebration of liturgy."

level the mission of Christ in the world.[30] According to this perspective, liturgical life was the vital center of the Christian life, providing a fundamental catechesis in the Christian life. Like Beauduin, they wanted

> Catholics to find in their parish church and its liturgical life the epicenter of the Christian life itself . . . . The parish Mass was to be reverenced as the great assembly meeting of God's people where, through the action of the visible priesthood, humans, already joined in ties of fraternity were steadily converted into a fuller sharing of Christ and a deeper fraternity with each other.[31]

Active participation in the liturgy gave Christians a deeper understanding of the Christian life and a greater share in divine life, thus enabling them to carry on Christ's mission in the world.[32]

American liturgists founded the Liturgical Conference under the influence of Pius XI, the pope of Catholic Action. On March 14, 1937, in his encyclical, *Mit brennender Sorge*, "On the Condition of the Church in Germany," Pius XI called for the closest union of the apostolate and the liturgy.

> It is not enough to be counted a member of the Church of Christ. One must be also a living member of this Church—in spirit and in truth. . . . And only in this way can it be proved to the present generation, and especially to the adversaries of the Church, that the salt of the earth has not lost its savor, that the leaven of Christendom has not become stale, but is capable and ready to bring to the people of today . . . the spiritual renewal and rejuvenation of which they stand . . . in greater need than ever before. . . . In the final analysis, every true and lasting reform has proceeded from the sanctuary; from humans who were inflamed and driven by love of God and their neighbor.[33]

---

30. See John La Farge, "Progress and Rhythm in the Liturgical Movement," *Liturgy for the People, Essays in Honor of Gerald Ellard, 1894–1963à*, ed. William J. Leonard (Milwaukee: Bruce Publishing Co., 1963), p. 3.

31. Romey P. Marshall and Michael J. Taylor, *Liturgy and Christian Unity* (Englewood Cliffs: Prentice-Hall, 1965), pp. 126–127. See Lambert Beauduin, *Liturgy: the Life of the Church*, trans. Virgil Michel (Collegeville: Liturgical Press, 1926), pp. 9–16.

32. See Hillenbrand, "The Social Nature of Grace in the Mystical Body of Christ," June 25, 1947, lecture. UNDA, CMRH8/4.

33. Pius XI, "On the Condition of the Church in Germany," in *Sixteen Encyclicals of Pope Pius XI* (Washington: National Catholic Welfare Conference, 1937), pp. 14–15.

At the first National Liturgical Week in Chicago, Archbishop Stritch reflected this same connection between liturgy and the apostolate, when he acknowledged that "without intelligent, vigorous liturgical action, there can be no real Catholic Action."[34]

If one unites the above encyclical with Pius XI's previous injunctions about the laity not being "mute spectators" (*Divini Cultus*) and the liturgy being the "most important organ of the ordinary teaching power of the Church" (Quas Primas), one finds the rationale behind Hillenbrand's positions on the liturgy:

> Liturgy is the corporate prayer of the Church, by which divine life streams from the head to the members. Corporate worship is the great need of our times, the cure of our evils, the rallying point of the spiritual forces of the world.[35]

Therefore, people must learn the lesson the liturgy teaches: that they possess divine life, that they are part of Christ's Body, and that they have the power to create a new world in Christ.[36]

Like Beauduin, Hillenbrand emphasized the transforming nature of our sharing in Trinitarian life.

> It is the life of God, transplanted, grafted on to us, inviscerated . . . into our own human flesh, into our own human nature which gives us the capacity of activity properly divine, to adopt the views of God, the knowledge of God.[37]

Like Michel, Ellard, or Hellriegel, Hillenbrand was confidant that our sharing in Trinitarian life at the liturgy inspired activity that would cure the evils of the world. In this conviction, these pioneers also reflect the influence of Columba Marmion who taught that "grace

34. Samuel Stritch, "Foreword," in *National Liturgical Week 1940* (Newark, NJ: Benedictine Liturgical Conference, 1941), p. ix.

35. Hillenbrand, Liturgy Course Notes. UNDA, CMRH 29/13. See Columba Marmion, *Christ the Life of the Soul*, trans. Nuns of Tyburn Convent (St. Louis: B. Herder Book Co., 1922), pp. 18–19.

36. See Hillenbrand, "The New Life," in *National Liturgical Week 1948*, pp. 28–35.

37. Lambert Beauduin, *Cahier Brun* (one of Beauduin's notebooks, probably dating from the late 1930s and early 1940s), in Sonya Quitslund, *Beauduin, A Prophet Vindicated* (New York: Newman Press, 1973), p. 274. See Kenneth R. Himes, "Eucharist and Justice: Assessing the Legacy of Virgil Michel," *Worship* 62 (1988), p. 208.

American liturgists believed that the reform of the liturgy would revitalize the life of the community. Pictured here are the leading American liturgists planning Liturgy Week, 1948. Msgr. Hillenbrand is seated in the front, on the left. *Archives of the University of Notre Dame.*

is a source of actions and operations which are supernatural, and tend towards a divine end. . . ."[38]

American liturgists believed that the reform of the liturgy would revitalize the life of the community.[39] For the liturgy "is the greatest means of the formation of a social conscience, because it is a corporate prayer."[40] Moreover, the Eucharistic liturgy is the great textbook of the Church. As members of Christ our great purpose is to reproduce his image in us. To do this we need contact with his life as he lived it. For that reason the Mystical Body reproduces his life each year: his birth, his manifestation, his passion, his resurrection, his

---

38. Columba Marmion, Christ the Life of the Soul, p. 16.Columba Marmion was the Benedictine abbot of Maredsous Abbey, Belgium, whose writings on the Gospels, Pauline theology, grace, liturgical texts, patristic sources, and Thomistic theology influenced many liturgists.

39. See John J. Egan, *Liturgy and Justice: an Unfinished Agenda* (Collegeville: Liturgical Press, 1983), p. 4.

40. Hillenbrand, 1946 Liturgy Course Notes, Pius X School. UNDA, CMRH 29/8.

second coming, etc. . . . . There is no surer way of making us one with Christ than the liturgy. Frequently, the pioneers made reference to the Thomistic teaching that the effect of receiving the Eucharist is union with the Mystical Body.[41]

For the liturgy enables us to discover the fundamental truth about our human nature: that we are made for union with God and God's people. As Odo Casel explains, "the decline of the concept of the worshiping congregation was associated with a similar decline in the feeling of fellowship on the part of the local church (be it parish or diocese)."[42] A proper presentation of the liturgy develops the communal nature of our human personalities (the fellowship) according to the pattern of Christ's life.

American liturgists considered the liturgy to be a school of Christian living, which transformed people into other Christs, capable of bringing redemption to a sinful world. They desired to bring to the United States the insights of European liturgists, who had long maintained this position. Like Romano Guardini, they believed:

> When persons continue to live with others, simultaneously though also with Christ, their relations to the others will change, if only in that they become increasingly patient, more understanding, kinder, but also more alert, less gullible, and better able to judge character and worth, whatever their natural limitations maybe . . . . Persons are changed by their daily contact with Christ, becoming more and more similar to their model.[43]

Hillenbrand expressed much the same sentiment when he said: "the more I participate in the liturgy, the more I reproduce Christ in myself and the more he lives in me."[44]

---

41. See Hillenbrand, Liturgy Course Notes. UNDA, CMRH29/12; Ellard, *Christian Life and Worship*, p. 75; Hellriegel-Jasper, "The True Basis of Christian Solidarity," pp. 2425; and Michel, *Our Life in Christ* (Collegeville: Liturgical Press, 1939), pp. 50–51.

42. Odo Casel, "The Liturgical Movement in the Catholic Church," in *Twentieth-Century Theology in the Making, Vol.III: Ecumenicity* and Renewal, ed. Jaroslav Pelikan (New York: Harper & Row, 1971), p. 404.

43. Romano Guardini, *The Lord*, trans. Elinor Castendyk Briefs (Chicago: Henry Regnery Company, 1954), p. 446.

44. Hillenbrand, Liturgy Course Notes. UNDA, CMRH 29/12. See Massey H. Shepherd, Jr., "Liturgy and Mission," in *Liturgy is Mission*, ed. Frank S. Cellier (New York: Seabury Press, 1964), p. 62: "In our own day the liturgy is still a school of Christian living, and we are all enrolled in this school, so to speak, by our baptism. But nowadays a good many of us don't understand the course!"

American liturgists emphasized the personal calling God gave to every baptized member to play an active role in the up-building of the Body of Christ. For baptism is a vital rebirth, which not only makes one a member of Christ's Body but gives one a share in the priestly ministry of Christ. Confirmation is the sacrament of maturity, the sacrament of Catholic Action, empowering one to build up the body of Christ. As Hillenbrand explained:

> [Confirmation] conveys a new seal and is an intensification of the priesthood of Christ, and a fuller consecration to bring the effects of that priesthood of redemption to the world . . . .[45]

Of course, the ultimate effect was expressed in terms of the restoration of the social order and the fulfillment of our vocation as Christ's apostles.[46]

Each time we participate in the Eucharist we renew this desire to bring the redemption to the world.

> We cannot stand at that renewal [of redemption] and not be interested in bringing the effects of that renewal into all of life . . . . The Mass is the action, the redemption, the renewal of the world and it is exactly that which is Catholic Action. All supplementary apostolic action is derivative. Therefore, we can't act with Christ at Mass without translating that act into life through the apostolate.[47]

However, Hillenbrand knew that people disagreed with this. And so, he reminded them that in *Mystici Corporis*, Pius XII had condemned the purely "spiritual approach" to worship that "confines the redemption to the four walls of the Church, as if it had no connection with life itself."[48]

---

45. Hillenbrand, "The Theological Bases of the Apostolate," August, 1948 lecture. UNDA, CMRH 12/30. See September 1969 lecture on baptism. UNDA, CMRH 29/14.

46. See Marmion, *Christ the Life of the Soul*, p. 18 and Hillenbrand, "Marmion and Liturgical Renewal," *American Benedictine Review* 14 (1963), pp. 3–4.

47. Ibid. See Hillenbrand, Liturgy Course Notes. UNDA,CMRH 5/21: "Through the liturgy the people become conscious of the Mystical Body, become accustomed to communal action, are impregnated with justice and charity, and are fired to set things right because they are members one of another."

48. Ibid. See Pius XII, Mystici Corporis, nos. 44, 65, 87, 98 and Hillenbrand, "Catholic Action," June 17, 1947, lecture. UNDA, CMRH 8/36: "We have to sense Christ in the world today and realize that we are one with him. He does his work through us and he won't get his work done without us. We learn this in the liturgy."

What Hillenbrand did through the Liturgical Conference and the Specialized Lay Apostolate was to mobilize the resources (especially, the laity) of the Church to bring everything to a head in Christ, to restore the unity of the human family.[49]

> Our Lord wanted a unity which would respond to the fact that we were divinely related to him, sharing his divine life as God . . . . This is what he prayed for the night before he died: that his apostles and we might be one with him, as his Father and he were one.[50]

The most hopeful sign that the Church would succeed in its work was the restoration of the laity to their rightful place in the work of Christ, the work of the Mystical Body.

Of all the exciting things that happened since the beginning of the twentieth century, Hillenbrand considered the most exciting thing to be the emergence of the lay apostolate and the fact that the laity has discovered their necessary and proper role in the work of the Church. In 1958, he boldly claimed:

> This . . . in one sense is much more exciting even than the great sacramental work of the Church, which is connected with the lay people— the fact that they have come to receive Christ so frequently and to receive him so early. It's more exciting . . . than the effort to make the Mass interesting and vital to people. And so much depends upon . . . the lay apostolate for the future.[51]

For the lay apostolate is intimately related to the work of evangelization in the world. People "need Christ so badly and all the things that Christ in the Church and the Mystical Body can offer to them."[52]

---

49. See Jeremy Hall, *The Full Stature of Christ, the Ecclesiology of Virgil Michel* (Collegeville: Liturgical Press, 1976), pp. 52–54. Many of these same points are also found in Michel's writings. See Michel, "The Liturgy, the Basis of Social Regeneration," *Orate Fratres* 9 (1935), pp.536–545; "Frequent Communion and Social Regeneration," *OrateFratres* 10 (1936), pp. 198–202; "The Scope of the Liturgical Movement," *Orate Fratres* 10 (1936), pp. 485–490.

50. Hillenbrand, "The Lay Apostolate," August 28, 1961 talk on WBBM radio. UNDA, CMRH 8/5.

51. Hillenbrand, "The Mass and the Lay Apostolate," August 25, 1958, lecture. UNDA, CMRH 12/28.

52. Ibid. See Leonard Doohan, *The Lay Centered Church, Theology and Spirituality* (Minneapolis: Winston Press, 1984).

The result of the Mystical Body's efforts to spread redemption in the world would be a more just society, a society that respected the great dignity of the human person, a society that understood the true meaning of life. Among contemporary liturgists, Mark Searle captured the spirit of the liturgical pioneers, when he wrote:

> The power of God's justice, which lifts up the lowly and undermines the pretensions of the powerful, was recognized both in the shape of the community's worship and in the shape of its common life. The two were not separable: both liturgy and the events of daily life were equally occasions for bearing generous and faithful testimony to the fact that God's merciful justice finds its scope in human history.[53]

For liturgical renewal and the renewal of society were really two sides of the same saving reality: the complete Christ active in the world.[54]

LITURGICAL ACTION AND CATHOLIC ACTION

The sacramental principle was a fundamental part of Hillenbrand's synthesis on liturgy and life, liturgy and the apostolate. In the liturgy, Christ reveals the mysteries of the Kingdom through concrete, physical realities. Like Virgil Michel, Hillenbrand saw the liturgy revealing the basic truths of our faith: divine life, the Mystical Body, Christ the redeemer. These truths are expressed

> in palpable terms, the invisible in visible signs, the divine in human forms, always in imitation, nay in continuation, of Christ Himself, God-man, the Word made flesh. The liturgy teaches the mind through the senses, the heart through the emotions, the individual by aid of the social, the human through the divine. It answers the whole human, body and soul, heart and mind—and is the one complete and genuine form of the holy grail so earnestly sought today: religious experience.[55]

---

53. Mark Searle, "Serving the Lord with Justice," in *Liturgy and Social Justice* (Collegeville: Liturgical Press, 1980), p. 19.

54. Hillenbrand demonstrates this connection by challenging all the members of the Mystical Body to use their gifts to eliminate injustice in industrial life, hatred in interracial life, irresponsibility in political life, the breakdown in married life, and extreme nationalism in international life. A good example of this is his talk, "The Family and Catholic Action," in *National Liturgical Week 1946* (Highland Park, Ill.: Liturgical Conference, 1947), pp. 128–136.

55. Virgil Michel, "The Liturgical Apostolate," *Catholic Educational Review*, 25 (1927), pp. 56; See Marx, p. 222 and Hall, pp. 3844.

People do not worship like angels, but require external signs and symbols to express invisible, spiritual realities.[56]

A truism of neo-scholastic theology was that grace builds on nature, that divine life does not destroy but ennobles our natural life. At birth, one receives natural life and at baptism (rebirth), one receives eternal (supernatural) life. The Eucharist is the sacrament of our unity in the one life of Christ. And so, "divine life is begun, recovered, enriched, sustained, and maintained by the Mass and the sacraments, i.e., the liturgy."[57] Divine life makes us sharers of the divine nature, which is a community of three persons. Hence, all human beings, created in the divine image, find fulfillment (redemption) by being part of a community, the Mystical Body of Christ.

Passive participation, which can make the liturgy a backdrop for personal devotion, may impoverish the communication of divine life and the experience of belonging to the Mystical Body. Liturgy is an action, a corporate action of the entire Mystical Body.

> We belong together; we must act together. . . . Corporate worship is at once humbling, because in it we are only one of many; and exalting, because it endows us with the sense of corporate strength; it brings home to us the human community, the human family, which is so necessary for full human thinking and living.[58]

For too long the redemptive work of Christ was hindered by a passive laity, unaware of their rightful place as baptized members of Christ's body.

Too many Catholics suffered from a distorted or partial vision of Christ, the Church, and the liturgy. Hillenbrand attempted to change their vision by introducing them to the concept of an "incarnational spirituality." An "incarnational spirituality" referred to the fact that

> God became incarnate . . . and thrust himself into human life and into human affairs. . . . He dealt with flesh and blood, and with actual situations. And that's the kind of spirituality we must have, an incarnate spirituality,

---

56. See Hillenbrand, Liturgy Course Notes. UNDA, CMRH5/21 and Michel, *The Liturgy of the Church*, pp. 80–81.

57. Hillenbrand, 1946 Liturgy Course Notes, St. Pius X School. UNDA, CMRH 29/18. See Pius XII, *Mystici Corporis*, no. 18.

58. Hillenbrand, "The Meaning of Liturgy," in *National Liturgical Week 1941*, p. 22.

like our Blessed Lord: thrust into life, dealing with people, dealing with human authority, dealing with flesh and blood.[59]

Unfortunately, there were far too many "crippled Christians" who failed to make the connection between what they did in church and the way they lived in the world.[60] Ideally, participation at Mass gave the baptized person the desire "to do something about bringing the redemptive influence of Christ to bear upon the world."[61] And so, the apostolate was seen as an extension of the altar, of the giving of self celebrated at the Eucharist.

> The fact that the Mass is an action should drive us to apostolic action. Otherwise, we leave our religion, and the greatest thing it has, Mass, in the realm of the "purely spiritual," with no resulting action.[62]

In the liturgy and in the lay apostolate the same dynamic was at work: the creation of apostles according to the pattern of Christ's life.

The liturgical pioneers addressed the need to connect daily prayer to a vigorous apostolic life. H. A. Reinhold expressed this well, when he challenged Christians to discover

> a coherence between life outside and within us, Christ and the world, our mind and the economy of salvation, our person and the Church. When we begin to see this, to experience the truth and the fact, we then are part of a divine man, consciously living members of the living Christ, the Church. Then we realize that the sacraments and the liturgy are functions of Christ, who becomes mysteriously contemporaneous to us, veiled and

---

59. Hillenbrand, "The Spirituality of the Young Worker," August 1951 lecture. UNDA, CMRH 8/38.

60. See Lawrence E. Mick, *To Live as We Worship* (Collegeville: Liturgical Press, 1984), p. 13: "For too many people the spiritual life is a compartment of their experience, carefully defined and neatly tucked away so that it can neither contaminate nor be contaminated by the rest of their lives. Spiritual matters have to do with God, church, and religion; they have no significant connection with politics, economics, professional responsibilities, career opportunities, recreation, entertainment, cultural events, family interactions, or anything else that really matters in their lives."

61. Hillenbrand, "The Mass as the Source and Center of the Lay Apostolate," in *National Liturgical Week, 1955* (Elsberry, Mo.: Liturgical Conference, 1956), p. 176.

62. Ibid., p. 179. See Mick, *To Live as We Worship*, pp.5051: "The liturgy stands as a constant corrective to the tendency to over spiritualize religion, to shun the human and the created as unworthy, sinful, or inherently evil."

disguised under appallingly plain symbols—bread, wine, water, oil, words, actions, and fellow humans.[63]

Hillenbrand saw his ministry of training lay apostles as away to make Christ contemporaneous to the people of his day.

From the earliest days of his involvement in the National Liturgical Weeks, Hillenbrand was convinced of the need for the specialized, organized training of lay apostles. He stated this position quite plainly at the 1945 National Liturgical Week:

> We shall never get on with the liturgy as we should until we create the specialized, organized Catholic Action movements. Its members inevitably come to see that they must have the liturgy or otherwise their formation and their work will be hindered.[64]

The reason why they saw the need for the liturgy is because their specialized training exposed them to the type of ecclesiology and liturgiology which we have just described.

In 1946, Hillenbrand became even stronger in his call to foster the specialized lay apostolate. In fact, he claimed that one cannot bring people to the liturgy

> except through the effort of Catholic Action apostles. The movement will create the people who are ready for the liturgy and eager for it and who will interest others as well . . . .[65]

Of course, there was a bit of rhetorical excess in the claim that the efforts of Catholic Action apostles was the only effective way to bring people to the liturgy. In addition, the numbers of trained lay apostles never reached the levels that Hillenbrand had originally envisioned. Nonetheless, they were a highly significant group prior to Vatican II and in the period of transition that followed the Council.

One of the reasons why Hillenbrand became involved in the specialized lay apostolate was due to the concern that Pius XI raised

---

63. H. A. Reinhold, "More or Less Liturgical," *Orate Fratres* 13 (1939), pp. 154–155. See Joel Patrick Garner, "The Vision of a Liturgical Reformer: Hans Ansgar Reinhold, American Catholic Educator," Ph.D. dissertation (New York: Columbia University, 1972), p. 49.

64. Hillenbrand, "The Liturgical Revival Today," in *National Liturgical Week 1945* (Peotone, Ill.: Liturgical Conference, 1946), p. 11.

65. Ibid.

over the inadequacy of the clergy to counter the threats of secularism and individualism. For the hierarchical apostolate

> inevitably needs to multiply its own activity by many hands, many arms, many lips, many wills, as Our Lord did in his own day, when he sent his own disciples ahead of him, to prepare the ways for his own evangelization.[66]

The solution to the losses in church members due to secularism and individualism was to heed Pius XI's call to "recruit and train auxiliary soldiers of the Church."[67]

In Europe, the foremost leader of the Catholic Action movement was Joseph Cardijn of Belgium, the founder of the JOC. As we discussed, his movement was ecclesiastically recognized, yet lay-oriented. It forged a bond between the challenges of living in the world and the worker's main contact with the church: the liturgy.

> To these new masses . . . the Church was bringing what Cardijn had taught from the beginning: a living relationship between liturgical and sacramental life and the daily sacrifice of their hands and muscles on the altar of industrial work. The Mass is ended: go and make your day a continual Mass in union with the Mass offered by the Pope, the bishops, the priests, the Mass whose effects are confirmed in your lives.[68]

What Cardijn did for the European Jocist Movement, Hillenbrand attempted to do for the Specialized Lay Apostolate in the United States.

Hillenbrand recognized the commonality in theology and goals between the liturgical and social action movements. This is why he could say without hesitation that

---

66. Pius XI, "Speech to the Directors of Roman Catholic Action," April 19, 1931, in Luigi Civardi, *A Manual of Catholic Action*, trans. C.C. Martindale (New York: Sheed & Ward, 1943), p. 115. This statement inspired Hillenbrand's frequently quoted passage: "You are the hands of Christ . . . where you work, Christ works. You are the feet of Christ . . . wherever you go, Christ goes. You are the heart of Christ; wherever you go the love of Christ is found because you love people. You are the lips of Christ; whatever you articulate, you are articulating for Christ." Cited in John N. Kotre, *Simple Gifts, The Lives of Pat and Patty Crowley* (Kansas City: Andrews & McMeel, 1979), p. 43.

67. Pius XI, *Quadragesimo Anno*, no. 141.

68. Michael De La Bedoyere, *The Cardijn Story, A Study of the Life of Msgr. Joseph Cardijn and the Young Christian Worker's Movement Which he Founded* (London: Longmans, Green, & Company, 1958), p. 182.

Catholic Action is rooted in the liturgy. Indeed, it is an extension of the liturgy. Why? Because it happens to be rooted in Christ. . . . That is the complete Christ—Christ still in the world, one living thing with his members, acting through them and with them.[69]

For the liturgy and Catholic Action are both ways in which Christ is carrying on his redemptive action in our world.

Quadragesimo Anno was a springboard for a great deal of social activism in the Church. As such, it came at the right time, with unemployment and the turmoil in family life graphically demonstrating the failure of the secularized social order and the need to reconstruct society on the organic model of the Mystical Body. One cannot pray in comfort in our churches, while one's brothers and sisters were being victimized by racial hatred, economic exploitation, or international violence. One must be active not only in the liturgy but in the extension of the liturgy in the world: the apostolate.

The early history of the Liturgical Conference reflected the strong convictions which American liturgical reformers had regarding the connection between liturgy and life. Of course, many of these connections were based on ideals originally developed by leaders of the European liturgical and social action movements. Nonetheless, there was a strong emphasis in the American liturgical movement on the relationship of liturgy to social justice. In part, this emphasis was due to the efforts of people like Hillenbrand who devoted their lives to training lay apostles to bring Christ's redemption, his justice, and his peace to the world.

---

69. Hillenbrand, "The Family and Catholic Action," *National Liturgical Week 1946*, p. 134. This quotation relates to Hillenbrand's fundamental conviction that "the liturgy isn't just a form of prayer, but it is an activity, the most important activity of the day, the most important thing that we do." From an August 7, 1964, letter of Hillenbrand to Bishop Ernest Primeau, critiquing a draft of the *Decree on the Laity*. UNDA, CMRH 9/4.

Chapter 7

Lay Spirituality, Apostolic Formation, and the Liturgy

LAY SPIRITUALITY AND THE APOSTOLATE

As we have seen, Reynold Hillenbrand had perhaps his greatest impact on the spirituality and formation of the laity. We have examined in detail his role as a liturgical reformer. In this chapter we will look at his vision of the laity in the Church through the lens of the liturgy.

Hillenbrand's approach to the topic of spirituality was based on the fundamental principles of his liturgical theology: anthropology, divine life, ecclesiology, Christology, and liturgiology. For Hillenbrand defined human beings in terms of their sharing divine life. He defined the purpose of the Church in terms of its sharing in the mission of Christ. He defined the liturgy as a celebration of what it meant to be, to become, and to build up the church.

Since Hillenbrand defined the Church as the Body of Christ committed to bringing the redemptive action of Christ to the world, his definition of Christ necessarily emphasized the central act of redemption, Christ's suffering and death on the cross. Since he defined the Mass as Christ's death renewed, then the source, the center, and the inspiration of the Christian life was obviously the Mass. In these convictions, Hillenbrand reflected the Christ-centered base given to the liturgical movement by European leaders such as Columba Marmion, Lambert Beauduin, or Romano Guardini.[1]

Hillenbrand rejected the mechanical understanding of grace "popping into us at baptism, popping out of us through mortal sin,

---

1. Hillenbrand, "Marmion and the Liturgical Renewal," *American Benedictine Review* 14:1 (1963), pp. 2–3 and Ephrem Boularand, "The Christocentric Quality in Dom Marmion," in *More About Marmion* (St. Louis: B. Herder, 1949), pp. 89–110.

popping back into us through Confession."[2] Instead, he preferred defining grace, as Marmion did, in relational terms, as sharing the Christ life, the life and the love of the Trinity. In other words, grace makes us sharers in the divine nature so that we become capable of knowing, loving, and acting as God acts.[3] And so, spirituality describes this sharing of the Christ life, this oneness in Christ.

> Spirituality simply means our closeness to Christ. It means living more completely in Christ. Perhaps the best way to express it is to say that spirituality means Christ-likeness. This term is very personal.[4]

For spirituality describes the intimate relationship of a life lived in Christ.

Like Marmion, Hillenbrand defined holiness in terms of the communication of divine life by Christ to God's children. Holiness was experiencing the great privilege

> . . . of being born into the very existence, and at the very hub of God, so that the life which courses in the Trinity and the love which courses in the Trinity, courses also into us.[5]

In other words, holiness is who you are ontologically. Since we are God's children, our very existence is a continuation of the existence of God, who is three in one. Holiness is not something you earn, but it is something you are in God. For too long, people were taught that holiness is achieved by keeping the commandments, saying their prayers, receiving Communion frequently, etc.[6] While behavioral holiness produced many good actions, it failed to grasp the relational character of divine life. Like the sacraments, holiness is primarily God's action in us, moving us to recognize our God-given dignity and live in the world like Jesus. Since grace builds on nature and action follows being, once people understand the social nature

---

2. Ibid., p. 4.

3. See Columba Marmion, *Christ the Life of the Soul*, trans. by a nun of Tyburn Convent (St. Louis: B. Herder Book Company, 1922), p. 15.

4. Hillenbrand, "Spirituality of YCW Leaders," July 1952 lecture. UNDA, CMRH 8/38.

5. Ibid., p. 4.

6. Hillenbrand, "Spiritual Formation of the Lay Apostle," August 1950 lecture. UNDA, CMRH 8/38.

of their being, they will either do something about their situation or frustrate their nature.[7]

Hillenbrand's understanding of spirituality as "Christ-likeness" reflected the positive evaluation of human nature, which was implied in the doctrine of the incarnation, in the fact that Christ became human. In the 1930s and 1940s, spirituality was associated with a negative evaluation of the world and an escape from its problems. Hillenbrand rejected the attempt by some in the Church to impose a monastic spirituality upon lay people, treating them like "second class" citizens in the church. In fact, some even claimed that "one cannot save one's soul or, at least, make spiritual progress, if one's life is spent in our industrial system."[8] Yet it is precisely in the world that a Christian finds their likeness to Christ, that a Christian is challenged to continue the redemptive activity of Christ, to participate in Catholic Action.

Pius XI saw Catholic Action as inseparable from Catholic life. Since action follows being, being a Christian inevitably involved taking action to solve life's problems. "In reality . . . it is the sacraments of baptism and confirmation themselves that impose, among other obligations, that of the apostolate, of spiritual assistance to our neighbor."[9] Each member of the Body of Christ must share with others the life of the Trinity, the life Christ came to bring to earth. "And consequently, every Christian ought to pour out this life upon others who do not possess it, or who possess it only in a too feeble measure, or only in appearance."[10] For the life of the Trinity exists in Christians not for themselves, but "for its diffusion, that is, the active life, action, the apostolate."[11] Thus, the apostolate (or Catholic Action) is a continual manifestation and proof of our sharing divine life.

---

7. In these convictions, Hillenbrand reflects the thought of Marmion, *Christ the Life of the Soul*, pp. 14–23 and Yves M. J. Congar, *Lay People in the Church, A Study for a Theology of the Laity*, trans. Donald Attwater (Westminster: Newman Press, 1957), pp. 106–111.

8. Hillenbrand, "The Spirituality of YCW Leaders," July 1952 lecture. UNDA, CMRH 8/38.

9. Pius XI, "Ex officiosis literris," (November 10, 1933 letter to Cardinal Cerejeira, Patriarch of Lisbon), cited in Theodore M. Hesburgh, *The Theology of Catholic Action* (Notre Dame: Ave Maria Press, 1946), p. 32.

10. Ibid.

11. Pius XI, "Address to the Pilgrimage of Feminine Catholic Youth (Aveyronnaise)," September 20, 1933, cited in Hesburgh, p. 30.

We must evaluate Hillenbrand's emphasis on redemptive activity and the diffusion of divine life in the light of the then-emerging theology of world transformation that surfaced as a result of the liturgical and social action movements.

> In the theological position of world transformation, the lay person is not only *in* the world but *for* the world. But this world does not correspond to the way God willed it; rather, it is a world in process of becoming in Christ what it is capable of being. It is not enough to view the world statically; it must be approached with an awareness that we are called to change it—to redeem it to the glory of God.[12]

In other words, Christians are agents of the consecration of the world to God in Christ, a consecration that embraces every area of human existence.[13]

When he spoke of lay spirituality, Hillenbrand frequently referred to the completeness of Christ's redemptive work. He would quote John 12:31–32, where Christ said: "Now has judgment come upon this world, now will this world's prince be driven out, and I— once I am lifted up from earth—will draw all to myself."[14] In Ephesians 1:22–23, this process is described in terms of the economy of salvation wherein all things are placed under Christ's feet and he is exalted as "head of the church, which is his body: the fullness of him who fills the universe in all its parts."

---

12. Leonard Doohan, *The Lay-Centered Church, Theology and Spirituality* (Minneapolis: Winston Press, 1984), p. 13. See Yves Congar, *Christians Active in the World*, trans. P.F. Hepburne-Scott (New York: Herder & Herder, 1968); Johannes B. Metz, *Theology of the World* (New York: Herder & Herder, 1969); and Richard P. McBrien, "A Theology of the Laity," *American Ecclesiastical Review* 160 (1969), pp. 73–86.

13. Ibid., pp. 14, 23. See Stanislas Lyonnet, "La rédemption de l'univers," *Lumière et Vie* 48 (1960), pp. 43-62 and B. de Margerie, "Le Christ, la sécularisation et la consécration du monde," *Nouvelle Revue Théologique* 91 (1969), pp. 370–395.

14. In a January, 1954 lecture on "The Mystical Body of Christ," Hillenbrand compared this passage to St. Irenaeus' doctrine of the recapitulation of all things in Christ: "Lifted up on a cross, Christ draws all things to himself, as St. Irenaeus says, 'He recapitulates in himself the long history of men and women, 'summing us up' and giving us salvation, that we might receive again in Christ Jesus what we have lost in Adam, that is, the image and likeness of God.' (*Adversus Haereses* III.xviii)." This doctrine is central to Hillenbrand's theology of divinization. UNDA, CMRH 10/35.

Therefore, the redemptive influence of Christ must reach every area, every province of life, nothing exempted. The redemptive influence must reach domestic life, racial life, economic life, political life, and international life.[15]

Because these areas are the laity's sphere of influence and responsibility, the laity must be taught that Christ depends on them to bring redemption to these areas of life.

Hillenbrand's global vision was expressed in terms of his understanding of the Mystical Body. As members of the Body of Christ, "we believe in one person present, living, acting, and loving in many people."[16] In Christ that person is the Holy Spirit. Consequently, the Body of Christ shares in the life of the Spirit, who empowers us to act like Christ, hindered only by our sinfulness. We begin this new life in Christ at baptism, when we become part of Christ's body, receive a share in divine life, and become a new creation. After baptism, we no longer live for ourselves but live in Christ, sharing his spirit and his ministry.[17]

The spirituality of the church is basically a baptismal spirituality.[18] If baptism is the fundamental moment in the Christian life, then any true Christian spirituality must explicate this moment. For too long, individualism has affected even our understanding of baptism.[19] Yet baptism is meant not only to redeem and renew one individually, but to give birth to a new people, who will live like the Trinity in the world.[20] Sharing the life of the Trinity with the world is really what the apostolate (or Catholic Action) is all about. "This is what makes us holy. This is Christ's desire and his charge to us."[21]

---

15. Hillenbrand, "The Theological Bases of the Apostolate," August 1948 lecture. UNDA, CMRH 8/34.

16. Doohan, p. 70.

17. Hillenbrand, "The Christian in Action—in the Home," March 2, 1951, lecture. UNDA, CMRH 31.

18. This approach has triumphed since Vatican II. See Don E. Saliers, *Worship and Spirituality* (Philadelphia: Westminster Press, 1984), p. 58: "Baptism initiates the double journey into our own humanity and into life with God. Baptismal spirituality therefore requires our humanity at full stretch in relation to God and to the whole human community. In this way, baptism into Jesus' dying and rising is the charter for all ministry in his name."

19. See Gerald Ellard, *Christian Life and Worship*, pp. 246–251, 265–270 and Virgil Michel, *The Christian in the World*, pp. 22–30.

20. Hillenbrand, "Lay Spirituality," August, 1956 lecture. UNDA, CMRH 8/38.

21. Hillenbrand, "Spirituality of CFM, Part II," February, 1966 lecture. UNDA, CMRH 10/19.

Baptism makes one part of a "chosen race, a royal priesthood, a holy nation, a people God claims for his own to proclaim the glorious works of the one who called you from darkness to light" (1 Peter 2:9). Consequently, baptism not only redeems humans but forms them into a priestly people.[22] "In baptism, Christ gave you a share in his priesthood which is the seal of Baptism. He impressed upon your soul the likeness of himself as the priest."[23] In this belief, Hillenbrand reflected the common teaching of various popes and theologians.[24]

Confirmation is the sacrament of Christian maturity, the sacrament that completes our baptism. In both baptism and confirmation, we receive the Holy Spirit. In baptism, the emphasis is on our personal sharing in divine life. In confirmation, the emphasis is more social. Like Thomas, Hillenbrand taught that confirmation strengthens the baptized person to profess his or her faith before the world, to give witness to Christ, to be an apostle. As he says:

> Seen in this light, confirmation is the sacrament of adult, mature Christians, equipping lay apostles for their great task in the world—to bring the fruits of the Redemption to all.[25]

Thus, Hillenbrand improved the old Thomistic synthesis with insights drawn from the doctrine of the lay priesthood that was popularized by leaders in the social action and liturgical movements.[26]

The liturgical pioneers reintroduced the doctrine of the common priesthood by explaining what Thomas taught about character. According to Thomas, "sacramental character consists in a certain participation in Christ's priesthood present in the faithful."[27] The proper office of a priest was to be a mediator, to unite those in need

---

22. Hillenbrand, "The Role of the Laity," August, 1953 lecture. UNDA, CMRH 9/15. See 1961 CFM Inquiry Program. UNDA, CMRH 10/37.

23. Hillenbrand, "The Mass and the Lay Apostolate," May 3, 1955, lecture. UNDA, CMRH 8/36.

24. See Jeremiah Newman, *What is Catholic Action? An Introduction to the Lay Apostolate* (Westminster: Newman Press, 1958), pp. 58–62.

25. Hillenbrand, "Lay Spirituality," August, 1956 lecture. UNDA, CMRH 8/38. See Thomas Aquinas, *Summa Theologica*, III, q. 72, a. 5.

26. See Gerald Ellard, "The Meaning of the Priesthood," in *National Liturgical Week 1941* (Newark: Benedictine Liturgical Conference, 1942), pp. 29–43 and Luigi Civardi, *A Manual of Catholic Action*, trans. C.C. Martindale (New York: Sheed & Ward, 1943), pp. 58–17.

27. Thomas Aquinas, *Summa Theologica*, III, q. 63, a. 5.

of reconciliation. Consequently, apostolic action became a form of priestly mediation (bringing God to the world and the world to God).[28] Moreover, priestly mediation was further refined in terms of the Augustinian doctrine of sacrifice (every work done with the aim of uniting us with God in holy fellowship).[29]

The acceptability of the doctrine of the common priesthood was immensely improved under the pontificate of Pius XII. While being careful to separate the priesthood of the ordained from the common priesthood, in *Mediator Dei*, Pius XII makes it clear that

> By the waters of baptism, as by common right, Christians are made members of the Mystical Body of Christ the priest, and by the "character" which is imprinted on their souls, they are appointed to give worship to God. Thus they participate, according to their condition, in the priesthood of Christ.[30]

Often Pius XII praised the good work done by the laity, who are in the front line of the Church's life, who literally are the Church in the world.[31]

Hillenbrand believed "the age of the laity" was just dawning.[32] In fact, the most exciting thing in the twentieth century was "the emergence of the laity into their rightful and full status in the Church."[33] Like Pius XII, he made the usual distinction:

> The lay apostolate in a general sense includes all apostolic Catholics and apostolic organizations. The apostolate in the strict sense means that lay

---

28. See Theodore M. Hesburgh, *The Theology of Catholic Action* (Notre Dame: Ave Maria Press, 1946), p. 65: "The mediatorial mission of Christ the Priest was entrusted to the Church, and in the supernatural organism of his Body, his priestly mediation is continued, participated variously by all his members, who through his life-giving sacraments partake of the influence of the greatest sacrament of all: his sacred humanity, the 'source of all priesthood.'"

29. See Yves M. J. Congar, *Lay People in the Church*, trans. Donald Attwater (Westminster: Newman Press, 1957), pp. 143–171.

30. Pius XII, *Mediator Dei*, no. 88.

31. See *Pius XII Speaks on the Lay Apostolate* (Rome: Permanent Committee for International Congresses on the Apostolate of the Laity, 1955). Great impetus was given to the lay apostolate as a result of the First World Congress on the Lay Apostolate held in Rome from October 1–14, 1951, and the Second World Congress held from October 5–13, 1957. Pius XII spoke at both Congresses, affirming the necessity of lay participation in the work of the Church.

32. Hillenbrand, "Doctrine of the Church on the Formation of Lay Apostles," August 21, 1961 lecture. UNDA, CMRH 9/2.

33. Hillenbrand, "Lay Spirituality," August, 1956 lecture. UNDA, CMRH 8/38.

people undertake tasks deriving from the mission entrusted by Christ to his Mystical Body.[34]

The laity's task was to give a Christian, a redemptive note to civilization and to make their role in the Mystical Body the dominant force in their lives.[35]

Frequently, Hillenbrand repeated the papal thesis that the breakdowns in the extension of Christ's redemptive work occurred in the areas of life that were the responsibilities of lay people: domestic life, racial life, economic life, political life, international life. The solution to these problems was to bring them under the influence of Christ. This can happen only if lay Christians accept the challenge to live their identity in Christ. Like Virgil Michel, Hillenbrand believed the ultimate purpose of the apostolate was to overcome those social conditions that make living one's life in Christ's Body difficult and to promote those conditions that foster the growth of that life.[36]

"Lay spirituality means working with life's problems. It is a growth in grace through action."[37] Lay apostles grow in grace by bringing Christ to others, by exercising their roles as priestly mediators. In giving Christ to others, they also find Christ themselves, thus deepening their union with him. And so, the intensification of divine life and the ability to act are mutually related. The stronger the divine life grows within us, the more Christians are empowered to engage in the apostolate. Consequently, their spirituality is an incarnate spirituality, thrusting them into the events of daily life, challenging them to continue the work of Christ in the world. It is a realistic spirituality that tries to "see the world as our Blessed Lord saw it."[38]

According to Hillenbrand, lay spirituality is achieved through associations with people, through meeting with people. It is a spirituality of communion, recognizing our common unity with others.

---

34. Hillenbrand, "Doctrine of the Church on the Formation of Lay Apostles," August 21, 1961, lecture. UNDA, CMRH 9/2.

35. Hillenbrand, "Introduction" to the 1959 CFM Program, *Politics & Christian Life* (Chicago: CFM, 1959). UNDA, CMRH 10/34.

36. See Marx, pp. 196–197.

37. Hillenbrand, "The Spirituality of YCW Leaders," July, 1952 lecture. UNDA, CMRH 8/38.

38. Hillenbrand, "The Spirituality of the Young Worker," July 6, 1954, lecture. UNDA, CMRH 8/38.

Our associations with others is a strong self-sacrifice out of charity. It is a love of others because we see Christ in them. . . . When you love a person, it is Christ loving through you. This is what the Mystical Body means. . . . It is not just a question of saving my soul, but of knowing what part to play in the Mystical Body, in the great plan of God.[39]

Hillenbrand explained our part in the great plan of God in terms of a sacrifice (making our lives a gift-offering to God).[40] Of course, the inspiration for this description was the sacrifice of the Mass, the supreme instrument of formation in the Christian life.

APOSTOLIC FORMATION AND THE LITURGY

In the 1940s, the spiritual life of the average Catholic centered around the rosary, devotional prayers, benediction, and the occasional novena. Hillenbrand and other liturgical leaders sought to change traditional piety by making the liturgy the "foremost and indispensable fount of the true Christian spirit."[41] Like Lambert Beauduin, they believed that the liturgy was an act of a different order and on a different level than the usual methods of personal prayer.

Through them (the acts of the liturgy), Jesus Christ fulfills the work of His priestly mission; the Holy Spirit acts on souls; the Church puts into play the full efficacy of her priestly powers: in them we reach the source of supernatural life. The more we participate, with body and soul, the more we draw life from this source.[42]

Like Beauduin, Hillenbrand often spoke of the full efficacy of active participation in the liturgy.

Hillenbrand's work in training lay apostles was grounded in a fundamental appreciation of the Mass as the source and center of

---

39. Hillenbrand, "The Spirituality of YCW Leaders," July 1952 lecture. UNDA, CMRH 8/38. In his August 17, 1956 lecture, "Lay Spirituality," Hillenbrand explained: "If only we could see this added dimension of what we're doing to others, what we're doing to Christ. We don't have to worry about our love of God, if we can say that we love our neighbor sufficiently." UNDA, CMRH 8/38.

40. For a fuller explanations of sacrifice as self-giving, see pp. 245 -247.

41. Pius X, *Tra le sollecitudini.*

42. Lambert Beauduin, *Liturgy: the Life of the Church,* trans. Virgil Michel (Collegeville: Liturgical Press, 1929), p. 81.

our spiritual lives.[43] Respected theologians like Alexander Schmemann also saw the need to educate people to make the connection between liturgy and life. As Schmemann explains:

> The essential role of liturgical education is to show how through participation in the *leiturgia*, the corporate and official worship of the Church, we can become witnesses to Christ in our private and public life, responsible members of the Church, or, in short, *Christians* in the full meaning of this word.[44]

Hillenbrand saw himself as providing the type of liturgical education, which Schmemann and many others saw as essential to the renewal of the life of the church.

Hillenbrand believed that the laity's knowledge about the liturgy was inadequate and hindered their becoming apostles. People were more interested in what they could do for themselves (e.g., obtain grace or the forgiveness of their sins) rather than in what they were doing for God: offering the whole Christ, head and members, to God.[45] Mass had become human-centered rather than God-centered. As Hillenbrand said:

> The primary thing about the Mass is that Christ gives himself to the Father, and that we give ourselves to the Father. The primary thing is what we do for God: that we adore God, praise God, and love God.[46]

This theology of self-offering was quite common and continues to be used today.[47]

For Hillenbrand, the essence of the Mass was the consecration, in which the offering of the same victim and priest as on Calvary takes place. Thomas taught that the consecration was the re-presentation of Calvary in an unbloody manner. On the cross our redemption was accomplished. In the Mass, the fruits of that redemption are applied

---

43. In this conviction, Hillenbrand frequently quoted Pius XII, *Mediator Dei*, no. 201: "The Mass is the chief act of divine worship; it should also be the source and center of Christian piety."

44. Alexander Schmemann, *Liturgy and Life: Christian Development through Liturgical Experience* (New York: Dept. of Religious Education, Orthodox Church in America, 1974), p. 23.

45. See James W. King, *The Liturgy and the Laity* (Westminster: Newman Press, 1963), pp. 58–61.

46. Hillenbrand, "The Priests' Spirituality," July 29, 1960, lecture. UNDA, CMRH 11/28.

47. See John H. Miller, *Fundamentals of the Liturgy* (Notre Dame: Fides, 1959), pp. 214–219.

or renewed.[48] In *Mediator Dei*, Pius XII repeats this theology and concludes that the merits which flow from the cross are imparted to Christians, who are co-offerers of the Mass.[49] Therefore, "the lay apostle who sees through faith Christ's redemptive action renewed in the Mass must leave the altar, bent upon bringing redemption to all."[50]

The offering of self was not limited to the time spent in Church. It characterized the way Christians should live their lives in the world, so that

> . . . a desk in an office, a table in a kitchen, a machine in a factory, a sales counter in a store, or a mangle in a laundry become in a feeble but helpful sense, an extension of the altar, because it is upon these that the lay apostles are carrying out the offering they made of themselves at Mass.[51]

In this conviction, Hillenbrand popularized in the United States an understanding of liturgy that Joseph Cardijn had fostered in the European Jocist movement.[52]

Hillenbrand defined the Mass as the great expression of the Mystical Body, the great sacrament of our unitive consciousness. People "eat the one Christ, in whom they are one. By that very eating they are forever forged more closely to Christ and each other."[53] The Mass was a great teacher of the sense of unity and corporateness, essential to motivating Christians to act like Christ in the world.[54] Yet when people merely attended Mass, it was easy to loose the corporate sense of being co-offerers of the sacrifice. "People need at Mass not only a vivid faith in their oneness but an experience of it."[55] Hillenbrand centered this experience of oneness especially in the consecration, the

---

48. Thomas Aquinas, *Summa Theologica*, IIIa, q. 74. a. 1; q. 76, a. 2, ad 1; q. 80, a. 12, ad 3.

49. Pius XII, *Mediator Dei*, no. 77. See *The Assisi Papers* (Collegeville: Liturgical Press, 1957), p. 229: at the Assisi Conference, on September 22, 1956, Pius XII states: "Even if the consecration takes place without ceremonial and in a simple fashion, it is the central point of the whole liturgy of the sacrifice."

50. *Fundamentals of the YCW* (Chicago: YCW, 1963), p. 1.

51. Hillenbrand, "The Mass as the Source and Center of the Lay Apostolate," in *National Liturgical Week 1955* (Elsberry, Mo.: Liturgical Conference, 1956), p. 178.

52. See Joseph Cardijn, *Challenge to Action*, ed. Eugene Langdale (Chicago: Fides, 1955), pp. 40–41, 62–63, 118–119.

53. Hillenbrand, "The Mass as the Source and Center of the Lay Apostolate," p. 179.

54. Hillenbrand, "The Spiritual Formation of the Lay Apostle," August 1950 lecture. UNDA, CMRH 8/38.

55. Hillenbrand, "The Mass as the Source and Center of the Lay Apostolate," p. 180.

moment in which the Head and the members offer their gift to the Father.[56]

While Hillenbrand placed a great deal of emphasis on sacrifice and self-offering, he also recognized the redemptive power unleashed with the proclamation of Scripture. The liturgy of the Word was the didactic or teaching part of Mass, whose goal was to form an image of Christ in his members. Hillenbrand was convinced that the scriptures not only deepened our knowledge of Christ, but turned us into apostles. "We can't look upon our Blessed Lord without his having an affect upon our life."[57] The better one understands the scriptures, the more spiritual resources one will have. The more spiritual resources one has, the better an apostle one can be.

In *Christ in His Mysteries*, Abbott Marmion provided the inspiration for the synthesis Hillenbrand developed on the impact of reading scripture.

> Each of these [biblical] incidents contains its own teaching, bears its special light, and is for our souls the sources of a particular grace of which the object is to form Christ within us. The actions of Jesus have this characteristic that they are ours as much as they are his.[58]

Therefore, Hillenbrand encouraged (and gave) a daily homily as a necessary ingredient enabling the Mass to become "the most effective teaching instrument the Church has."[59]

Hillenbrand related the reception of Communion to the offertory and the consecration. He saw this relationship as an exchange of gifts: "at the offertory we give God bread and wine, and God takes

---

56. Hillenbrand, "The Mass as the Source and Center of the Lay Apostolate," p. 180. See Joseph Jungmann, *The Mass of the Roman Rite, Vol. I*, trans. Francis A. Brunner (Westminster: Christian Classics, 1986), p. 190: "Never is the Church so closely bound to her master, never is she so completely Christ's spouse as when, together with him, she offers God this sacrifice . . . . The action which brings this about . . . is the consecration."

57. Hillenbrand, "The Five Essential Qualities of a Chaplain of a CFM, YCW, YCS Group," April 28, 1958, lecture. UNDA, CMRH 10/19.

58. Columba Marmion, *Christ in His Mysteries*, cited in *For Happier Families, Fifth Edition* (Chicago: CFM, 1957). See Hillenbrand, "Marmion and the Liturgical Renewal," *American Benedictine Review* 14:1 (1963), pp. 6–1.

59. Hillenbrand, "Specialized Lay Apostolate," May 1, 1964 article. UNDA, CMRH 9/18. In this article Hillenbrand quoted the *Liturgy Constitution*, par. 33, as agreeing with him about the teaching function of the Mass. Hillenbrand gave a daily homily throughout his priestly career.

these gifts, changes them into Christ, and gives them back to us."[60]
At the time of Christ, people commonly ate the sacrifice offered
to God. In a similar way, Communion is the meal part of the sacrifice
which unites us to God and one another.

> Communion increases life in us each time we receive the Lord. Communion
> unites us more closely with Christ and the other members of the Mystical
> Body. The more divine life we have, the closer we are to Christ and
> to others. Whenever we receive Christ, we draw the Mystical Body
> closer together.[61]

This explanation seeks to overcome the vertical (God and me)
spirituality that became more prevalent in practice in the years prior
to Vatican II and replace it with a more balanced, a more realistic
Incarnate spirituality.[62]

Ignorance of the scriptures and the meaning of the liturgy led
to the problem of the double conscience—people doing and hearing
one thing at the liturgy, but acting another way in the world.

> A person might be a weekly communicant, even a daily communicant, and
> yet in their place of work sit in isolation, refusing to join a [trade] union.
> A person might be a daily communicant, yet come election day be so
> apathetic as not to think of coming out to vote. A person might be a daily
> communicant, but when the subject of the UN comes up, says: "our job is
> to get the US out of the UN and the UN out of the US.[63]

Yet no one who understands the scriptures and the liturgy
can live with a double conscience. For the liturgy increases the sense
of oneness, giving one the mind of Christ and reproducing in one
the life of Christ.

---

60. *For Happier Families, Fifth Edition* (Chicago: CFM, 1957).

61. Ibid. See Pius XII, *Mediator Dei*, no. 120: "The Church of Jesus Christ needs no other bread than this to satisfy fully our souls' wants and desires, and to unite us in the most intimate union with Jesus Christ, to make us "one body," to get us to live together as brothers (and sisters) who, breaking the same bread, sit down to the same heavenly table to partake of the elixir of immortality."

62. See Joseph Jungmann, *The Mass: an Historical, Theological, and Pastoral Survey*, trans. Julian Fernandes (Collegeville: Liturgical Press, 1976), p. 140: "For the recipient, it (communion) is a pledge of eternal life, of participation in the life of the God-man . . . . The reception of Christ's sacramental body constitutes as well as confirms anew the recipient's incorporation into the Mystical Body."

63. Hillenbrand, "Double Conscience," July 6, 1954, lecture. UNDA, CMRH 8/38.

Hillenbrand's synthesis on the Eucharist was typical of the theology fostered at National Liturgical Weeks until the 1960s. Hillenbrand embodied his synthesis in numerous lectures and essays as well as in all the publications of the Specialized Lay Apostolate. Since it appeared so often in print and was spread throughout the United States by the YCW, YCS, CFM, and the Liturgical Conference, it is useful to summarize it here. This summary is also an accurate reflection of the liturgical theology in use in the United States prior to Vatican II:

1. The Mass is Calvary, the sacrifice of Christ's death renewed— same victim, same priest, same sacrifice.
2. Though the same sacrifice, there is a difference between Calvary and Mass—bloody/unbloody distinction, more faith required of those at Mass.
3. The most important moment is the consecration: the moment when Christ renews the sacrifice of his death.
4. Sacrifice means giving a gift to God: bread, wine, Christ, our lives.
5. With the gift we must offer ourselves. Mass is a sacrifice of the whole Christ.
6. Mass is an offering and a meal. Christ feeds us, increases life in us, unites us to others each time we receive him.
7. Mass is our great act of love. Giving a gift to God at Mass shows our love and Christ's great love, giving himself completely on the cross.
8. Mass is something we watch (see the priest consecrate the elements) and do (offer Christ with the priest by virtue of the seals of baptism/confirmation).
9. Mass is something we do together, a corporate action, not a private act.
10. Mass is a great teacher, enabling us to know Christ and become like Christ.
11. Communion is related to the offertory (God gives us a gift back, we eat the sacrifice as the priests did of the Old Testament) and to the consecration (the special moment when we unite our self-offering with Christ).

12. Mass teaches through the feasts, which appeal to the whole human: emotions, senses, as well as mind. The feasts not only instruct us in the truths of faith but form a Christ-likeness in us.
13. We must take an active part in the Mass, making it a truly human action with our bodies (standing, sitting, singing, eating, etc.).
14. The dialog Mass conforms to the very structure of the Mass and is a more perfect form of participation.
15. Sung Mass is a more active form of participation than the dialog Mass.
16. Weekday Mass is necessary if we are to live as more effective apostles.
17. Mass reminds us to bring redemption into all of life, all relationships.[64]

While Hillenbrand, like the other liturgical pioneers, spent the bulk of his time educating people about the Eucharist, he also had a healthy sense of the richness of the Church's tradition of affective prayer.[65] In numerous lectures, Hillenbrand referred to the staples of the spiritual life: Mass with Communion, mental prayer, confession, mortification, devotion to Mary, spiritual direction, evenings of recollection, and spiritual reading. If liturgical renewal was to achieve its full impact on the life of the church, the full resources of the spiritual life needed to be recovered and revitalized.[66]

While Hillenbrand believed daily Mass with Communion was the most important thing in our spiritual formation, he recommended mental prayer (meditation) as "absolutely indispensable for anyone in a specialized Catholic Action movement."[67] In fact, he encouraged people to include time for mental prayer in their days of renewal rather than a Eucharistic devotion like Benediction.[68]

Hillenbrand was convinced that mental prayer more effectively developed an identity in Christ than saying the popular devotional

---

64. See *For Happier Families, Fifth Edition* (Chicago: CFM, 1957). UNDA, CMRH 10/13.

65. See H. A. Reinhold, ed. *The Soul Afire: Revelations of the Mystics* (New York: Pantheon, 1944).

66. See Joseph P. Chinnici, "Virgil Michel and the Tradition of Affective Prayer," *Worship* 62 (1988), pp. 225–236.

67. Hillenbrand, "Lay Spirituality," August 17, 1956, lecture. UNDA, CMRH 8/38.

68. Hillenbrand, "The Five Essential Qualities of a Chaplain of a CFM, YCW, YCS Group," April 28, 1958, lecture. UNDA, CMRH 10/19.

prayers of his day. By reflecting on Christ's life (he hungered, thirsted, grew weary, worked, was happy, was disappointed, showed sympathy, wept, prayed, etc.), one strengthened one's identity in Christ by surrendering oneself to him in love and seeking his direction for one's life. In this way, Hillenbrand sought to overcome the individualism and subjectivism of an a liturgical piety, which had developed as a result of the fact that liturgy no longer served as the source and center of the people's spiritual lives.[69]

THE METHODOLOGY OF
THE SPECIALIZED LAY APOSTOLATE

As was discussed in Part I, the meetings in the Specialized Lay Apostolate all followed the same basic format. There was a discussion of a portion of the Gospel, a discussion of the liturgy, a review of the previous week's apostolic effort, and the social inquiry which subjects the problems of the student, the worker, the family to the See-Judge-Act methodology.

Hillenbrand saw the purpose of these meetings as the forming an identity in Christ, as the training for life-long participation in the apostolate.

> The Gospel discussion brings the historical Christ's words and actions into our minds; the liturgy discussion shows them Christ in the Mystical Body, active now, bringing the redemption to our time; the social inquiry can be summed up in Christ—seeing the departure from Christ in some problem (e.g. immorality in dating, hostility to labor unions, etc.), judging it according to the doctrine of Christ, and acting for Christ to set it right.[70]

While this method of training lay apostles was grounded in a more contemporary understanding of Scripture, liturgy, and Church, it did call for action, regardless of how much formation had occurred.[71]

---

69. See Gabriel M. Braso, *Liturgy and Spirituality*, trans. Leonard J. Doyle (Collegeville: Liturgical Press, 1971), pp. 160–164.

70. Hillenbrand, "Spiritual Formation of the Lay Apostle," August, 1950 lecture. UNDA, CMRH 8/38.

71. See Bernard F. Meyer, *The Mystical Body in Action, a Workbook of Parish Catholic Action* (Herman, Penn.: Center for men of Christ the King, 1947) and Eugene S. Geissler, *Training of Lay Leaders* (South Bend: Apostolate Press, 1944). Meyer and Geissler both explain the Cardijn method.

Some members of the Specialized Lay Apostolate questioned the necessity of action as an essential part of each year's inquiry program. Such criticism is reflected in a 1963 article by Andrew Greeley, who claimed that "CFM programs of recent years have often seemed very unconducive to significant action."[72] In this, Greeley touches on one of the weaknesses in Hillenbrand's interpretation of the Cardijn method. However, Hillenbrand never gave up on his conviction that formation takes place simultaneously with action. "What is accomplished is by the way. It's primarily for formation."[73] It is primarily to form the apostle in the image of Christ. Just as the sacraments have their proper effect *ex opere operato*, Hillenbrand thought the meetings of the Specialized Lay Apostolate had the effect of creating lay apostles.

Lay apostles were sent by Christ into the world to continue his saving work (see John 20:21).

> The work means some action. . . . And what we must be convinced of . . . is that when we take an action in the fields which Christ has entrusted into the hands of the laity . . . you are doing something that makes you holy. . . . This is the will of God for us. This is Christ's desire and his charge to us. This is our love for others and therefore is our love for God and this makes us like Christ.[74]

In order to be holy, in order to live like Christ, one must be involved with others. Therefore, if one is to advance spiritually, one must deal with the problems of life.

Hillenbrand believed the method of the Specialized Lay Apostolate produced a "complete" spirituality. He taught that traditional spirituality was often incomplete or faulty. It emphasized unduly the vertical dimension of one's relationship with God and failed to identify the horizontal implications for one's life in community. The goal of apostolic formation is to know Christ, to think like

---

72. Andrew Greeley, "A Sociologist Looks at the CFM." An example of the type of program Greeley criticized was the 1962 program on "Christianity and Social Progress," inspired by John XXIII's encyclical, *Mater et magistra*. Originally written for the October, 1963 issue of *Marriage*, this article was withdrawn at the request of the Archdiocese of Chicago. Copy in: UNDA, CMRH 10/17.

73. Minutes of the Winter Meeting of the Coordinating Committee, February 11, 1966. UNDA, CMRH 10/19.

74. Hillenbrand, "The Spirituality of CFM, Part II," February 11, 1966, lecture. UNDA, CMRH 10/19.

Christ, to act like Christ. It mattered little whether or not the action was of any great significance. What mattered most was that it was a "holy action, an action pleasing to God. We're doing something dear to Christ's redemptive heart and therefore, growing in holiness."[75]

Finally, Hillenbrand saw a principal effect of the Specialized Lay Apostolate's emphasis on liturgy was that it created in a whole generation of lay leaders a richer understanding of the true nature and effect of the liturgy.[76] For Hillenbrand believed that Jesus wanted "to revitalize our parishes through the layman's participation in the Mass."[77] If people only appreciated the liturgy for what it really is, they would have a complete spirituality and live like Christ in the world.

SUMMARY

Hillenbrand's approach to the topic of spirituality represented a creative application of the fundamental principles of his liturgical theology. Hillenbrand clearly embraced the Christ-centered thrust given to the liturgical movement by leaders such as Columba Marmion, Lambert Beauduin, or Romano Guardini. He combined their insights with those of Virgil Michel, Gerald Ellard, H.A. Reinhold, Joseph Cardijn, and the popes to produce an approach to apostolic formation that centered around the liturgy. The liturgy confronted people with their radical holiness in the Triune God. The liturgy increased the sense of oneness, giving one a complete spirituality that inspired one's life in the world.

Hillenbrand's incarnate spirituality took seriously the meaning of baptism and confirmation as a deputation for ministry. In advocating the common priesthood, Hillenbrand was quite progressive in his thinking. In addition, by building on Thomistic categories and the encouragement given by the popes to lay participation, Hillenbrand

---

75. Hillenbrand, "The Spirituality of the Layman," January 18, 1963 lecture. UNDA, CMRH 8/5.

76. See Kevin W. Irwin, *Liturgy, Prayer, and Spirituality* (New York: Paulist Press, 1984), chapter twelve: Liturgy and Mission, p. 311: "This approach to mission respects the liturgy for what it is—an experience of the mission of God to us in Christ and of the justice Christ came to bring. . . . Programs and strategies to accomplish these ends ought to find the liturgy a source of life, inspiration, and challenge."

77. Hillenbrand, "The Five Essential Qualities of a Chaplain of a CFM, YCW, YCS Group," April 28, 1958 lecture. UNDA, CMRH 10/19.

struck a balance between the classical approach and the historical-evolutionary approach to theology. His theology of the Eucharist was a faithful summary of the best insights of scholars working in the 1940s and 1950s. In fact, many of his best ideas (e.g., the Eucharist being a sacrament of unitive consciousness) are still in use today.

Chapter 8

The Parish, the Pastor, and the Liturgy

Reynold Hillenbrand was pastor of Sacred Heart Church for almost 30 years, from July 15, 1944, to May 7, 1974. During this period he implemented a vision of the "living parish," which he held in common with other liturgical and social action leaders. He shared his understanding of the role of the pastor in numerous workshops and training courses for the chaplains of the Specialized Lay Apostolate, in study weeks and days of renewal for seminarians and priests, and with the many organizations of which he was a member. In order to appreciate his vision of the parish and the pastor, this chapter will situate Hillenbrand's programs and ideals within the context of the larger renewal occurring in the Roman Catholic Church.

THE LIVING PARISH: THE MYSTICAL BODY IN MINIATURE

While Hillenbrand's lectures during the 1940s and early 1950s often identified various social problems as the greatest challenges facing the Church, in 1957 he began to emphasize the parochial problem. He became concerned that

> 50% of our people do not offer Mass regularly on Sunday. This goes back to the fact that the parish, as it is now, is hindered in doing what a parish ought to do. If the parish is not functioning as it should, then Christ is not able to do his work. And Christ's work is not only all necessary, but it is also all-powerful in people's lives.[1]

---

1. Hillenbrand, "The Parish is Christ," February 7, 1957, lecture. UNDA, CMRH 11/28.

Thus, people needed to renew their understanding of the true purpose of a parish and their part in achieving that purpose.

Hillenbrand criticized the attitude of people, who only attended Mass when they had some problem or faced some crisis in their lives. He also rejected the "gas station" approach to parish life, where people came to gain grace from God, but cared little about their neighbor. In some cases, he felt that parishes relied too much on secular approaches and were dominated by fund raising or social gatherings. In other cases, he felt the clergy held an outdated model of church, which unduly restricted the role of the laity.

In all this, Hillenbrand believed the basic problem was the loss of the sense in which the parish is the Mystical Body in miniature.

> It's a living thing, therefore, because Christ is living and because the parish ought to be pulsating more and more with life. The parish is Christ in space and time, Christ, our blessed Lord, contemporized. In brief, the parish is Christ working for his people through his people, in his people.[2]

However, for many people the parish was too often understood in institutional, individualistic terms rather than in the Christocentric vision Hillenbrand articulated.

Toward the last half of the 19th century, German theologian Johann Möhler identified the Church with Christ. As Möhler says: "The Church . . . is the Son of God himself, everlastingly manifesting himself among us in human form, perpetually renewed, and eternally young—the permanent incarnation of the Son of God."[3] At the beginning of this century, Lambert Beauduin further developed the idea that the parish is a realization in miniature of the mystery of the church.[4] Finally, this idea was strengthened with the issuance of Pius XII's encyclical, *Mystici Corporis*.

---

2. Ibid. See Martin Hellriegel, "The Parish in Practice," in *National Liturgical Week 1940* (Newark: Benedictine Liturgical Conference, 1941), pp. 30–38. Hellriegel says on p. 31: "The parish is for us, in all truth, the Mystical Body, or, if you will, a 'miniature' Mystical Body."

3. Johann Möhler, *A Symbolism or Exposition of the Doctrinal Differences Between Catholics and Protestants as Evidenced by their Symbolic Writings*, trans. James B. Robertson (London, 1906), pp. 258–259, cited in Emmanuel Cardinal Suhard, *The Church Today, Growth or Decline?* trans. James J. Corbett (Chicago: Fides, 1948), p. 36.

4. See Lambert Beauduin, "L'esprit paroissial dans la tradition," in *Les Questions liturgiques*, II (1911–12), pp.16–26, 80–90, 305–11 (reprinted in Cours et Conférences des Semaines liturgiques, Vol. IV, *Louvain*, 1926, pp. 11–42), cited in Yves Congar, *A Gospel Priesthood*, trans. P. F. Hepburne-Scott (New York: Herder & Herder, 1967), p. 177.

In *Mystici Corporis*, Pius XII identified the biblical and patristic sources behind the statement: the church is Christ. He says Saint Paul in 1 Corinthians 12:12

> . . . calls the Church "Christ," following no doubt the example of his master who called out to him from on high, when he was attacking the Church: "Saul, Saul, why do you persecute me?" Indeed, if we are to believe Gregory of Nyssa, the Church is often called simply "Christ" by the apostle, and you are familiar . . . with that phrase of Augustine: "Christ preaches Christ."[5]

Thus, the concept that "the parish is Christ" was both a traditional and yet fresh approach to defining the nature of the parish and its mission.

On February 20, 1946, Pius XII addressed a group of newly made cardinals on the necessity of the Church fulfilling its mission in the world.

> More energetically than ever she must repulse that narrow and false conception of her spirituality and inward life which would confine her, blind and dumb, to the recesses of the sanctuary. The Church cannot shut herself up, inactive, in the privacy of her churches and thus neglect the mission entrusted to her by divine providence, the mission to form humans in their fullness and so ceaselessly to collaborate in building the solid basis of society. This mission is of her essence.[6]

Thus, Hillenbrand's understanding of parish was very much inspired by and a response to the papal mandate to make the church relevant to contemporary life.

In February of 1948, Cardinal Emmanuel Suhard, Archbishop of Paris, wrote a famous pastoral letter, *The Church Today, Growth or Decline?*, which embodied the above mentioned theology of church. This letter was often called the Catholic intellectual's Magna Carta, because it asserted the legitimate autonomy of competent, contemporary research. In addition, Suhard recognized the need for an objective evaluation of urban civilization with its many injustices and called for a new synthesis (beyond Thomism or Augustinianism) capable of

---

5. Pius XII, *Mystici Corporis*, no. 53.

6. Pius XII, February 20, 1946 message to new cardinals, cited in Yves Congar, *Laity, Church, and World*, trans. Donald Attwater (Baltimore: Helicon Press, 1960), p. 49.

reforming society. He asserted that the mission of the Christian is not only an apostolate, but "it is the convergence of three simultaneous actions: religious, civic, and social."[7] Hillenbrand was one of the intellectuals who responded to Suhard's challenge to develop a new synthesis that embraced the religious, civic, and social needs of society.

Hillenbrand believed he found such a synthesis in the liturgical and social action movements, which attacked the problem of the passive participant in church life. The problem of people in the parishes was that they

> . . . had fallen into a spiritual routineness and apathy. . . . The trouble is not the assault from the outside. The real trouble are the indifferent and apathetic Catholics who are in the Church and those who are forever drifting away.[8]

Parishioners had lost interest, because they were not allowed to participate in the ways proper to them. The solution was to reintroduce people to the true nature of the parish and help them to make the connection between liturgy and life.

Hillenbrand certainly recognized that the church is hierarchically organized and not a democracy.[9] There is functional subordination of organ to organ as in a living body. However, "it is not necessary to stress hierarchy all the time—we can stress equality, while recognizing the subordination of function."[10] Yet striking the proper balance was always a difficult task for Hillenbrand to accomplish. Too much input from Hillenbrand led to the charge that he was domineering and too little input made some people feel that Hillenbrand did not support them.

---

7. Emmanuel Cardinal Suhard, *The Church Today, Growth or Decline?*, pp. 101–108.

8. Hillenbrand, "The Parish is Christ," February, 1957 lecture. UNDA, CMRH 11/28. See Daniel Callahan, *The Mind of the Catholic Layman* (New York: Charles Scribner's Sons, 1963), p. 123: "Lay apathy and indifference are present in the American Church; many laymen have no desire at all to serve the Church; to understand their faith more intelligently, to assist the clergy or hierarchy . . . ." Virgil Michel makes a similar point in "Liturgy and Catholic Life," cited in Jeremy Hall, *The Full Stature of Christ*, p. 33.

9. Hillenbrand, "Participation in View of Pius XII's Decree," August 26, 1959, lecture. UNDA, CMRH 11/28.

10. Hillenbrand, Notes from July 27, 1960 lecture by Gustave Weigel on "The Role of the Layman in the World," CFM Area Chaplains Meeting, Denver, Colorado. UNDA, CMRH 9/21.

To be a member of a parish means to live in Christ. To live in Christ means we share his life, power (kingship), priesthood, mission, victimhood. "If we are one in these, we are one with him in his resurrection, ascension, and glory."[11] Hillenbrand understood that the role of the hierarchy is to coordinate the work of the Church, the work of Christ. The power to do the work of Christ comes from our baptism and confirmation. The ordained priest is certainly not the only one called to do Christ's work. If people have this idea, they will not participate and the parish will not function properly. "We have to sense Christ in the world today and realize that we are one with him. He does his work through us and he won't get his work done without us."[12]

One must regard the parish as Christ living in the midst of his people, doing for his people today what he did in his own day: worshipping the Father, divinizing his members, teaching them, redeeming them.[13] Yet too often parishes developed a narrow "parochialism" that inhibited the spread of Christ's redemption to the larger community outside the parish. Hillenbrand challenged people

> . . . to be interested in all the communities to which you belong. Whether it's your parish, or village or city or this great nation of ours or the world. No individual, no family, no group of families lives in isolation . . . .This is the great thing that inhibits the apostolate. Unless we overcome it, our blessed Lord's redemptive influence is simply not going to radiate through the world as He wants it to radiate.[14]

This same conviction was expressed by well-known liturgists such as Virgil Michel or H. A. Reinhold as well as famous ecclesiologists such as Yves Congar and Henri de Lubac.[15]

---

11. Ibid.

12. Hillenbrand, "Catholic Action," June 17, 1947, lecture. UNDA, CMRH 8/36.

13. Hillenbrand, "The Church—the role of the Laity in the Church," September 3, 1956, lecture, UNDA, CMRH 13/22.

14. Hillenbrand, "The Spirituality of CFM," January, 1955lecture. UNDA, CMRH 8/36 or CMRH 10/19.

15. See Yves Congar, *The Wide World, My Parish, Salvation and Its Problems*, trans. Donald Attwater (Baltimore: Helicon Press, 1961), pp. 19–26, and Henri de Lubac, *The Splendor of the Church*, trans. Michael Mason (Glen Rock: Paulist Press, 1956), pp. 93–119. The fast laws at that time dictated that if a person wanted to receive communion, he or she had to fast from midnight.

PRIORITIES OF THE PARISH

As discussed in Part I, Hillenbrand believed that the first priority in the renewal of a living parish was the restoration of active participation in the Mass. Partly because of the communion fast laws in force in 1957, "at some late Masses, the priest doesn't even distribute Communion."[16] Children were kept from participating at Mass because of the communion fast and the lack of a breakfast program in force in school.[17] The sung Mass had not been implemented to any extent in the United States. Worship for many had become simply an action of the mind and the will, often times many people attending Mass were oblivious of the rich appeal to the senses. Because they didn't always understand the action on the altar, people often became lost in their devotional prayers, while the priest and the organist, who made the sung responses, celebrated Mass in the background. In many parishes, preaching had degenerated into short moral exhortations and little attention was paid to implementing the liturgical year. "If we want to make the parish more effective, the first job is to make the Mass what it should be."[18]

The second priority was to train lay apostles in the parish.[19] In order to train lay apostles, one needed the type of methodology used by the Specialized Lay apostolate. Hillenbrand implemented lay ministry training programs for all ages: grammar school, high school, college, single and married adults. These types of groups generally did not spend all, or even a majority, of their time in the parish, since their areas of concern were economics, politics, international life, or marriage.[20]

---

16. Hillenbrand, "The Parish is Christ," February 7, 1957, lecture. CMRH, UNDA 11/28. The fast laws at that time dictated that if a person wanted to receive communion, he or she had to fast from midnight.

17. Much like Martin Hellriegel, Hillenbrand believed very strongly in the importance of a daily children's Mass. See Martin Hellriegel, *How to Make the Church Year a Living Reality* (Notre Dame: University of Notre Dame, 1955), p. 6.

18. Ibid. Hillenbrand went on to recommend lay leaders of song, the use of sung Mass booklets, the leaflet Missal, the dialogue Mass, frequent Communion, greater participation in baptism by implementing its stations, emphasis on lay priesthood, children's daily Mass, etc.

19. See Joseph Cardijn, *Laymen into Action* (London: Geoffrey Chapman, 1964), pp. 126–127: ". . . the parishes and the movements of the lay apostolate are, for me, inseparable and indivisible. The parish will always be the cradle both of individual and corporate work in the lay apostolate: it is there that the apostolate is born and nourished . . . . They are essentially 'one' in the Church and in Christ."

20. In this conviction, Hillenbrand reflected the agreement of social activists like Joseph Cardijn, popes like Pius XI and Pius XII, liturgists like Michel or Reinhold, and ecclesiologists

While traditional parish organizations like the Holy Name Society or the Altar and Rosary did not have the methodology to train apostles, they did have their place in the parish, as long they did not hinder the apostolic activity of the parishioners. In fact, Hillenbrand favored developing numerous small groups, wherever there was a worthwhile need: from making ceramics to studying scripture.[21] Joining these small groups was often the first step in a parishioner's becoming involved in the organized lay ministry training programs of the Specialized Lay Apostolate.[22]

The third priority was to make new converts. Lack of participation in Mass was all too often tied in with a loss of a missionary spirit, a loss of a desire to make converts.[23] Every other year at Sacred Heart Church, Hillenbrand offered "a series of lectures on doctrine for those who are not Catholic but may have an interest in the Church."[24] As early as 1952, Hillenbrand was describing the Easter Vigil as the privileged time to initiate converts into the Church.[25] In fact, Sacred Heart Parish was among the first parishes in the Archdiocese of Chicago to receive permission to celebrate the new Easter Vigil in 1952, at which time Hillenbrand baptized five converts. Hillenbrand was concerned that parishes make an effort to preserve the communal character of initiation into the Church.[26]

The fourth priority was the religious education of the children of the parish. Hillenbrand strongly supported the parish school. He

---

like Congar and De Lubac, who saw the world as the major field of the apostolate. See Hugo Rahner, ed. *The Parish, from Theology to Practice* (Westminster: Newman Press, 1958).

21. Hillenbrand, August 7, 1964, letter to Bishop Ernest Primeau on the *Decree on the Laity*. UNDA, CMRH 9/4.

22. See Yves Congar, *Faith and Spiritual Life*, trans. A. Manson and L. C. Sheppard (New York: Herder & Herder, 1968), p. 145: "The major element in the formation of an adult Christian life will consist of the discovery of one's exact position in the world and in the Church, a discovery to be followed by corresponding commitments." R. Kevin Seasoltz surveys the various groups dedicated to such self discovery, from Marriage Encounter to CFM, from the Cursillo Movement to the Movement for a Better World, etc. in "Contemporary American Lay Movements in Spirituality," *Communio* 6 (1979), pp. 339–364.

23. Hillenbrand, "Participation in View of Pius XII's Decree," August 26, 1959, lecture. UNDA, CMRH 11/28. See Francis X. Durrwell, *The Apostolate and the Church*, trans. Edward Quinn (Denville: Dimension Books, 1973), pp. 1–20.

24. Hillenbrand, 1957 Booklet on Sacred Heart Church.

25. Hillenbrand, April 7, 1952, letter to Sacred Heart Parish. UNDA, CMRH 35.

26. See Martin B. Hellriegel, "The Liturgical Movement and the Sacraments," *Orate Fratres* 10 (1936), pp. 504–505.

saw that the goal of a Catholic education was "to form the full human and the full Christian. Aside from this, no Catholic school justifies its existence."[27] Most important was religion class, which was the first class in the morning. Hillenbrand and his associate pastors taught in the parish school several times a week. In addition, he was convinced that daily Mass was "the most important class of the day."[28] Hillenbrand loved preaching at children's Masses and his personal papers contain a complete set of notes for children's homilies for all the various feasts and seasons of the liturgical year.

The fifth priority was to train lay people to take part in liturgical ministries. Hillenbrand began the dialog Mass and lay readers in 1945. In the 1950s he not only had a daily Mass for children, but he also involved them as readers at Mass.[29] He conducted regular training programs for all readers and ushers. He gave special homilies each year at all the Masses to educate the congregation on the meaning of the liturgy and their part in it. In all these efforts, Hillenbrand provided his parishioners with the baptismal spirituality that we spoke of in the last chapter, thus producing a high level of commitment to the parish and extra-parochial ministries.

The sixth priority was to welcome newcomers, including Non-Catholics, to the parish. Hillenbrand was concerned about creating a unity that was deeper than just the usual level of sociability found in most parishes. The success of a parish and its liturgy did not depend on everyone becoming friends of one another. Sacred Heart Church had a large cross section of people from lower middle class to upper class. And so, Hillenbrand cautioned against the

> . . . kind of overly-sentimental . . . approach, where you think you can get everybody socially together in a parish and everybody feeling at home. This is impossible where the parish is socially stratified. Those differences ought to be respected. You can't club people into feeling at home at a social function no matter what you do.[30]

---

27. Hillenbrand, 1957 Booklet on Sacred Heart Church.

28. Ibid.

29. In a 1957 Booklet on Sacred Heart Church, Hillenbrand wrote: "The children take part each week in three dialog and two sung Masses—all with the priest facing the congregation. The vested choir assists at all Masses. Boys are the readers at the dialog Masses, and one grade takes part in an offertory procession before the Mass begins. At intervals a priest acts as commentator during the Mass."

30. Hillenbrand, "The Parish is Christ," February 7, 1957, lecture. UNDA, CMRH 11/28.

For the unity of the parish was deeper than its social gatherings. It was the unity of the Mystical Body, a shared life in Christ.

The seventh priority was to implement the social teachings of the Church. Parish organizations must do something about providing information and assistance with childbirth, help for the poor and needy (e.g., tuition scholarships for high school), a babysitting service for families, a compassionate ministry to the sick and bereaved, a challenge of the racist attitudes of its members, a parish library to encourage continuing education, study clubs to examine the latest papal encyclical, etc.[31]

The eighth priority was to attend to the climate of hospitality. People need a spirit of friendliness, a willingness to talk to and work with each other. They need an openness to dialogue and opportunities to communicate with one another outside the liturgical assembly. Hillenbrand's great belief was that active participation in the liturgy would lead to active participation in the redemptive work of Christ in the world. In many ways, the true test of the liturgy's effectiveness was its ability to sustain lay apostles, by providing them with a hopeful and healing community, from which they were sent and in which they discovered a depth of human living not experienced in the world.[32] While people were experiencing the end of one age and the beginning of a new age, some folks stubbornly resisted change, thus making the renewal of the Church a slow and uneven process.[33]

The ninth priority was to create a worship space suitable for active participation, in which good art and the performance of good religious music had pride of place. Like Martin Hellriegel, H. A. Reinhold, or Maurice Lavanoux, Hillenbrand believed that the church building conveyed to the parish its priorities. And so, he emphasized the close connection between the font and the altar, tied the sanctuary to the nave by use of a free standing altar which stood close to the people, provided worthy art works created by qualified artists, installed

31. Ibid., and Hillenbrand, "A Pastor Looks at His Parish," *Ave Maria* 80 (1958), pp. 5–10.

32. Hillenbrand, "A Pastor Looks at the Parish," *Ave Maria* 80 (1958), p. 8. Hillenbrand believed what Congar asserted in The Wide World My Parish, p. 42: "Life's meaning is bound up with a right relationship between us creatures and God our creator. At the deepest level, this relationship consists in so conducting ourselves that we allow God to be really God in us, shining in and through us, fulfilling his will in and through us. To hinder God being God in us, for us, and through us . . . is sin."

33. Hillenbrand, "Lay Spirituality," April 13, 1961, lecture. UNDA, CMRH 11/28.

a Wicks pipe organ to foster congregational singing, and seated the choir in the front pews in order to lead the congregation in song."[34]

As we mentioned in some detail in Chapter 4, when Hillenbrand renovated Sacred Heart Church in 1957, he placed the font near the sanctuary (in the place of one of the old side altars), because baptism gives divine life and leads to Eucharist. "If you are baptized, you are able to offer the sacrifice and eat from the table of sacrifice. The position in front of Church is especially important at the Easter Vigil."[35] In addition, the vine and the branches sculpture behind the main altar reminded the parishioners that they were members of Christ's Body. Their lives produced no fruit unless they were attached to the vine and lived in Christ. Moreover, just like a vine was pruned in order to bring forth more fruit, so too Christ's members must expect trials and suffering, if they were to possess the same self-sacrificial love that lived in Christ. Yet never were human beings so united in Christ, as when they offered the priestly sacrifice of the Mass together.[36]

A moderately sized, movable (to allow for special ceremonies) lectern (or ambo) was placed near the altar.[37] Christ speaks to us both through the prayers at Mass as well as through the scriptures and the homily. Hillenbrand believed in a daily homily and saw the lectern as an extension of the altar, fulfilling the didactic purpose of the Mass. The homily was to be based on scripture, the liturgical season, or the feasts of Christ and the saints. It was an integral part of the celebration, to be carefully prepared and effectively delivered.[38]

Hillenbrand believed the main worship space should serve the needs of the liturgy and should not be devotional space. Consequently,

---

34. See Martin Hellriegel, "The Holy Sacrifice of the Mass," July 21, 1941, lecture at St. Mary of the Lake Seminary. UNDA, CMRH 28/23: "The holiest places on earth are the baptismal font and the eucharistic altar . . . . These two places must be dearest to us, and worthy of our most priestly care." Martin Hellriegel also seated the choir in the front of church. See Noel Barrett Hackmann, p. 182. Also see H. A. Reinhold, *Speaking of Liturgical Architecture* (Notre Dame: Notre Dame Liturgy Program, 1952), pp. 3–5.

35. Hillenbrand, "Redoing the Church," June 1957 Homily, Sacred Heart Rectory files on Church Renovation.

36. Hillenbrand, "Redoing the Church, The Vine and the Branches Sculpture," January 19, 1958, Homily, Sacred Heart Church Rectory files on Church Renovation. See Martin Hellriegel, *Vine and the Branches* (St. Louis: Pio Decimo, 1948).

37. The GIRM 2000 has stated that altars must be fixed in the sanctuary.

38. Hillenbrand, "A Pastor Looks at the Parish," *Ave Maria* 80 (1958), p. 8.

devotional art works like stations of the cross were placed in a side aisle, out of view from the nave.[39] However, Hillenbrand did retain a crucifix, designed by Ivan Mestrovic, which he suspended over the main altar. He explained that it is

> . . . not an ornament, but a symbol of what happens on the altar: the sacrifice of Calvary renewed. Confessionals were placed in the traditional place, near the entrance of church, to show that we recover divine life before approaching the sacrifice, if need be.[40]

In short, the design of the church was a visual demonstration of the unity of the Church: Christ, the priest, and the people offering one sacrifice around one altar.

Since he became a member of the Board of Directors of the Liturgical Arts Society on January 5, 1942, Hillenbrand was familiar with the goals of the Society. In fact, the renovation of Sacred Heart Church was done with these goals and the principles of the liturgical movement in mind.

> The sentimental fakery of neo-stylistic church buildings, with decorations "stuck on like band-aids on a cancer," which were so prevalent at the time of the Society's founding, were to be replaced by those which were honest, simple, and functional.[41]

As we have seen, when Hillenbrand renovated Sacred Heart Church, he eliminated many of the ornamental, "neo-gothic" decorations and implemented the honest, simple, functional approach fostered by the Liturgical Arts Society.[42]

Regular concerts of sacred music in church and religious art displays in school were part of the parish's commitment to its continuing appreciation of religious art and music. Hillenbrand took risks in sponsoring some religious art displays. He knew that

---

39. See H.A. Reinhold, *The Dynamics of the Liturgy* (New York: Macmillan Company, 1961), p. 81, where he recommends that the stations of the cross, shrines, and popular images belong "in a special chapel that provides the kind of atmosphere our people want for such occasions."

40. Ibid.

41. Susan J. White, "The Liturgical Arts Society (1927¬1972): Art and Architecture in the Agenda of the American Roman Catholic Liturgical Renewal," Ph.D dissertation (Notre Dame: University of Notre Dame, 1987), p. 293.

42. See Peter F. Anson, *Churches, Their Plan and Furnishing,* revised and edited y Thomas F. Croft Fraser and H.A. Reinhold (Milwaukee: Bruce Publishing Co., 1948) and J. B. O'Connell, *Church Building and Furnishing: The Church's Way, a Study in Liturgical Law* (Notre Dame: University of Notre Dame Press, 1955).

. . . some will find, perhaps, things that will disturb them. It seems to be a part of human nature that we tend to fear the new, the different, the unfamiliar.[43]

In addition, Hillenbrand believed that the employment of artists to provide good religious art was a matter of social justice.[44] Joseph O'Connell, who designed the vine and the branches sculpture and the baptismal font, reported that Hillenbrand "was very fair and understood the importance of paying artists justly. His social conscience was highly developed."[45]

When one affirms that the parish is Christ, one must also recognize that

the altar is the center of the parish. . . . Not the school, not the playfields, not the recreational activities for teenagers. The most important thing in the parish is the altar and people's participation in the Mass.[46]

The altar is Christ worshipping the Father through the consecration, sanctifying his people through Communion, and teaching them through the propers of the Mass, the Scriptures, and the homily.

The Mass is the key to parish life, the key to revitalizing the life of the parish. Hillenbrand was convinced that lack of participation in the liturgy was one of the principal reasons for the deterioration of parish life. On August 23, 1963, at the CFM National Convention, Hillenbrand explained this position quite plainly:

Unity in the parish is lacking, unless it has a good dialog Mass, which is improving. Mass offered mutely violates human nature, because we are not mute creatures at a social offering. (We need) to preach active participation, weekdays as well as Sunday. (We need) to encourage the reception of Communion at wedding and funeral Masses, to turn the altars around so people can see more, obtain lay readers for the Epistle and Gospel, provide leaflet missals with the propers and song-Mass booklets.[47]

43. Hillenbrand, Introduction to Booklet, "Contemporary Religious Art Exhibit," Sacred Heart School, March 3–17, 1957. UNDA, CMRH 25/1. See H.A. Reinhold, *Liturgy and Art* (New York: Harper & Row,1966), pp. 85–89.

44. See Susan J. White, pp. 318–320.

45. Joseph O'Connell to the author, April 1, 1988, College of St. Benedict, St. Joseph, Minnesota. See Appendix A for a complete description of the worship program and parish organizations at Sacred Heart Church in 1957.

46. Hillenbrand, "The Parish is Christ," February 7, 1957 lecture. UNDA CMRH 11/28.

47. Hillenbrand, "The Parish— Leaven of the Community," August 23, 1963, lecture, cited in *Chicago Observes* 8 (1963), p. 1. UNDA, CMRH 9/24.

Thus, prior to the issuance of the Liturgy Constitution, Hillenbrand had become a forceful advocate for many of the reforms that were soon to be adopted in the Church.

THE PASTOR: CHRIST UNITING HIS PEOPLE IN MINISTRY

If the parish is the altar and the altar is Christ worshipping the Father, sanctifying His people, and teaching them, then it is a logical deduction to maintain:

> The pastor is Christ because with Christ he makes the sacrifice possible. He teaches for Christ. He rules for Christ, that is, leads the people. Therefore, we ought to have an appreciation of a priest as a priest and not judge him by any other standards: whether he's a financial wizard . . . has good artistic judgment . . . good social appeal . . . a lot of diplomacy and tact . . . goes great with teenagers, or even because he preaches well. No these aren't the standards at all.[48]

Instead, one should evaluate a pastor by these standards: is he doing the priestly work that Christ wants done among his people— making the Mass the center of parish life, involving the people in the celebration of the sacraments, teaching the social gospel, training his people for the Apostolate.[49]

In his theology of parish and the parish priest, Hillenbrand was influenced by Ildefons Herwegen, the abbot of Maria Laach. Herwegen maintained that

> the purpose of the Christian religion is to assimilate human beings to God through Christ; to form humankind, therefore in the likeness of Christ. *Christianus alter Christus.* The Christian is another Christ.[50]

Like Herwegen, Hillenbrand saw the purpose of the Church was to deify or transform humans into other Christs. One of the chief methods of such transformation was the liturgy. "It is this transcendent

---

48. Hillenbrand, "The Parish is Christ," February 7, 1957, lecture. UNDA, CMRH 11/28.
49. Ibid.
50. Ildefons Herwegen, The Art-Principle of the Liturgy, trans. William Busch (Collegeville: Liturgical Press, 1931), pp. 15–16.

purpose that has brought out the inherent beauty of the liturgy and made it a consummate work of art."[51]

Hillenbrand's synthesis on the theology of parish and the pastor was invigorated by the research he did for the 1957 renovation of Sacred Heart Church. This renovation prompted him to see fresh connections between the liturgy and art, the liturgy and life:

> The liturgy is human life at its height, its most productive level. Only by intensifying our liturgical life will church art, sacred art, an ember now, burst into full flame.[52]

Hillenbrand bemoaned the use of "heavenly, sugared hack-work" which blurs the face of Christ, "just as surely as an unjust economic system with its grinding poverty blurs the image of Christ."[53] He challenged priests to preserve the honesty and simplicity of the worship space or weaken the effectiveness of the liturgy.

Hillenbrand fought to center people's spiritual lives on the liturgy. Catholics placed too much attention on the peripheral (lighting vigil lights or making the stations) and not enough attention on the central and essential aspects of their faith (the Mass and the apostolate).[54] Good art was a help toward restoring a proper focus in the spiritual life. Good liturgy was an art form, the most complete embodiment of the beauty of God, of the Trinity, of Christ, of his sacrificial, redemptive action, of the Mystical Body, of the sacraments and sacramentals, and of the divine office. The liturgy calls on the arts—drama, poetry, and music—to create an experience of life in all its fullness.[55]

In many ways, Hillenbrand's work on art and the liturgy caused him to reaffirm the beliefs he inherited from Lambert Beauduin and Virgil Michel on the sacramental principle.[56] Kilian McDonnell,

---

51. Ibid., p. 16.

52. Hillenbrand, "Art and the Liturgy," 1958 lecture. UNDA, CMRH 29/16.

53. Ibid.

54. See Pius XII, *Mediator Dei*, no. 189: "We deem it our duty to censure . . . those who emphasize special and insignificant practices, neglecting essential and necessary things."

55. Ibid. Hillenbrand explains: "The liturgy is the most complete embodiment of the beauty of the God it worships. It is truly the greatest form of art. For art is a window to the infinite. St. Thomas calls it a 'reflection of truth, goodness.' "

56. See Beauduin, *Liturgy: Life of the Church*, pp. 9–16, Marx, pp. 62–67, and Hall, pp. 38–44.

a monk of St. John's Abbey, expressed these same beliefs, when he described the incarnation as

> the sacramental law of the Church's greatness, the definition of her very essence. By virtue of the law of the incarnation the divine is made flesh in the human and the earthly, the essence of the Church is defined. She must daily act in accordance with the law of the incarnation and of her essence—*agere sequitur esse*. She must daily make Christ incarnate in the flesh of the world or lose her meaning—indeed, her existence.[57]

In order to be a good pastor, a priest had to do more than just count the number of hosts he distributed on Sunday. He had to take seriously the sacramental principle of the Church's life.

The sacramental principle (incarnating Christ in the world) complemented Hillenbrand's beliefs on the necessity of training lay apostles. The number of Catholics was increasing and the number of clergy was diminishing.[58] As early as November 9, 1945, Hillenbrand claimed that the old pastoral theology that the ordained priests can do it all was not sufficient for the needs of the apostolate.

> The work of Christ requires many more apostles in the world. So do what Christ did. Create apostles. This is as indispensable today as priestly ministry itself."[59]

Thus, we see that Hillenbrand certainly anticipated the thrust toward lay ministry that occurred after the Second Vatican Council.

As we discussed earlier, Hillenbrand was involved in many social action apostolates. If you consider his anthropology (humans are economic, political, familial, and religious creatures), his commitment to putting papal teachings into action, his convictions about the

---

57. Kilian McDonnell, "Art and the Sacramental Principle," *Liturgical Arts* 25 (1957), p. 92.

58. See Jay P. Dolan, "The American Catholic Parish, a Historical Perspective, 1820–1980" in The *Parish in Transition, Proceedings of a Conference on the American Catholic Parish*, ed. David Byers (Washington: USCC, 1986), pp. 40–41: Dolan notes that between 1930 and 1980 the number of Catholics increased dramatically, while the number of church personnel remained roughly the same. "The implications of this remain to be seen, but it is no coincidence that dioceses now devote substantial staff resources to workshops and training programs for laity."

59. Hillenbrand, "Obligations, Problems and Privileges of the Priest in Catholic Action," November 9, 1945, lecture. UNDA, CMRH 8/6. It is important to recall that Hillenbrand believed the training of lay apostles started in grammar school, continued through high school and college, matured after a person's choice of a career or a marriage partner, and hopefully resulted in a lifelong commitment to carrying on the redemptive work of Christ in the world.

organic nature of society, and his definition of the Mass as the
sacrament of unitive consciousness, then it is understandable why
Hillenbrand became an arbitrator of wage disputes, or served on the
Catholic Council on Interracial Life, the National Catholic Social
Action Conference, or the Winnetka Human Relations Committee.
These activities were a conscious acting out of his fundamental
principles in fulfilling his image of the good Christian and the
Christ-like pastor.

Hillenbrand was not afraid to challenge parishioners or clergy
on their awareness of the demands of the social Gospel. Often he
asked priests

> to teach not only truth which directly bears on salvation—certainly not
> just the barest ethical bones of the decalogue, mere moralizing, mere
> sweetness and light—but the teaching derived from the Church, which
> bears upon the grave problems of our times. . . . In the Church a gap
> exists between what the popes have taught and what people have heard.
> Preaching on the sins of immorality, on untruthfulness goes on, while we
> neglect immorality in economic life, discrimination in racial life, untruth-
> fulness in international life.[60]

Hillenbrand was very much aware of the weakness in Catholic
preaching, which is still a problem in the Church today.[61] "Mere
sweetness and light" was not the answer, if one wanted to make the
liturgy the center of the lay apostolate.

Before the promulgation of the *Decree on Ecumenism*,
Hillenbrand engaged in ecumenical cooperation in his community.
For example, he participated in the Winnetka Human Relations
Committee, an ecumenical group of ministers, priests, and a rabbi.
On April 6, 1964, this group produced a joint statement on the
necessity of openness to integration, which in a largely white, affluent
area was a risky thing to do.[62] Yet, they courageously maintained that

---

60. Hillenbrand, "Today's Mission—Catholic Viewpoint on the Lay Apostolate,"
August 3, 1965, lecture. UNDA, CMRH 9/2.

61. See Bishops' Committee on Priestly Life and Ministry, *Fulfilled in Your Hearing,
the Homily in the Sunday Assembly* (Washington: USCC, 1982).

62. This occurred at a time when many clergy were concerned about the passage of the
Civil Rights Act (1964) and marches in Washington, Mississippi, and Alabama were raising
the consciousness of the nation regarding racial segregation.

The coming of Negro families will enrich our community life and give us all an opportunity to put into practice our religious beliefs and our national principles . . . . We believe that the combination of respect for human dignity, concern for the national interest, and religious faith will lead us to a fuller realization of the basic unity that our Creator has established in the human family.[63]

In addition, Sacred Heart Church participated in the National Interracial Home Visit Week in April 1964.[64]

Hillenbrand was convinced of the importance of people of faith cooperating with each other.

We must talk with one another, work with each other, and, with God's help, heal the divisions in Christendom and heal the aloofness between Christians and the vast numbers who are not Christians. We must always assume that they have divine life, which assures them salvation, either through Christ in baptism or through an act of love of God.[65]

In many ways, his fundamental principles led him to seek that necessary understanding and cooperation, without which unity remains the impossible dream.

Hillenbrand's program for priestly life went well beyond the old sacramental theology, which defined the priesthood as "a sacred order, which gives power to consecrate the body and blood of Jesus Christ and to forgive sins."[66] Instead, his program was a combination

63. April 6, 1964, letter of the ministers, priests, and rabbi of the Winnetka Churches and temple to the Winnetka community, UNDA, CMRH 25, 20. This statement agrees with the 1964 position of the Catholic Interracial Council of Chicago, which stated that "there can be no lasting peace in our community without a foundation of complete inter-racial justice." UNDA, CMRH 29/26.

64. Hillenbrand, April 19, 1964, letter to Sacred Heart Parish, urging parishioners to visit black homes in Evanston and on the south side of Chicago to discuss human relations progress and problems. UNDA, CMRH 30/2.

65. Hillenbrand, "Today's Mission—Catholic Viewpoint on the Lay Apostolate," August 3, 1965, lecture. UNDA, CMRH 9/2. See Yves Congar, *Ecumenism and the Future of the Church*, trans. John C. Guinness (Chicago: Priory Press, 1967), p. 167: "For the past twenty years now, serious reflection on the internal mission of the Church has led to an understanding of it not as a unilateral giving, but as including a responsibility to acquire a certain receptivity, a welcoming openness to others, a willingness for exchange, for reciprocity, and ultimately for sharing."

66. Arthur Devine, *The Sacraments Explained, According to the Teaching and Doctrine of the Catholic Church* (New York: Benziger Brothers, 1905), p. 415. This is one of the texts used at St. Mary of the Lake Seminary, when Hillenbrand was a seminarian.

of the best ideas of the liturgical and social action movements. Simply stated, Hillenbrand recommended that priests

> Stay close to the Pope in everything he says. Have a well-rounded interest in the liturgy, labor, rural life, the race problem, peace. Stay rooted in the Mass, in the death of Christ, the great moment of history.[67]

To this list, one should add his frequent mention of the divine office, mental prayer, regular confession, and the use of a spiritual director. Consequently, Hillenbrand tempered his emphasis on the liturgy and social action with a healthy awareness of the demands of the interior life.[68]

SUMMARY

Hillenbrand's theology of the living parish, the Mystical Body in miniature, reflected the influence of numerous leaders from the liturgical and social action movements in the Catholic Church, especially Möhler, Beauduin, Cardijn, Pius XII, Suhard, and Hellriegel. In particular, the pastoral experiences of Martin Hellriegel provided as a model for Hillenbrand's leadership at Sacred Heart Church. Moreover, the development of his ideas on the role of the laity in ministry harmonized well with the thinking of such famous ecclesiologists as Yves Congar or Henri de Lubac. Finally, many of Hillenbrand's pastoral priorities were inspired by his basic belief that the liturgy was the key to revitalizing parochial life.

Hillenbrand's theology of the pastor as Christ, uniting his people in ministry, was a logical deduction from his theology of parish. Hillenbrand's 1957 renovation of Sacred Heart Church prompted new reflections on the influence of the environment on worship. In addition, it reaffirmed the fundamental sacramental principle that guided all ecclesial life. Many of Hillenbrand's concerns—ministry training, good preaching, ecumenical cooperation, and continued education— remain high priorities among pastors today. Finally, Hillenbrand fostered a healthy awareness of the necessity of a pastor attending to his own legitimate needs for growth in the spiritual life.

---

67. Hillenbrand, "Today's Mission—Catholic Viewpoint on the Lay Apostolate," August 3, 1965, lecture. UNDA, CMRH 9/2.

68. See Durrwell, *The Apostolate and the Church*, pp. 109–133.

Chapter 9

Vatican II: Preparation, Implementation, and Evaluation

Every age makes its own contribution to the understanding of faith. In the twentieth century, the biblical, patristic, liturgical, and social action movements in the Catholic Church redefined the nature and purpose of the liturgy and membership in the Church. The American liturgical movement implemented the synthesis about liturgy and life, liturgy and the apostolate that first arose in the European Church thanks to the efforts of leaders such as Lambert Beauduin, Pius Parsch, Joseph Cardijn, Romano Guardini, and others. In this chapter we will survey the elements out of which American liturgical reformers, as represented by Reynold Hillenbrand, forged a new understanding of liturgy and church. We will explore the ways Hillenbrand prepared for, implemented, and evaluated the teachings of Vatican II. We will conclude with a final assessment of Hillenbrand's place among the American liturgical pioneers.

REDEFINING LITURGY AND MEMBERSHIP IN THE CHURCH

Like the European movement, the American liturgical movement was concerned with the pastoral effectiveness of the liturgy. The goals of American liturgists went beyond training congregations to sing Gregorian chant or renovating churches to encourage active participation in the liturgy. As Godfrey Diekmann said,

> I have no right to judge others, but as for myself, if liturgical renewal since the mid-1920s had implied chiefly external changes in ritual or architecture

or whatever, I for one would not have wasted my life's efforts on it—and I am sure I speak for all the old pioneers.[1]

Instead, the efforts of American liturgists were aimed at redefining the nature and purpose of the liturgy and membership in the Church.

Under the influence of European leaders like Möhler, Marmion, Herwegen, Casel, Guardini, and Parsch, American liturgists adopted a new anthropology, which moved beyond Neo-scholasticism and embodied the insights of the biblical and patristic movements. These leaders, each in their own way, saw one's identity in Christ as crucial to understanding the meaning of one's life. Christ is the key to history and to understanding the mystery of life. As Hillenbrand said,

> Christ sums up all being. He sums up in himself God, because he is God. He sums up angels and humans because he has a human spirit. He sums up the bodies of humans and the whole range of the universe, because he has a body. Christ is the center of history. All history is the unfolding of Christ.[2]

Hence, in order to understand the meaning of human life, one must enter into the Mystery of Christ.

Where does one gain one's understanding of Christ? Like all the liturgical pioneers, Hillenbrand believed the "first and indispensable source of the true Christian spirit" is the liturgy. Like Odo Casel and Martin Hellriegel, Hillenbrand stressed the formative impact of the liturgical year.

> There is no better way to be formed in Christ—to be made a real and apostolic Christian (to achieve the highest human distinction: to be like Christ)—than the machinery of the liturgical year, which is the Church's own, matchless way of making her members the images of Christ, who is Head, firstborn of many creatures.[3]

Thus, participation in the liturgical year is the Church's "matchless" means of transforming us into other Christs.

1. Godfrey Diekmann, "Sunday Morning: Retrospect and Prospect," in *Sunday Morning: A Time for Worship,* ed. Mark Searle (Collegeville: Liturgical Press, 1982), p. 182.

2. Hillenbrand, "Doctrine of the Church on the Formation of Lay Apostles," August 21, 1961, lecture. UNDA, CMRH 9/2.

3. Hillenbrand, "The Need and Scope of the Lay Apostolate," August 17, 1946, lecture. UNDA, CMRH 8/13.

In the late nineteenth century, Johann Adam Möhler fostered the notion of the Church as the continuation of the incarnation, in reaction to the ecclesiology that defined the Church as "a perfect society established by God in virtue of the merits of Christ, endowed with all the means necessary to obtain its supernatural end."[4] He stressed the permanent, active presence of Christ in the world. Hillenbrand, of course, defined the liturgy as the actions of Christ in the world. As Hillenbrand said,

> It isn't enough to seek Christ's history, Christ in the past . . . . We have to sense Christ in the world today and realize that we are one with him. He does his work through us and he won't get work done without us. We get that in the liturgy.[5]

This oneness in Christ takes on an even deeper meaning, when seen in terms of a renewed appreciation of baptism.

Like the other liturgical pioneers, Hillenbrand saw membership in the church (through baptism) as providing one with a share in the priestly, prophetic, and kingly ministry of Christ. As he said,

> The Mystical Body teaches, rules, sanctifies, and all the members in some way share in those offices, in that work of Christ, each in their degree.[6]

Lay Christians teach by bringing the truth of Christ to others and sharing with them the doctrines of Christ.[7] They rule by "persuasion and appeal, by channeling human ideas and actions into conformity,

---

4. Edward J. Kilmartin, *Christian Liturgy: Theology and Practice* (New York: Sheed & Ward, 1988), p. 218.

5. Hillenbrand, "Catholic Action," June 17, 1947 lecture. UNDA, CMRH 8/36.

6. Hillenbrand, "The Theological Bases of the Lay Apostolate," August, 1948 lecture. UNDA, CMRH 8/36. See the Constitution on the Church, no. 31: "These faithful are by baptism made one body with Christ and are established among the People of God. They are in their own way made sharers in the priestly, prophetic, and kingly functions of Christ. They carry out their own part in the mission of the whole Christian people with respect to the Church and the world."

7. If people understand the truth of Christ, they would see the necessity of community. The prophetic witness of the Church's emphasis on community is clarified in Leonard Doohan, *Laity's Mission in the Local Church: Setting a New Direction* (San Francisco: Harper & Row, 1986), p. 22: "It is a faithful portrayal of oneness in Christ (see Gal 3:21–28). It is also a vision and challenge to those who consider change in our present world impossible. True community with all its demands and implications, offers a new type of society to a hate-filled world and "is in harmony with the most secret desires of the human heart" (*Constitution on the Church in the Modern World*, no. 21:8).

if not always into contact with Christ."[8] They sanctify by sharing in the priesthood through the seal of baptism, which etches into their souls the image of Christ the priest.

As we discussed in earlier chapters, lay Christians exercise their priesthood by offering the Eucharistic sacrifice with the ordained priest and by extending that sacrifice into the world through their willingness to live for others (their self-sacrificial love). Like other liturgists, Hillenbrand defined sacrifice as self-giving, as "the giving of a gift at an altar—a gift which symbolizes the giving of ourselves to God."[9] It was in the concept of sacrifice (or self-giving) that Hillenbrand found a crucial link between liturgy and life.

A Christian's self-giving does not end at the altar, which is why Catholic Action (or the apostolate) was defined as a necessary component of a life lived for others. In this conviction, Hillenbrand popularized in the United States one of the important insights, which contemporary scholars sought to reintroduce into Eucharistic theology. Moreover, this theology of self-giving continues to be influential, as is evidenced in its use by James F. White in his book, *Sacraments as God's Self Giving*:

> Through self giving, love becomes visible, audible, tangible, in short, capable of being perceived by another. Love demands some means of expression, and self giving provides the necessary signs of love.[10]

Thus, Hillenbrand frequently told people: "If others are to feel Christ's love, they must feel it through your heart. When you love a person, it is Christ loving through you."[11]

---

8. Hillenbrand, "The Theological Bases of the Lay Apostolate," August 1948 lecture. UNDA, CMRH 8/36.

9. Hillenbrand, "Statement of Principle," in *National Liturgical Week 1943* (Ferdinand, In.: Liturgical Conference, 1944), p. 103. See Jungmann, *Pastoral Liturgy*, p. 284: "For sacrifice is essentially a demonstrative action, the symbolic representation of inward readiness to give oneself."

10. James F. White, *Sacraments as God's Self Giving* (Nashville: Abingdon Press, 1983), p. 16. In the same book, see Edward Kilmartin's "A Catholic Response," p. 138: "The interplay between the liturgical experience of God's self giving as the basis and goal of all human self giving and the experience of the mediation of God's self giving in social action assures the vitality of authentic Christian communal worship and service in the world."

11. Hillenbrand, "The Spirituality of YCW Leaders," July, 1952 lecture. UNDA, CMRH 8/38. In this same lecture, Hillenbrand further explains: "Our associations with others is a strong self-sacrifice out of charity."

Frequently, Hillenbrand spoke of the Mass as Christ's death renewed, as one with the sacrifice of Calvary. The self-emptying love of Christ incarnated on Calvary is a revelation of God's own Trinitarian love.[12] Christ's oneness with the Father in the unity of the Holy Spirit is now a reality that Christians also share, especially in the Eucharist.

> Christ wanted a unity, which once more resembled the unity that he and the Father had. Oneness—that's why he died the following day. It was the last thing Christ did before he died. He sent the Holy Spirit to press these people [apostles] into a oneness, which the world had never dreamed, except that Christ had told us that it does exist.[13]

The work of the Holy Spirit that began at Calvary was to unite the members of Christ's Body to the head, to bind them together and give them life.[14] Thus, Hillenbrand saw an important connection between the Mass as the renewal of Calvary and the doctrine of Trinitarian love.

What Hillenbrand discovered through this connection between Calvary and Trinitarian love was an interpersonal ontology that views self-development in terms of a Trinitarian model. Hillenbrand's convictions about an interpersonal ontology continue "to be advocated by modern theologians like Robert T. Sears, who further explains the rationale for this position:

> The cross is then interpreted as dying to autonomous personhood for the sake of community growth. It is clear how community and Church are more essential in this view than with a more Subject-centered ontology.[15]

---

12. Contemporary theologians continue to discuss this doctrine. See Robert T. Sears, "Trinitarian Love as Ground of the Church," in *Why the Church?*, eds. Walter Burghardt and William Thompson (New York: Paulist Press, 1976), p. 116.

13. Hillenbrand, "The Mystical Body in Relation to Spiritual Charity," May 27, 1955, lecture. UNDA, CMRH 8/38.

14. Hillenbrand, "The Theological Bases of the Apostolate," August 1948 lecture. UNDA, CMRH 8/34. See Edward J. Kilmartin, Christian Liturgy: Theology and Practice, p. 109: "The Spirit is the bond of union between the primordial sacrament Jesus Christ and the Church. In virtue of the presence of the Holy Spirit, the Church is a mystery intrinsically related to the mystery of the incarnation."

15. Robert T. Sears, "Trinitarian Love as Ground of the Church," in *Why the Church?*, p. 115: "Being the fullness of the manifestation of God's Spirit, the cross is not seen as a single act but the culmination of a life of self-giving and the fruitfulness of this life in community formation."

While Hillenbrand was a pastoral liturgist and seldom concerned with explaining the intricacies of his theology, there is a depth to his work that contemporary theologians still find challenging.

Like most liturgists of his time, Hillenbrand frequently affirmed that the sacraments continue the redemptive action of Christ in the world. Through these saving encounters with Christ, divine life flows into us and the Trinity dwells within us.[16] This personal sense of encounter with Christ in the sacraments is a tremendous advance over the abstract concept, "the sacraments produce grace," that prevailed in the old manuals of theology. Yet convincing Americans to accept this new theology was no easy task and remains part of the unfinished agenda of the liturgical movement.

As was discussed in Part I, during the 1920s and 1930s, American theologians reacted to the condemnations of Modernism and Americanism by isolating themselves from the new theology, which emerged in Europe as a result of the biblical, patristic, liturgical, and social action movements. The American liturgists, led by Virgil Michel, brought the insights of these movements to the United States. The work of the Liturgical Conference during the 1940s was very much a crash course in the best of these insights. During the 1950s, the emphasis among American liturgists shifted to defining the sacraments as celebrations of the Mysteries of Christ and seeing them in the light of salvation history.

Undoubtedly, Edward Schillebeeckx's book, *De sacramentele Heilseconomi. Theologische bezinning op S. Thomas' sacramenteleer in het lict van de tradite en van de hedendaagse sacraments-problematiek* (1952) and Francis X. Durrwell's book, *La Résurrection de Jésus mystère de salut* (1954) influenced American liturgists. In addition, Schillebeeckx's book, *Christus, Sacrament van de Godsontmoeting* (1960), and Karl Rahner's book, *Kirche und Sakramente* (1961), paved the way for the triumph of the personalist/ecclesial approach to the sacraments at Vatican II.[17] There is implicit in Hillenbrand's theology, even from

---

16. See Edward Kilmartin, *Christian Liturgy: Theology and Practice*, p. 106, for a good example of the continued use of these concepts by contemporary theologians: "The saving grace, derived from the redeeming work of Christ, is mediated through the encounter with Christ in the liturgy. The encounter with Christ culminates in the bestowal of the Spirit and his gifts."

17. See John H. Miller, "Liturgical Studies," in *Theology in Transition*, ed. Elmer O'Brien (New York: Herder & Herder, 1965), pp. 174–183. While this paper lists works that Hillenbrand was familiar with, Miller gives a more comprehensive survey of the writings in

his days as rector at the seminary, much of the same type of personal encounter/church as sacrament of salvation theology, which the above mentioned works explicate so well. This emphasis is evident in Hillenbrand's seminary liturgy course and in all his lectures or writings, which drew upon this course for their core content.

From the period (1929–1931) during which Hillenbrand researched his doctoral thesis, *De Modo quo Deus Justificatos Inhabitat*, he became convinced that grace (divine life) was a comprehensive doctrine that described the work of Christ in the liturgy and in the world. Yet grace is a very difficult term to define and often ends up uniting itself to whatever doctrine is being discussed.[18] If one takes an experiential approach to defining grace, inevitably the discussion returns to Christ and the work of redemption.[19] Hillenbrand preferred the personal term, divine life, over the abstract term, grace, because

> It has been too easy to examine grace detached from the living reality and experience of people, as if grace were an abstract substance, found only in the theological laboratory but not in a natural state elsewhere.[20]

It is easy to resist an abstract notion, but harder to resist the offer of divine life coming from the person of Jesus Christ.

Hillenbrand's frequent assertions that we are the hands, lips, arms, legs, and heart of Christ[21] must be understood in the light of the growing awareness among theologians that the sacraments are the actions of Christ in the world today. A.-M. Roguet, whose works are often quoted in the inquiry programs of the Specialized Lay Apostolate, defined a sacrament as an act of God, which "reaches the human soul

---

this period. Hillenbrand recommended Durrwell's *The Resurrection* and Schillebeeckx's *Christ the Sacrament of the Encounter with God* in the bibliographies he produced for his Chaplain Training Courses in the mid-1960s.

18. See Thomas F. O'Meara, *The Future of Catholicism* (Notre Dame: University of Notre Dame, 1986), p. 14: "Grace is ultimately only a code word. The theologian must labor to express concretely what the poet St. John Perse called 'the mystery of the real.'"

19. See Jeffrey Hopper, *Understanding Modern Theology II: Reinterpreting Christian Faith for Changing Worlds* (Philadelphia: Fortress Press, 1987), pp. 149–152.

20. James F. White, *Sacraments as God's Self Giving*, p. 27.

21. Hillenbrand, "The Mass and the Lay Apostolate," August 25, 1958 lecture. UNDA, CMRH 12/28. In this lecture, Hillenbrand says: "Why did Christ make his Mystical Body? He made it so that these members, wherever they are, could do a little portion . . . of the mighty work, the all-necessary work Christ wants done in the world, the redemptive work."

by way of a whole chain of intermediaries, instruments operating on the soul through the body."[22]

The first of these intermediaries is Christ, who acts upon humans through the medium of his humanity, which acts through the Church and priests, who work through the sacraments, which reach the soul through a last instrument, the human body of each recipient.[23] And so, it is a "perfectly accurate, albeit abridged, statement of the truth to say that it is Christ who acts in every sacrament: Christ baptizes in every baptism, absolves whenever absolution is given."[24] Hillenbrand understood the sacraments in this way and embodied these ideals in all the written materials of the Specialized Lay Apostolate.

Until the 1960s Hillenbrand's liturgical theology was quite ahead of its time and drew upon the best works of European and American scholars. However, it was in the pastoral realm that he spent the bulk of his efforts and where he had his greatest effect. For Hillenbrand's most important contribution to the American liturgical movement was to take seriously the connection between the sacramental encounter in church and the extension of that encounter (the apostolate or Christ's work of redemption) in the world by forming lay apostles through his involvement with the Specialized Lay Apostolate.[25]

Hillenbrand saw the apostolate as an extension of the altar, of the self-giving celebrated in the Eucharist.[26] Baptism and Confirmation gave the laity a share in Christ's priestly ministry (the apostolate) as

---

22. A.-M. Roguet, Christ Acts through the Sacraments, trans. Carisbrooke Dominicans (Collegeville: Liturgical Press, 1954), p. 12.

23. See James F. White, *Sacraments as God's Self-Giving*, p. 30: "Unfortunately, most sacramental theology in recent centuries was more concerned about matters of how to achieve a valid and regular sacrament so that God's grace was conferred . . . . Sometimes, we do need to know the bare minimum—no water, no baptism. But something far more important could easily be overlooked: the humanity of the sacraments. The sacraments communicate within a community of flesh and blood."

24. Ibid.

25. See Joseph A. Jungmann, *Liturgical Worship*, trans. by a monk of St. John's Abbey (Collegeville: Liturgical Press, 1941), p. 28: "One must have a proper understanding of what the Church is—the community or communion of those who are united to Christ, of those who are called to work for the spreading of his life and his prayer on earth. Thus understood, the liturgy will never grow slack or become torpid."

26. Hillenbrand, "The Mass as the Source and Center of the Lay Apostolate," in National Liturgical Week 1955 (Elsberry, Mo.: Liturgical Conference, 1956), p. 176.

well as gifts to serve God's people.[27] The lay apostolate consisted in the laity "undertaking tasks deriving from the mission Christ entrusted to his Church."[28] The place where the Church celebrated its willingness to carry on Christ's mission was the liturgy.[29]

The constant emphasis on liturgy as "corporate worship" must be understood as an expression of a renewed understanding of Church, based on a baptismal spirituality.[30] We find such an understanding of Church in Joseph Jungmann, a European liturgical theologian and historian whom Hillenbrand read, quoted, and recommended to others. Joseph Jungmann wanted people to recapture the sense that the people who carry out the liturgy

> . . . are not in the first place this or that particular people with its peculiarities. . . . Before anything else, they are the People of God. They are the *plebs sancta*, a holy people, who have emerged from the baptismal waters.[31]

What the liturgical movement sought to recover was the sense of a corporate identity in Christ, the sense in which one's whole approach to life is a living out of a baptismal identity, which we share with God's holy people.

When Hillenbrand stressed the need to develop the awareness that the sacraments are the action of Christ, the whole Christ in the world, he was reflecting the growing consensus among liturgists regarding the need to perceive the inner meaning of the liturgical act. Like Romano Guardini, Hillenbrand was concerned that the discussion get beyond the externals, the need for active participation or greater

---

27. Hillenbrand, "The Theological Bases of the Apostolate," August 1948 lecture. UNDA, CMRH 8/36.

28. Hillenbrand, "The Lay Apostolate," April 13, 1961 lecture. UNDA, CMRH 11/28. Hillenbrand sees the nature of the church as a continuation of Christ's mission. To fail to carry on this mission is to fail as a member of the church.

29. See Doohan, *The Lay-Centered Church*, pp. 80, 82: "In fact, the laity's awareness of their responsibilities is largely the result of the pastoral leadership and formation work of visionary clerics and religious . . . . The importance of all the baptized was not fully appreciated until the Church rediscovered . . . 1) that we are all community, 2) called to reincarnate the Lord's message, 3) through our shared ministry, 4) which leads to the liberation of the world."

30. See *The Liturgy Constitution*, no. 2: "The liturgy is the outstanding means by which the faithful can express in their lives, and manifest to others, the mystery of Christ and the real nature of the true church."

31. Jungmann, *Liturgical Worship*, p. 58.

use of the vernacular.[32] And so, his efforts in the movement went beyond external reforms to something more important: defining the full nature of the liturgical act.

People frequently approached worship as an act of the mind and will, an intellectual experience rather than a contemplative action.[33] In order to understand Hillenbrand properly, when he speaks of the need for a stronger sense of Christ Mystic, one must recognize how the liturgy is simultaneously a human, a symbolic, and a contemplative action.

> It's not enough to see Christ historically, but you have to sense him in the world as he is today—in his great corporate reality, in his great redemptive action, in the extension and application of that redemption, which is his sacramental activity.[34]

Thus, it was out of an appreciation of the full implications of the liturgical act that Hillenbrand evolved much of his synthesis regarding liturgy and life, liturgy and social action.[35]

THE TRANSITION AFTER VATICAN II

In the light of the above discussion on liturgy and church, we can better evaluate the numerous practical steps taken by the liturgical pioneers prior to Vatican II. While in Part I of this book, we outlined the specific reforms (dialog Mass, daily homily, singing, lay readers, Mass facing the people, etc.) that Hillenbrand espoused, we will now describe the many ways Hillenbrand's theology triumphed at Vatican II. In particular, there are three areas that merit closer attention: the nature of liturgy, ministerial formation, the connection between liturgy and life.

---

32. Romano Guardini, "A Letter from Romano Guardini," April 1, 1964, letter to the Mainz Liturgical Congress, reprinted in Assembly 12 (1986), pp. 322–324. Guardini sees the liturgy as a contemplative action of self-surrender to God by means of its symbolic actions and words.

33. Hillenbrand, "The Parish is Christ," February 7, 1957, lecture. UNDA, CMRH 11/28.

34. Hillenbrand, "The Need and Scope of the Lay Apostolate," April 17, 1946, lecture. UNDA, CMRH 8/13. See Jennifer Glen, "A Reflection on the Liturgical Act," Assembly 12 (1986), pp. 325–328.

35. Many liturgists today reflect these same convictions. See Mark Searle, "On the Art of Lifting up the Heart: Liturgical Prayer Today," Studies in Formative Spirituality 3 (1982), p. 406: "To join in the celebration of liturgy is to acknowledge that we belong to the world that God is redeeming, that we share the common human condition and that the whole of humanity is the object of his reconciling and redeeming love."

The Constitution on the Sacred Liturgy (*Sacrosanctum Concilium*) was the first completed work of the Vatican Council. "It was in the provisions of the Constitution on the Sacred Liturgy more than anywhere else that the *aggiornamento* which John XXIII had demanded of the Council assumed visible and incisive forms."[36] The static, clerically dominated, more passive model of liturgy was replaced by a pastoral model of liturgy in which "the full and active participation by all the people is the aim to be considered before all else" (no. 14). It says, "such participation by the Christian people as a "chosen race, a royal priesthood, a holy nation, a purchased people . . . is their right and duty by reason of their baptism" (no. 14). However, the section on "The Nature of the Sacred Liturgy and its Importance in Church Life" (nos. 5–13) fails to adequately explains the doctrine of Paschal Mystery and opens itself to conflicting interpretations.

Hillenbrand read the Constitution on the Sacred Liturgy and claimed that it was in continuity with *Mediator Dei*. In some ways, he was correct. Constitution on the Sacred Liturgy is built upon the foundation established by Mediator Dei:

> In the liturgy full public worship is performed by the Mystical Body of Jesus Christ, that is, by the Head and His members" (no. 7). "By offering the Immaculate Victim, not only through the hands of the priest, but also with him, they should learn to offer themselves too. Through Christ the Mediator, they should be drawn day by day into ever closer union with God and with each other, so that finally God may be all in all" (no. 48).

However, the Constitution went well beyond *Mediator Dei* in defining the nature of the liturgy.[37]

The problem with the Constitution is that it was the first document approved by the Council. The full ecclesiology and Christology necessary to interpret it is found in the Dogmatic Constitution on the Church, the Pastoral Constitution on the Church in the Modern World, the Dogmatic Constitution on Divine

36. Josef Jungmann, "Constitution on the Sacred Liturgy," in *Commentary on the Documents of Vatican II*, ed. Herbert Vorgrimler (New York: Herder & Herder, 1967), p. 1. Jungmann surveys the numerous developments in this century that ultimately produced the Constitution on the Sacred Liturgy. See Teresa Berger, " 'Sacrosanctum Concilium' and 'Worship and the Oneness of Christ's Church,' Twenty-Five Years Later," *Worship* 62 (1988), pp. 299–316.

37. See Kevin W. Irwin, "The Constitution on the Sacred Liturgy, *Sacrosanctum Concilium* (4 December 1963)" in *Vatican II and its Documents, an American Reappraisal*, ed. Timothy O'Connell (Wilmington: Michael Glazier, 1986), pp. 9–38.

Revelation, the Decree on Ecumenism, and the Decree on the Apostolate of the Laity. If one based their evaluation of the teachings of the Council mainly on the Constitution on the Sacred Liturgy, one could find in it sufficient references to sacrifice or self-offering (nos. 2, 5, 6, 7, 10, 47, 48, 49) to justify the conclusion that the Constitution has not superseded the basic theology of Mediator Dei.[38] However, if one interpreted the Constitution in the context of the previously mentioned documents, one could not maintain this position.

    Mediator Dei asserted the link between liturgy and daily life. It saw the liturgy as the expression and formation of the Church.[39] In these assertions, the Constitution on the Sacred Liturgy agreed with *Mediator Dei*. However, when Hillenbrand defined sacrifice in terms of the moment of consecration, it was at that point he separated himself from the inadequate, but still workable, explanation of Paschal Mystery that the Constitution espoused. Had Hillenbrand been able to accept the sacrificial nature of the Eucharist as a form of prayer, he could have avoided a sharp conflict with the Chicago Archdiocesan Liturgical Commission over the Archdiocesan Directory.

    Hillenbrand's scholarship was never weaker than when he attacks the "sacrament of a sacrifice" theory espoused by Salvatore Marsili and Gerard Broccolo.[40] As he said,

> I have re-read *Mediator Dei* and nowhere does it present the Mass in this way. It constantly insists on sacrifice, or Christ's death, or the consecration. Jungmann's *Mass of the Roman Rite* overwhelmingly stresses the consecration as a sacrifice and Communion as a meal.[41]

---

    38. Hillenbrand to Albert Cardinal Meyer, November 13, 1964, letter. UNDA, CMRH 7. See Hillenbrand's annotated copy of the Liturgy Constitution. UNDA, CMRH 28/15.

    39. See Edward J. Kilmartin, "Theology of the Sacraments: Toward a New Understanding of the Chief Rites of the Church of Jesus Christ," in *Alternative Futures for Worship, Vol.I: General Introduction*, ed. Regis A. Duffy (Collegeville: Liturgical Press, 1987), pp. 133–137.

    40. Salvatore Marsili, "The Mass, Paschal Mystery and Mystery of the Church," in *The Liturgy of Vatican II, Vol. II*, ed. William Barauna (Chicago: Franciscan Herald Press, 1966), p. 4: "Even the very title (art. 47 of the) 'On the Most Holy Mystery of the Eucharist,' without wishing to abolish the scholastic distinction of *sacrament* and *sacrifice* does not emphasize the distinction, but prefers to present a more unified concept of the Eucharist." See Henry Govert, "The Eucharist—a Sacrament of a Sacrifice," in *Let us Give Thanks, Explanation and Texts of the New Eucharistic Prayers*, ed. Gerard Broccolo and Mary Jo Tully (Chicago: Liturgy Training Program, 1968), pp. 23–34.

    41. Hillenbrand to Albert Cardinal Meyer, November 13, 1964 letter. UNDA. CMRH 7. See David Power, *The Sacrifice We Offer* (New York: Crossroad, 1987), pp. 15–21 on the new doctrinal and ecclesial context in which sacrifice needs to be interpreted.

However, Jungmann developed his idea of sacrifice from the time he wrote *Mass of the Roman Rite* (1939–1948) to an even more nuanced position, based on an understanding of the institution narrative as a part of the memorial prayer, in *The Eucharistic Prayer, A Study of the Canon of the Mass* (1952–1953).[42]

Hillenbrand's emphasis on sacrifice as verified in the consecration of the Mass should not obstruct his more important recognition that the whole life of the Christian was a sacrifice offered to God (See Romans 12:1).[43] Moreover, he associated his theories on sacrifice and redemptive activity with the importance of lay ministry and ministerial training. These later emphases, coupled with his theory on lay spirituality, were affirmed numerous times in the documents of Vatican II. However, Hillenbrand's major disappointment with the documents was that the Constitution on the Sacred Liturgy missed the connection between liturgy and social justice.[44]

The Dogmatic Constitution on the Church (*Lumen Gentium*), no. 33, clearly supported Hillenbrand's position on the lay apostolate:

> The lay apostolate is a participation in the saving mission of the Church itself. Through their baptism and confirmation, all are commissioned to that apostolate by the Lord himself.

Moreover, many of Hillenbrand's recommendations to Bishop Ernest Primeau about the role of the laity[45] were adopted. These include the need for lay participation in evangelization (Missions 36, Church 31, 35, Liturgy 6), family ministries (Church 35, Church Today 48, 52, Education 3), human development (Church Today 23–32, 53, 60–64, 75), world transformation (Liturgy 9, Church 36),

---

42. See Josef Jungmann, *The Eucharistic Prayer: A Study of the Canon of the Mass*, trans. Robert L. Batley (London: Burns & Oates, 1956), p. 40: "The Mass is indeed a sacrifice of propitiation, as the Council of Trent emphasizes, but it is primarily the sacrifice of thanksgiving: *Gratias agamus*." Jungmann was a fairly conservative theologian. He did not make statements such as the above without recognizing the fact that he was reinterpreting the old doctrine of sacrifice in the light of contemporary research into the Eucharistic prayer.

43. Hillenbrand, "The Spirituality of YCW Leaders," July, 1952 lecture. UNDA, CMRH 8/38. Hillenbrand says, "our associations with each other is a strong self-sacrifice out of charity."

44. *The Decree on the Apostolate of the Laity* does make this connection (nos. 2–5, 1–8, 11).

45. See Chapter 4 for the list of recommendations, pp. 116–117.

ministry training (Laity 20–23, 30–32), and internal Church life (Liturgy 10, 26–32,).[46]

While the Cardijn method was not specifically mentioned, apostolic training, beginning with a child's earliest education, was forcefully recommended (Laity 30–32). Catholic Action organizations were earnestly endorsed (Laity, 20). Hillenbrand must have been encouraged when Bishop Ernest Primeau responded to his recommendations on the Decree on the Laity:

> Your comments and animadversions on the Schema "De Apostolatu Laicorum" have reached me. With a covering letter, I sent them on to the Commission. George Higgins, who is a peritus on the subject, agrees with me that your remarks are excellent and deserve to be heard where they can do the most good.[47]

Consequently, Hillenbrand enjoyed a great amount of satisfaction that his fundamental vision of the lay apostolate was clearly endorsed by the Council and made part of the documents of Vatican II.

Unfortunately, Hillenbrand's strict understanding of encyclical teachings as binding in conscience hindered his ability to adapt his methodology to the new possibilities presented in the Council documents.

> When the Roman pontiffs go out of their way to pronounce on some subject which has hitherto been controverted, it must be clear to everybody that, in the mind and intention of the pontiffs concerned, this subject can no longer be regarded as a matter of free debate among theologians.[48]

And so, Hillenbrand attempted to harmonize past encyclical teachings with the Council documents. He dismissed contemporary theology, whenever it seemed to disagree with previous papal positions.

---

46. See Leonard Doohan, *The Lay-Centered Church* (Minneapolis: Winston Press, 1984) and *Laity's Mission in the Church* (San Francisco: Harper & Row, 1986).

47. Bishop Ernest Primeau to Hillenbrand, September 1964 letter. (Bishop Primeau was originally a priest of the Archdiocese of Chicago and the former rector of the Chicago House of Studies in Rome. In 1960, he became the Bishop of Manchester, New Hampshire.) UNDA, CMRH 9/3. See Chapter 4, note 39. In particular, Hillenbrand's recommendations that references to the Cardijn "like ministering to like" principle (no. 13) and to the importance of Catholic Action groups (no. 20) be maintained were adopted in the final draft. UNDA, CMRH 9/3.

48. Hillenbrand, "The Social Encyclicals," May 25, 1951 lecture. UNDA, CMRH 8/37. See Johannes-Baptist Metz & Edward Schillebeeckx, eds., *Concilium 180: The Teaching Authority of Believers* (Edinburgh: T. & T. Clark, 1985).

A weakness in Hillenbrand's methodology was that papal encyclicals are summaries of where the Church has been and how far it can go at that particular point in time. They do not stop the growth of theology. They only set limits on the positions the church is willing to accept. They remind us that liturgical change is meant to be a continuation of the past, not a rupture or break with past tradition. In holding on to the whole corpus of previous encyclicals (especially, *Mystici Corporis*, *Mediator Dei*, and *Quadragesimo Anno*) and failing to integrate the new approaches advocated in the documents of Vatican II, Hillenbrand restricted his ability to deal with current issues. Moreover, his theological synthesis began to be questioned, when he failed to address the alternative methods of apostolic formation that sprang up after the Council.

The Vatican Council advocated a more eclectic approach to apostolic formation than Hillenbrand was ready to accept. Cardijn Methodology (See-Judge-Act) had accomplished a great deal of good in the first half of the twentieth century. However, people were looking for something new that would make use of the latest insights of the biblical and patristic movements, new ways of living in community, and greater respect for personal charisms. They wanted a leader who could synthesize the insights of the Vatican Council and introduce them to the next step in their growth as baptized Catholics committed to implementing the "Pastoral Constitution on the Church in the Modern World." By refusing to integrate new insights from theology and the behavioral science into his methodology, and by neglecting the directives found in the documents of Vatican II, Hillenbrand unwittingly looked like a leader who was out of step with the modern Church envisioned by the Council.

After the Council, some of the laity, especially leaders in the Specialized Lay Apostolate, reacted to Hillenbrand's stress on the papal encyclicals as a form of clerical domination. The Council told the laity that they were the Church, the people of God. After the Council, many of the lay leaders felt the time had come to claim their "independence." As we discussed earlier, in 1967, the CFM voted to cease submitting its programs to Hillenbrand for censorship. YCS and YCW lost members as new ministries began to compete with these older forms of the lay apostolate.

Vatican II called priests and laity to new styles of participation in the life of the Church: collaboration, mutual accountability, shared leadership in liturgical celebration, etc.[49] While Hillenbrand had long advocated that greater responsibility be given to the laity, it was probably difficult to see his authority challenged. When his parish voted in 1973 against his policy on a daily Mass for children, he began to question the fruitfulness of his ministry. As someone trained in the administrative style of Cardinal Mundelein, Hillenbrand found the post-Conciliar transition to be quite a strain.

Concern over the pace of change after the Council was voiced by many people. One of Hillenbrand's long-time allies in the liturgical movement, William Busch, wrote Hillenbrand about his apprehensions:

> I rejoice, of course, at what the Second Vatican Council has done in the *Liturgy Constitution*. But I think that in carrying out its wishes we have moved too rapidly and have tried to do everything at once, whereas I would prefer a gradual procedure. Moreover, I am distressed at some of our young priests, who, with no depth of understanding, have assumed the role of "reformers" both in thought and in action.[50]

In some ways, Busch was correct. There were many strange experiments that occurred after the Council. Books were published with experimental Eucharistic Liturgies. "Underground churches" sprang up in numerous parishes.

Hillenbrand opposed priests using their own or unofficial English translations of the Latin Mass. He deplored the lack of vestments, the use of non-scriptural readings, Communion in the hand at a time when it was not permitted. He was annoyed when priests took it upon themselves to eliminate parts of the Mass that they no longer considered relevant—names of unfamiliar saints, prayers at the foot of the altar, the Last Gospel, etc. At the same time, Hillenbrand was clearly in favor of simplifying and making more intelligible the

---

49. See Doohan, *Laity's Mission in the Church*, pp. 32–37.

50. William Busch to Hillenbrand, February 21, 1965, letter. UNDA, CMRH 36, Correspondence, 1965.

parts of the Mass.[51] Moreover, he had fought long and hard to bring the vernacular into the liturgy.[52] It was the attack on papal authority and the scandal to the laity that most bothered him, when people did these things.[53]

Undoubtedly, the pace of change had produced its excesses. However, Hillenbrand's reaction was quite different from that of William Busch. Hillenbrand's theory was that formation took place simultaneously with action (change). The people only needed a short explanation and then they should experience the new liturgy. If one did the liturgy properly, eventually people would understand its inner nature and purpose. In addition, follow-up catechesis would resolve most of people's difficulties.

The minutes of the Archdiocesan Liturgical Commission reported that

> Msgr. Hillenbrand found no fault with the pace of change that has been set by Rome. He felt that an adequate preparation of the people, who participate in the liturgy, would indicate a pace, with lags between documents designed as pauses for reflection.[54]

At Sacred Heart Church, Hillenbrand implemented every change in the liturgy as soon as it was possible.[55] While the response of his parish was excellent, Sacred Heart Church had almost 20 years of liturgical catechesis prior to the changes authorized by Vatican II.

---

51. See the list of "Recommended Changes" that he presented to the Archdiocesan Liturgical Commission: all the Mass in the vernacular, improved translations of biblical and prayer texts, English chants, change "and with your spirit" to "and also with you," improve the Preface dialogue, be more precise about the Word/word distinction, use good English words instead of Latin derivatives (e.g., reader instead of lector), never place a processional cross in front of the altar, eliminate the joining of the fingers after the consecration, give the offertory prayers to the people. UNDA, CMRH 22/6.

52. See Chapter 4, note 38. UNDA, CMRH 37, Correspondence, 1963–1965.

53. CFM Executive Committee Meeting Minutes, February 11-13, 1966. UNDA, CMRH 10/8.

54. Archdiocesan Liturgical Commission, September 19, 1967 Minutes. UNDA, CMRH 28/2.

55. Often, he spoke at all the Masses, personally summarizing the changes already achieved and then introducing the newest rite (e.g., Funeral Rite, Penance Rite, Communal Anointing, etc.) and its theology.

HILLENBRAND'S PLACE AMONG THE LITURGICAL PIONEERS

Hillenbrand played an important role in the American liturgical movement. As rector of St. Mary of the Lake Seminary, he trained a whole generation of priests to see the connection between liturgy and life, liturgy and the apostolate. He inspired countless numbers of people in the Specialized Lay Apostolate to define their membership in the Church as lay apostles, whose lives were an extension of the liturgy they celebrated. He played a crucial role in the founding of the Liturgical Conference and the Vernacular Society. His contacts with European and American liturgists and his acquaintance with the writings of Beauduin, Marmion, Herwegen, Casel, Guardini, Parsch, Jungmann, Roguet, and others were reflected in the synthesis he developed and spread throughout his long years as a Catholic priest.

While Hillenbrand's synthesis was derived from some of the best sources available in his day, it does have a problem. It becomes quite repetitive after awhile. For Hillenbrand saw clearly the connection between anthropology, divine life, Christology, ecclesiology, liturgiology, and social action. No matter what concern he was asked to address, he usually did so by addressing all or at least most of these areas. While his focus might be on social justice, for example, the way he deals with it is to carefully lead his audience or reader through his fundamental principles. Certainly, his Neo-scholastic training at St. Mary of the Lake Seminary accounts for some of this desire to foster a comprehensive theological system. In fact, some of the repetitiveness of this book is due to this characteristic in Hillenbrand's lectures and writings, which ordinarily were written for popular audiences and journals rather than scholarly groups and publications.

Certainly, Hillenbrand's Eucharistic theology had its weaknesses, especially in his interpretation of the doctrine of sacrifice. However, much of his synthesis (anthropology, divine life, Body of Christ, the centrality of Christ, an appreciation of contemplative dimensions of the liturgical act) is still being used today! While Hillenbrand was mainly a popularizer of the insights of European and American liturgists, he was undoubtedly one of the more successful liturgists to champion the cause of social justice. In many ways, he continued the legacy of Virgil Michel, who saw so clearly the necessity

of a pastoral liturgical movement. Unfortunately, his rigid adherence
to past directives from Pius XII rather than the new directives of
Paul VI and the Vatican Council as well as his poor physical health
resulted in his becoming a relatively minor figure in the liturgical
movement in the United States after Vatican II.

Much of what Hillenbrand stood for represented the best
insights of European and American liturgists. His liturgical program
at Sacred Heart Church was modeled on the work done in St. Louis
by Martin Hellriegel and Ermin Vitry. His commitment to a daily
homily was inspired by Pius Parsch. His beliefs in the pastoral nature
of liturgy were clarified by Gerald Ellard and Romano Guardini. His
approach to building and renovation was influenced by H. A. Reinhold.
His leadership of the Specialized Lay Apostolate was based on the
theology and methodology of Joseph Cardijn. His concern for social
justice issues was stimulated by the Central Verein and activists like
John A. Ryan, Francis Haas, and Dorothy Day. Hillenbrand was
a product of his times. He was staunchly loyal to papal teachings,
dismissing too easily the new insights of modern theologians. He held
a classical approach to doctrine and a historical, evolutionary approach
to social problems.

Hillenbrand made a tremendous contribution to the American
liturgical movement in the written publications of the Specialized Lay
Apostolate, which he edited, and the education in ministry and
liturgy that he gave to thousands of lay Christians across the nation
prior to Vatican II. Hillenbrand's incarnate spirituality and vision
of parish, pastors, and lay apostles not only captured the imaginations
of many people, but are still very much in evidence today. While the
transition after Vatican II was a painful one for Hillenbrand, there is
ample proof that his ideals live on in the Church.

Unfortunately, Hillenbrand was too sick to attend the Second
Archdiocesan Liturgical Conference that took place in Chicago in
1978. If he had attended the Conference, he would have heard Gerard
Broccolo, the associate director of the Chicago Office for Divine
Worship, commend his pioneer work throughout our nation. He would
have especially enjoyed Broccolo's synthesis on the "Chicago Parish":

The parish has come to mean the base from which we are Church, the base from which we minister to others, whether from within or beyond our local Christian community. . . . The parish now has become a ministerial formation center, a center by which we form people to go out and be church, to go out and minister to others. . . . Real ministry is being my fullest self in a way that calls others forth to be their fullest selves.[56]

Broccolo states well the Hillenbrand legacy: it is a vision of parish and people ministering to one another.

Godfrey Diekmann, the editor of *Orate Fratres*, worked with Hillenbrand for many years and valued his contributions to the liturgical movement. As Diekmann says,

In any historical overview of the Catholic Church in the United States in this century, Monsignor Hillenbrand would certainly have to be numbered among the top dozen who influenced its apostolic developments. In fact, I cannot think of more than three or four others who could rank with him in this respect. He inspired several generations of priests and laity with his vision of the social gospel rooted in the community-formative dynamic of the Mass.[57]

Hillenbrand definitely had a fruitful ministry. Yet, like all people, he had his drawbacks. By stubbornly holding to one methodology (formation through action, SEE-JUDGE-ACT, papal encyclicals), he eventually lost his position as a leader of the Modern Church during the post-conciliar era.

The inspiration for Hillenbrand's ministry was the liturgy. Hillenbrand loved the Mass and truly made it the source and center of his spiritual life. Msgr. John J. Egan, his old student and eventual partner in ministry, explains:

The strongest passion in Reynold Hillenbrand's life was reserved for the liturgy. The sacrifice of the Mass was the center of his life, the core of his spirituality. If there is any area of study to which he devoted total concentration, it was to understand more and more of the beauty, the meaning, the depth of the "Mysterium Fidei." . . . It was the liturgy which animated his work in social action, in the family life apostolate, and in seminary renewal.[58]

---

56. Gerard Broccolo, "The Chicago Parish: Gathering us into Ministry," September 24, 1978, lecture. NCR Cassettes.

57. Godfrey Diekmann, "Msgr. Reynold Hillenbrand," *Liturgy 70* 10 (1979), p. 2.

58. John J. Egan, "Msgr. Reynold Hillenbrand," *Liturgy 70* 10 (1979), p. 3.

Hillenbrand's liturgical theology truly provided the base for his personal and ministerial involvements. His example challenges ministers today to integrate the liturgy ever more completely into their spiritual life.

In Ephesians 4:11–13, there is a passage that captures Hillenbrand's beliefs about Christ, Church, and ministry:

> It is Christ who gave apostles, prophets, evangelists, pastors, and teachers in roles of service for the faithful to build up the Body of Christ, till we become one in faith and in the knowledge of God's Son, and form that perfect creature, who is Christ come to full stature.

Hillenbrand has been described as many things: from the American Cardijn to Chicago's version of Martin Hellriegel, from a social activist to a liturgical pioneer. Yet I suspect the one title that best describes Hillenbrand is the one found in the above passage from Ephesians: he was an apostle, whom the Lord called to build up the Body of Christ.

Appendix

Sacred Heart Church (Winnetka, Illinois) 1957 Worship Program

In 1957, on the occasion of the completion of the renovation of the parish Church, Hillenbrand composed a booklet, in which he described the worship program and parish organizations, existing at Sacred Heart Parish in 1957:

> Sacred Heart parish has had active participation in the Mass by the laity since 1945 . . . . All Masses have this participation. On Sunday there is one sung Mass . . . and four dialog Masses. On weekdays the 6:15 Mass is congregationally sung, the 6:55 is a dialog Mass.
>
> The Sung Mass on Sundays at 9:30 is the Parish Mass. Parishioners alternate with the vested boys' choir. The vested men's choir sings the propers and joins the boys' choir in polyphonic music. A fine tradition carries on when a family has representation at this Mass, because it is the Parish Mass.
>
> At the dialogue Masses, a lay reader cues in the people, and reads the epistle and Gospel. Masses are preceded and ended with English hymns.
>
> A feature, rarely experienced in parishes, is the Mass "facing the congregation." Parishioners find this Mass visually more interesting and gripping.
>
> The sung Mass—the Parish Mass—is always offered this way, as well as Masses on holydays and the weekday children's Mass.
>
> There is a striking tradition in our parish of receiving Christ each time parishioners offer Mass. The changes in the fasting laws have made Communion so much more accessible.
>
> Your priests will be glad to bring Our Lord in Communion every week to anyone who is unable to go to Mass, whatever his disability is.

You should receive Christ at wedding and funeral Masses. These are great events in human life and apt occasions to receive the Lord of life.

On weekdays, parishioners come to the front of the Church to make participation possible. For this reason cords are placed on the rear pews. Adults are welcome at the weekday children's Mass at 11:00 o'clock.

On Sunday, all parishioners are provided with a leaflet missal and need not, therefore, bring missals.

Masses start promptly on the moment. Parishioners should continue the tradition—the only right tradition—of being in church when Mass begins and not leaving until the priest returns to the sacristy.

The Sunday Masses are kept to three quarters of an hour. The sung Mass takes a little longer.

Announcements are held to a minimum. You may read these in our weekly news folder, the "Tower," distributed after Mass. The financial matter of contributions is confined to the barest minimum. Except for the diocesan collections, money is rarely mentioned from the pulpit.

The ushers are efficient and eager to help in any way.

Holy Week, in which we relive with Christ the most important events of our redemption, is carried out with the greatest effectiveness and beauty.

On the Second Passion Sunday, the blessing of palms takes place in the school, and the congregation moves in procession to the church.

During the Mass, the Passion is read by three men, and the people take the part of the crowd who cried for Christ's death.

On Holy Thursday, the Mass of the Lord's Supper is at 6:00 PM in the evening. The washing of the feet is a ceremony in this Mass and deepens its meaning.

On Good Friday, the services with Communion are also at six in the evening.

The climax of Holy Week is the Easter Vigil Service, the most striking and beautiful of the year. It is held at the appropriate hour, determined by the church—10:30 at night—and it concludes with Easter Mass. The Easter Vigil with its Mass is an unforgettable experience. Nothing else can do as much for us as Christians.

Baptism. This sacrament would be better called rebirth or second birth, which Our Lord actually called it. Baptism in our parish is an attractive ceremony with which you will be pleased. It begins in the vestibule of the church and ends at the baptismal font next to the high altar.

Confession. Next to offering Mass and eating Christ's flesh, we can do nothing better than giving Christ the opportunity to step into our lives by the sacrament known as Confession or Penance, better called repentance.

Confirmation. This sacrament, which matures the divine life in those who were only children by Baptism, is given in May in alternate years. Adults who are not confirmed should call the parish house so they will not be overlooked at the next Confirmation.

Marriage. It is almost unthinkable that there would be a Catholic marriage without Mass. All Catholics in the wedding party should receive Christ in Communion. All Catholics at the wedding should be invited to receive Communion, and this might be mentioned as an enclosure in the invitation.

The Sacrament of the Sick. This is the more helpful name of Extreme Unction or the Last Anointing . . . . This sacrament is meant for the seriously sick, and most of its prayers plead for a return to health.

The School aims to do what every Catholic school must do, to form the full human and the full Christian . . . . The most important class of the day is Mass at which Christ is the teacher. At Mass there is a three-minute talk.

The Parish has a number of organizations: Men's Club, Council of Catholic Women, Mother's Club, Women's Sodality, Christian Family Movement, Young Christian Students (elementary and high school), Confraternity of Christian Doctrine, Men's choir, Boys' choir, Readers, Ushers, Library Committee, Contemporary Religious Arts Foundation, Sarto Foundation (to aid needy).

Other Parish Activities: annual retreat for men and women, monthly evenings of recollection, vigil of prayer on Fridays, lecture series on Catholic doctrine for converts and interested parties, parish library, concerts of religious music, Mistletoe Market, Founders' Day party, newcomers buffet dinner and party, annual parish dance, two sports awards nights.

This description of parish life is remarkable especially for the high priority placed upon active participation in the liturgy. Undoubtedly, the liturgy is the most important activity in the parish.

Bibliography

PRIMARY SOURCES

The listing of Msgr. Reynold Hillenbrand's books, pamphlets, articles, and lectures will stand in chronological rather than alphabetical order. In this way, his contribution to the development of the liturgical movement and the Specialized Lay Apostolate will be more clearly seen. The majority of these materials are part of the Msgr. Reynold Hillenbrand Collection in the University of Notre Dame Archives, University of Notre Dame, Notre Dame, Indiana.

I. *Book*

De Modo quo Deus Justifactos Inhabitat, Unpublished S.T.D. Dissertation. Mundelein: St. Mary of the Lake Seminary, 1931.

II. *Articles and Lectures*

1936

"Seminary Social Thoughts," Fall, 1936 lecture notes, St. Mary of the Lake Seminary, UNDA, CMRH 3/25.

1938

"Christian Principles Applied to the Printing Trades." In: *Proceedings of the National Catholic Social Action Conference in Milwaukee, May 1–4, 1938,* pp. 260–265. Milwaukee: Archdiocese of Milwaukee, 1938. Also in UNDA, CMRH 7.
"Communism: Dialectical Materialism: Theory of Class Struggle," and "The Priest's Work According to the Encyclicals." In: *Summer School of Social Action for Priests, July 18–August 12, 1938, Vol. 4,* pp. 410–418, 419–423. Mundelein: St. Mary of the Lake Seminary, 1938.
"Liturgy Course Notes." St. Mary of the Lake Seminary Lecture Notes from Hillenbrand's Liturgy Course, 1938–1943. UNDA, CMRH 4/12, 4/13, and 29/13.

1940

"Introductory." October 21, 1940, lecture, National Liturgical Week, Chicago, Illinois. In: *National Liturgical Week 1940,* pp. 5–13. Newark: Benedictine Liturgical Conference, 1941.

1941

"The Meaning of Liturgy." October 7, 1941, lecture, National Liturgical Week,
St. Paul, Minnesota. In: *National Liturgical Week 1941*, pp. 20–28. Newark:
Benedictine Liturgical Conference, 1942.

1942

"The Mystical Body." August 9, 1942, lecture, Summer School of Liturgy for
Seminarians, Conception, Missouri. UNDA, CMRH 35.

1943

"The Mass, Parts I & II." Summer, 1943 lectures, The Grail, Doddridge Farm,
Libertyville, Illinois. UNDA, CMRH 4/9.
"Catholic Action." September 16, 1943 lecture, LaCrosse Diocesan Clergy Conference,
LaCrosse, Wisconsin. UNDA, CMRH 7/29 and CMRH 36.
"Liturgy and Catholic Action." October 6, 1943, lecture, Priests' Study Week
on Catholic Action, Childerly Retreat House, Wheeling, Illinois. UNDA,
CMRH 7/28.
"The Spirit of Sacrifice in Christian Society, Statement of Principle." October 13,
1943, lecture, National Liturgical Week, Chicago, Illinois. In: *National Liturgical
Week 1943*, pp. 100–109. Ferdinand, IN: The Liturgical Conference, 1944.

1944

"In Pursuit of Peace." February 1, 1944, lecture, University Catholic Club, University
of Pittsburgh, Pennsylcania. UNDA, CMRH 36.
"The Family Spirit." June 1944 lecture, Study Week for Catholic Action Students,
St. Mary's College, Notre Dame, Indiana. UNDA, CMRH 7/25.
"The Life of the Liturgy." *Liturgical Arts* 12 (1944), pp. 53–55.
"Present Status of the Business Girl." July 2, 1944, lecture, Catholic Action Business
Girls' Study Week, Childerly Retreat House, Wheeling, Illinois. UNDA,
CMRH 7/25.
"The Word in the Mystical Body." October 4, 1944, lecture, National Liturgical
Conference, St. Meinrad's Abbey. UNDA, CMRH 28/24.
"The Mass." December 29, 1944, lecture, The Grail, Doddridge Farm, Libertyville,
Illinois. UNDA, CMRH 29/12.

1945

"The Mystical Body, Divine Grace, and Worship." June 10, 1945, lecture, St. Bernard's
Woman's Club, Chicago. UNDA, CMRH 36.
"The Liturgical Revival" and "Summary and Prospects." August 28 and August 31,
1945, Lectures, Maritime Liturgical Conference, Charlottetown, P.E.I. UNDA,
CMRH 8/6 and 29/13.
"Obligations, Problems, and Privileges of the Priest in Catholic Action." November 9,
1945, lecture, Catholic Action Conference, Saskatoon. UNDA, CMRH 8/6.

"The Liturgical Renewal Today." December 12, 1945, lecture National Liturgical Week, New Orleans, Louisiana. In: *National Liturgical Week 1945*, pp. 9–14. Peotone, Ill.: The Liturgical Conference, 1946.

"The Liturgical Movement." December 1945 Lecture, Sheil School of Social Studies, Chicago. UNDA, CMRH 8/6.

"Liturgy as Corporate Worship," "Mass as Center of Christian Life and Source of an Apostolic Spirit," and "World Vision of the Apostolate." December 29–31, 1945, lecture, Grailville, Loveland, Ohio. UNDA, CMRH 37.

1946

"The Mystical Body." July 1946 lecture, Newman Club Convention, Manhattanville College of the Sacred Heart, New York City. UNDA, CMRH 42.

"The Need and Scope of the Lay Apostolate," "The Function of the Liturgy," and "The Holy Sacrifice of the Mass." August 17, 20, and 22, 1946 lectures, Catholic Action Study Week, Grailville, Loveland, Ohio. UNDA, CMRH 7 and 8/13.

"The Meaning of Mass and Catholic Action." August 29, 1946, lecture, Seminarians' Catholic Action Study Week, Notre Dame. UMDA, CMRH 7/25.

"Oneness in the Mystical Body." October 3, 1946, lecture, Sacred Heart Church, Hubbard Woods, Illinois. UNDA, CMRH 22/11.

"The Family and Catholic Action." October 16, 1946, lecture, National Liturgical Week, Denver, Colorado. In: *National Liturgical Week 1946*, pp. 128–136. Highland Park, Illinois: The Liturgical Conference, 1947.

"Employer-Labor Relations and the Encyclical, *Quadragesimo Anno*." December 9, 1946, lecture, Catholic Conference on Industrial Problems, Neil House, Columbus, Ohio. UNDA, CMRH 24/9.

1947

"Sacred Heart Church, Hubbard Woods, Illinois, 1891–1947." Booklet written by Hillenbrand for Sacred Heart Church Founder's Day Celebration, 1947. UNDA, CMRH 8/36.

"Catholic Action." June 17, 1947, lecture, Sacred Heart Convent, Greenwich, Connecticut. UNDA, CMRH 8/36.

"Supernatural View of Society." June 24, 1947, lecture, Seminarians' International Study Week, Montreal, Canada. UNDA, CMRH 7/25.

"The Social Nature of Grace in Mystical Body of Christ." June 25, 1947, lecture, YCW International Study Week, Montreal, Canada. UNDA, CMRH 8/4.

"The Place of Liturgy in Catholic Action," "The Divine Life," "The Central Position of the Mass," and "The Liturgy as the Restorer of a Sense of Corporateness." July 1–10, 1947, course (4 lectures), University of Notre Dame Summer School. UNDA, CMRH 28/27 and 28/13.

"Job Equality." August, 1947 lecture, Marshall Field's, Chicago. UNDA, CMRH 8/6.

"Social Problems of Today." August 5, 1947, lecture, Catholic Action Study Week for Priests, Notre Dame. UNDA, CMRH 7/28.

"Social Problems Today." August 14, 1947, lecture to YCW Chaplains, Catholic Action Study Week for Priests, Notre Dame. UNDA, CMRH 8/36.

"With One Another At Mass." August 19, 1947, lecture, National Liturgical Week, Portland, Oregon. In: *National Liturgical Week 1947,* pp. 60–66. Boston: The Liturgical Conference , 1948. See also UNDA, CMRH 29/13.

"A Pastor's Standpoint on the Spiritual Life of College Students." December 8, 1947, lecture, St. John's University, Collegeville meeting of representatives of the Catholic Colleges and Newman Centers in Minnesota. UNDA, CMRH 35.

1948

"Oneness." March 1948 Lecture, CIO Industrial Council, Chicago. UNDA, CMRH 8/6.

"The Mass and Marriage." August 1948 lecture, Cana Conference Convention, Our Lady of Mt. Carmel High School, Chicago. UNDA, CMRH 29/12.

"The Challenge to Catholic Faith." August 1, 1948, lecture, School of Medicine, Loyola University, Chicago. UNDA, CMRH 7.

"The New Life." August 3, 1948, lecture, National Liturgical Week, Boston, Massachusetts. In: *National Liturgical Week 1948*, pp. 28–36. Conception, Missouri.: The Liturgical Conference, 1949.

"Man: His Nature and Supernature." August 8, 1948, lecture, School of Medicine, Loyola University, Chicago. UNDA, CMRH 7.

"The Theological Bases of the Apostolate." August 1948 lecture, Catholic Action Priests' Study Week, Notre Dame. UNDA, CMRH 8/34 and 12/30.

"The Extension of Christ: The Mystical Body." September 3, 1948, lecture, School of Medicine, Loyola University, Chicago. UNDA, CMRH 7.

1950

"Spiritual Formation of the Lay Apostle." August 1950 lecture, Catholic Action Conference, St. Louis, Missouri. UNDA, CMRH 8/38.

"The Interior Life of the Apostle." November 20, 1950, lecture, Catholic Art Association Convention. UNDA, CMRH 31.

1951

"The Lay Apostolate." January 1951 lecture, Coordinating Committee Meeting, Fatima Retreat House, Notre Dame. UNDA, CMRH 9/5.

"The Christian in Action—in the Home." March 2, 1951, Easter Sunday Lecture, the "Christian in Action Series" sponsored by the National Council of Catholic Men on ABC Radio. The NCCM published this Lecture in a Booklet by the same name in 1951. UNDA, CMRH 31.

"The Social Encyclicals." May 25, 1951, lecture, Sheil School of Social Studies, Chicago. UNDA, CMRH 8/38.

"The Spirituality of the Young Worker." August 1951 lecture, YCW Study Week, Notre Dame. UNDA, CRMH 8/38.

"The Priesthood and the World." August 21, 1951, lecture, National Liturgical Week, Dubuque, Iowa. In: *National Liturgical Week 1951,* pp. 161–173. Conception, Missouri: The Liturgical Conference, 1951. Also found in *Worship* 26 (1952), pp. 49–58 and in *YCW Bulletin for Priests* 10 (1952), pp. 1–9. Longer Version in UNDA, CMRH 8/5.

"Spiritual Formation." September 29, 1951, lecture, Chicago Catholic University Discussion Club, Childerly Retreat House, Wheeling, Illinois. UNDA, CMRH 31.

"Specialized Catholic Action Groups and the CYO." October 18, 1951, lecture, Third National Catholic Youth Conference, sponsored by the Youth Department of the NCWC, Cincinnati, Ohio. UNDA, CMRH 12/30 and CMRH 31.

"The Mission of the Church Today." December 8, 1951, lecture, Third Annual Advent Symposium of the National Catholic Action Study Commission. UNDA, CMRH 31.

1952

"Freedom, Democracy, and the Church." February 2, 1952, lecture, YCS Study Day, Crossroads Student-Center, Chicago. UNDA, CMRH 40.

"The Meaning of the Mass." May 25, 1952, lecture, CFM Group, Chicago. UNDA, CMRH 11/27.

"The Theology of Catholic Action" and "The Spirituality of Catholic Action." June 18, 1952, lectures, YCW Study Week on Catholic Action for Priests and Seminarians, Sacred Heart Scholasticate, Lebret, Saskatchewan. UNDA, CMRH 7 and CMRH 21/13.

"Social Doctrines of the Church" and "The Spirituality of YCW Leaders." July 1952 lectures, YCW Training Course, Notre Dame. UNDA, CMRH 8/38.

"The Stroke of Genius." *Act* 5 (July 1952), pp. 1–2.

"Our Blessed Lady and the Mystical Body." August 26, 1952, lecture, YCW Day of Recollection, Chicago. UNDA, CMRH 3/36.

"The Liturgy and the Lay Apostolate" and "The Sacred Liturgy: Essential Nature and Qualities." September 1, 1952, lectures, Seminarian's Catholic Action Study Week, St. Augustine's Seminary, Toronto, Canada. UNDA, CMRH 31.

"The Inquiry." *YCW Bulletin for Priests* 10 (October 1952), pp. 1–6. Also reprinted March 1952 in *Catholic Action Reprints*.

"The Spiritual Formation of the Layman." November 28, 1952, lecture, Cardijn Center, Milwaukee, Wisconsin. In: *Bulletin of the National Catholic Action Study Commission* (January 1952). UNDA, CMRH 31.

"The Job Ahead." November 20, 1952, lecture on the occasion of the tenth anniversary of Friendship House in Chicago. UNDA, CMRH 8/12.

1953

"Objections to the Easter Vigil." *Worship* 27 (1953), pp. 203–304.

"The Priest's Work." January 1952 Lecture, YCW Chaplain's Meeting, Chicago. UNDA, CMRH 8/27.

"The Apostle is Never Shunted." *Act* 6 (1953), pp. 1, 3.

"Pius XII on Democracy." May 1, 1953, lecture, Cardijn Center, Milwaukee, Wisconsin. UNDA, CMRH 7/32.

"A New Day is Dawning for the Church." June 28, 1953, lecture, CFM National Convention, Notre Dame. UNDA, CMRH 11/10.

"Family Movement Need More Depth." *Act* 7 (1953), pp. 4–6. Excerpts from the June 28, 1953, lecture at the CFM National Convention, Notre Dame.

"Sacraments, Wellsprings of CFM." *Act* 7 (1953), pp. 4–6.
"The Role of the Laity." August 1953 lecture, CFM Area Convention, Portland, Oregon. UNDA, CMRH 9/15.
Liturgical Life in the Home—What Can We Do?" August 20, 1953, lecture, National Liturgical Week, Grand Rapids, Michigan. UNDA, CMRH 28/29.
"What the Lay Apostolate Means." *Act* 7 (1953), p. 2.

1954

"The Mystical Body." January 1954 lecture, CFM Coordinating Committee Meeting, Fatima Retreat House, Notre Dame. UNDA, CMRH 9/5.
"New Inquiries to Stress 'Oneness'." *Act* 7 (1954), pp. 1–2.
"Pope Pius X." February 5, 1954, lecture, Serra Club, Chicago. UNDA, CMRH 28/29.
"The Spiritual Impact of Newmanism or Catholicism, on the Life and Environment of the University." February 24, 1954 lecture, Chicago Region Newman Federation, Northwestern University, Evanston, Illinois. UNDA, CMRH 37.
"The Mass as the Source and Center of our Spiritual Life." February 28, 1954, lecture, CFM Evening of Recollection, Longwood Academy, Chicago. UNDA, CMRH 40.
"The Christian Concept of Career." March 31, 1954, lecture, Barat College, Lake Forest, Illinois. UNDA, CMRH 7/32.
"Reasons Why Christ Created the Mystical Body." *Act* 7 (1954), pp. 3–4.
"The Mass and Spiritual Formation." June 1954 lecture, East Coast CFM Convention, New York. UNDA, CMRH 9/17.
"Economics." June 26, 1954, lecture, CFM National Convention, Notre Dame. Tape and UNDA, CMRH 10/19, 11/11.
"Double Conscience" (also titled: "The Spirituality of the Young Worker"). July 6, 1954, lecture, YCW National Study Week, University of Notre Dame. UNDA, CMRH 8/5, 8/38, 14/5.
"Christ's Sacrifice and Ours." August 16, 1954, lecture, National Liturgical Week, Milwaukee, Wisconsin. UNDA, CMRH 28/25.
"Lay Spirituality." August 23, 1954, lecture, YCW Study Week, San Francisco, California. UNDA, CMRH 9/17.
"Social Teachings of the Church." August 24, 1954 lecture, The Apostolic Week, San Francisco, California. UNDA, CMRH 8/16 and 9/17.
"The Role of the Chaplain." August 28, 1954, lecture, CFM Chaplains Meeting, San Francisco, California. UNDA, CMRH 8/16 and 9/17.
"A New Day for the Church." August 29, 1954, lecture, CFM Convention, San Francisco, California. UNDA, CMRH 8/16, 9/17, 9/27.

1955

"The Spirituality of CFM." January 1955 lecture, Coordinating Committee Meeting, Fatima Retreat House, Notre Dame. UNDA, CMRH 10/19.
"Training Apostles through the Social Inquiry: Judge." February 1, 1955, lecture, CFM Chaplains' Study Day, St. Mary of Perpetual Help Church, Chicago. UNDA, CMRH 11/27.

"Judge." *Apostolate* 2 (1955), pp. 10–17. Reprinted with some minor changes in
    Chaplain's Notes (November, 1964), pp. 1–5.
"The Interracial Apostolate and the Need for a Strong Spiritual Life and Spiritual
    Motivation." February 20, 1955, lecture, Chicago Catholic Interracial Council,
    Chicago. UNDA, CMRH 31.
"Who Belongs to the Mystical Body," *Chaplain's Notes* (June 3, 1955), pp. 1–2.
    Reprinted in *Chaplain's Notes* (November 1960), pp. 1–2.
"The Mass and the Lay Apostolate." May 3, 1955, lecture, North Shore Serra Club,
    Chicago. UNDA, CMRH 8/36.
"The Mystical Body in Relation to Spiritual Charity." May 27, 1955, lecture,
    North Shore Serra Club, Chicago. UNDA, CMRH 8/38.
"Christ and People." June 8, 1955, lecture, YCW Midwest Study Week, Camp Don
    Bosco, Missouri. UNDA, CMRH 13/23.
"The Spirituality of the YCW." June 25, 1955, lecture, YCW Study Week, St. Joseph
    College, Rensselear, Indiana. UNDA, CMRH 14/9.
"Five-Pint Social Program." August 21, 1955, lecture, CFM National Convention,
    Notre Dame. UNDA, CMRH 8/37, 8/38, and 11/12 (where this lecture is
    given the title "The Social Doctrine of the Church"). Excerpts in: *Apostolate* 3
    (1955): 11–24. This article was first published in *Realities, Significant Writing
    from the Catholic Press,* edited by Herr, Dan and Lane, Clem, pp. 162–176.
    Milwaukee: Bruce Publishing Company, 1958. CFM, YCW, YCS also published
    it as a separate booklet. Excerpts appear as "The Economic Problem." *Act* 12
    (1959), pp. 8, 11.
"The Mass as the Source and Center of the Lay Apostolate." August 25, 1955m
    lecture, National Liturgical Week, Worcester, Massachusetts, in: *National
    Liturgical Week 1955,* pp. 175–185. Elsberry, Missouri: The Liturgical
    Conference, 1956. Reprinted in 1955 in *Catholic Action Reprints.*
"The Specialized Lay Movements: YCW, YCS, and CFM." August 27, 1955, lecture,
    Social Action Conference on "The Lay Person in the United States in 1955,"
    Worcester (Spencer), Massachusetts. UNDA, CMRH 8/17 and CMRH 32.
"The Social Doctrine of the Church." *Act* 8 (September 1955), pp. 1–2.
"About Mixed Groups." *Chaplain's Notes* (September 15, 1955), pp. 1–2.
"The Role of the Chaplain." *Chaplain's Notes* (December 1955), pp. 1–2. This article
    appeared in the YCW Booklet, *Introducing YCW.* Chicago: YCW, 1955.

1956

"The Spirituality of the Lay Apostle." January 1956, First Sunday of the Month
    Priests' Meeting, Chicago. UNDA, CMRH 9/20.
"Mass and the Apostolate." March 3, 1956, lecture, Gateway Grail Center, Detroit,
    Michigan. UNDA, CMRH 8/13.
"Lay Spirituality." May 11, 1956, lecture, Chaplains' Study Day, Buffalo, New York.
    UNDA, CMRH 9/20.
"The Mystical Body and the Lay Apostolate." July 3, 1956, lecture Sisters of the
    Immaculate Heart of Mary, Monroe, Wisconsin. UNDA, CMRH 32.
"Why the World Needs Student Apostles?" August 16, 1956, lecture, YCS
    Convention, Notre Dame. UNDA, CMRH 8/6, 8/16, and 12/8.

"The Purpose and Importance of Programming in CFM." August 16, 1956, lecture,
CFM Chaplains' Meeting, CFM National Convention, Notre Dame. UNDA,
CMRH 9/20.

"Lay Spirituality." August 17, 1956, lecture, CFM National Convention, Notre Dame.
UNDA, CMRH 8/38. 1956 Tape is titled "The Spiritual Life." Excerpts in:
Act 10 (1956), pp. 3–4, 12–14.

"Getting More out of Worship." August 21, 1956, lecture, North American Liturgical
Week, London, Canada. In: *North American Liturgical Week 1956*, pp. 36–44.
Elsberry, Missouri: The Liturgical Conference, 1957.

"The Church—The Role of the Laity in the Church." September 3, 1956, lecture,
College YCS Midwest Regional Study Week, Camp Don Bosco, Missouri.
UNDA, CMRH 13/22.

"Christian Aspects of Contemporary Problems." September 21, 1956, lecture,
Milwaukee Teacher's Institute. UNDA, CMRH 32.

"The Liturgical Apostolate and the YCS." November 1, 1956, lecture, YCS Study
Day, St. Patrick High School, Chicago, Illinois, UNDA, CMRH 12/8.

1957

"The Mystical Body." *Chaplain's Notes* (January–February 1957), pp. 1–2.

"The Parish is Christ." February 7, 1957, lecture, Coordinating Committee Meeting,
Fatima Retreat House, Notre Dame. UNDA, CMRH 11/28. 1957 Tape is
titled "The Parish." UNDA.

"The Importance of Next Year's Program." *Act* 10 (1957), pp. 1, 4–6. Excerpts from
February 8, 1957, lecture, Coordinating Committee Meeting, Fatima Retreat
House, Notre Dame.

"The Missionary and International Spirit" (also titled "Basic Principles of International
YCS"). August 1957 lecture, Chaplains' Meeting, Chicago in preparation for
the 1957 YCW Pilgrimage to Rome. UNDA, CMRH 8/27 and 9/6.

"The Gospel Discussion." August 22, 1957, lecture, YCS Chaplains' and Regional
Assistants' Meeting, Notre Dame. UNDA, CMRH 12/28.

"The Spirituality of the Lay Apostolate." August 22, 1957, lecture, YCS National
Study Week, Notre Dame. UNDA, CMRH 13/3, 13/22, and 13/24.

"History of Sacred Heart Church, 1891–1957." UNDA, CMRH 41.

"Lay Spirituality." December 28, 1957, lecture, Winter Meeting, High School YCS,
Lisle, Illinois. UNDA, CMRH 12/15.

1958

"The Purpose of Economic Life." *Act* 11 (1958), pp. 4–5. Excerpts from January 31,
1958, lecture Coordinating Committee at Fatima Retreat House, Notre Dame.

"The Mass: Source and Center of our Spiritual Lives." March 1958 lecture to priests,
St. Paul, Minnesota. UNDA, CMRH 24/22.

"Five Points for an Effective Chaplain." March 3, 1958, lecture, Milwaukee,
Wisconsin. UNDA, CMRH 11/28 & CMRH 32.

"The Holy Sacrifice of the Mass." March 16, 1958, talk, Day of Recollection for the
Officers of the Milwaukee Federation of the YCW. UNDA, CMRH 32.

"The Books and Authors I Have Cherished." March 23, 1958, lecture, Adult
    Education Centers of Chicago, Chicago Federation Headquarters. UNDA,
    CMRH 14/9.
"The CFM Apostolate." April 27, 1958, lecture, CFM Convention, Tulsa, Oklahoma.
    UNDA, CMRH 9/17.
"The Theology of the Lay Apostolates" and "The Five Essential Qualities of a
    Chaplain of a CFM, YCW, YCS Group." April 27 and April 28, 1958, lectures,
    Chaplains' Meeting, Benedictine Heights College, Tulsa, Oklahoma. UNDA,
    CMRH 9/21 and 10/19.
"The Effect of YCS on Its Members Spiritually." May 4, 1958, lecture, Chicago YCS
    Federation Leadership Training Course, Chicago, Illinois. UNDA, CMRH 12/8.
"Contemporary Church Art." May 8, 1958, lecture, Fine Arts Festival, Clarke College,
    Dubuque, Iowa. UNDA, CMRH 36.
"Understanding the Liturgy as a Meaningful and Necessary Part of Christian Life."
    June 8, 1958, lecture, College YCS National Study Week, Camp Villa Marie,
    Pistakee Bay. UNDA, CMRH 13/23.
"The Mystical Body" and "Lay Spirituality." June 25, 1958, lectures, High School YCS
    Day of Recollection, Marillac House, Chicago. UNDA, CMRH 32.
"The Mass and the Lay Apostolate." August 25, 1958, lecture, First Southern Regional
    YCS Study Week, Memphis, Tennessee. UNDA, CMRH 12/25 and 12/28.
"The Mystical Body," "The Inquiry and the Liturgy," and "Review of the Essential
    Work of the Chaplain." August 27, 28, and 29, 1958, lectures, CFM Chaplains'
    Meeting, Notre Dame. The tape of the August 29, 1958, lecture is titled "The
    Ways of Loving." UNDA, CMRH 8/5, 9/21, and 10/28.
Readers, Sacred Heart Church. Winnetka: Sacred Heart Church, 1958.
Ushers, Sacred Heart Church. Winnetka: Sacred Heart Church, 1958.
"A Pastor looks at the Parish." *Ave Maria* 80 (1958), pp. 5–10. Unedited version of
    this interview from August 30, 1958, in UNDA, CMRH 30/11. were
    Exceppiated in *Chaplian's Notes* (September, 1965), pp. 1–4.
"The Liturgical Movement and the Lay Apostolate." November 30, 1958, lecture,
    Chicago Catholic University Club, Sacred Heart Church, Hubbard Woods,
    Illinois. UNDA, CMRH 32.

1959

"Double Conscience." January 24, 1959, lecture, Coordinating Committee, Fatima
    Retreat House, Notre Dame. Tape also available. UNDA, CMRH 9/27
    and 11/28.
"Recent Liturgical Documents and Their Significance for the Newman Chaplains."
    January 26, 1959, lecture, National Newman Chaplain's Advisory Board
    Meeting, Notre Dame. UNDA, CMRH 32.
"What is YCW?" February 8, 1959, lecture, YCW Study Weekend, Oklahoma City,
    Oklahoma. UNDA, CMRH 32.
"The Parish Is Christ." February 1959 lecture, CFM group, Chicago. UNDA,
    CMRH 24/13.
"Right to Work Laws, the Economy, and the Church." February 13, 1959, lecture,
    Lake County Regional CFM Meeting, St. Raymond's Parish, Mt. Prospect,
    Illinois. UNDA, CMRH 9/17.

"The Mass. February 26, 1959, talk, YCW Day of Renewal, Sacred Heart Church, Hubbard, Woods, Illinois, UNDA, CMRH 32.

"The Social Doctrine of the Church." March 7, 1959, lecture, College YCS, St. Mary's College, Notre Dame, Indiana. UNDA, CMRH 32.

"Problems in U.S. Economic System" and "How to Create a Dynamic on Social Doctrine." March 13, 1959, lectures, YCW Training Sessions at Marillac House, Chicago. UNDA, CMRH 32.

"Spiritual Direction." April 19, 1959, talk, Chaplains' Afternoon of Renewal, Cardijn Center, Milwaukee, Wisconsin. UNDA, CMRH 32.

"Lay Spirituality or the Theological Basis of the Lay Apostolate." April 19, 1959, talk, CFM, YCS, YCW Evening of Recollection, Cardijn Center, Milwaukee, Wisconsin. UNDA, CMRH 32.

"Full Participation in the Holy Sacrifice of the Mass." May 5, 1959, lecture, National Catholic Music Educators Convention, Chicago. UNDA, CMRH 32.

"What Does Our Lord Expect from Us and from Our Efforts?" May 17, 1959, lecture, Leadership Training Session for the Filipino Students FIXCA Meeting, St. George High School, Evanston, Illinois, UNDA, CMRH 32.

"God and Life." June 17, 1959, talk, CFM Evening of Recollection, Sacred Heart Church, Hubbard Woods, Illinois. UNDA, CMRH 9/24.

"The Mystical Body." June 22, 1959, lecture, YCS Training Course, Chicago. UNDA, CMRH 12/32.

"The Economic Problem: The Most Acute Problem in the World." *Act* 12 (July 1959), pp. 8–11. Excerpts from the August 21, 1955, lecture, "Five-Point Social Program."

"Participation in View of Pius XII's Decree." (also titled "Why We Participate in the Mass.") August 26, 1959, lecture, Chaplains' Meeting, CFM National Convention, Notre Dame. Also published in *The Catholic Messenger* (September 1959). UNDA, CMRH 11/16 and 11/28.

"The Christian Family Apostolate." October 11, 1959, lecture, Social Life Conference, Canadian Catholic Conference, Social Action Department, Sudbury, Ottawa, Canada. UNDA, CMRH 32.

"The Bishops' Program of Social Reconstruction." November 22, 1959, lecture, Catholic Council on Working Life, Loyola Union House, Chicago. UNDA, CMRH 8/6.

"The Christian Concept of Person." December 29, 1959, lecture, YCS National Committee Meeting, University of Notre Dame. UNDA, CMRH 13/2 and 13/10.

1960

"Foreword." In: *The YCW Chaplain*, John J. Hill. Chicago: Young Christian Workers, 1960.

"The Spirituality of CFM" (also titled: "The Spirituality of the Lay Apostle"). January 22, 1960, lecture, Coordinating Committee Meeting, Fatima Retreat House, Notre Dame. UNDA, CMRH 9/27 and 11/28.

"The Importance of Action in International Life." April 30, 1960, lecture, Congress on International Life, Edmond, Oklahoma. UNDA, CMRH 32.

"Liturgy, the Parish, and the College Graduate." May 5, 1960, lecture, fourteenth annual Wisconsin Catholic Action Convention, sponsored by SUMA (Sodality Union of the Milwaukee Archdiocese), Milwaukee, Wisconsin, UNDA, CMRH 32.

"Motivation to Attend Mass and Receive Holy Communion." May 22, 1960, lecture, Loyola Academy Sodality, Wilmette, Illinois, UNDA, CMRH 32.

Apostolic Vocation of the Layman" (also titled: "The Layman's Role in the Crisis of the Modern World") and "The Role of the Chaplain." July 24–25, 1960, lectures, YCW Conference, St. John's Seminary, Omaha, Nebraska. UNDA, CMRH 8/16.

"The Priests' Spirituality." July 29, 1960, lecture, Chaplains' Meeting , CFM Convention, Denver, Colorado. Tape also available. UNDA, CMRH 9/21, 10/29, 11/28, and 21/15.

"Growing with CFM." July 30, 1960, lecture, Rocky Mountain Area CFM Convention, Denver, Colorado. UNDA, CMRH 9/21.

"Why Participate at Mass," August 10, 1960, lecture, YCW Convention, St. Joseph College, Rensselear, Indiana, UNDA, CMRH 15/1.

"The Spirituality of the Layman." August 20, 1960, lecture, Friendship House Meeting, Childerly Retreat House, Wheeling, Illinois. UNDA, CMRH 32.

"The Mystical Body" and "The Mass. August 22, 1960, lectures, North Area Leadership Training Course, Catholic Action Federation, Chicago. UNDA, CMRH 32.

"International Affairs" (also titled: "The Lay Apostolate") and "The Chaplains' Role in CFM" (also Titled: "The Priest and CFM—the Second Decade"). August 26, 1960, lectures, Chaplains Meeting, CFM Regional Convention, St. Xavier College, Chicago, Illinois. Tape of "International Affairs" is titled: "The Social Mission of the Church." UNDA, CMRH 9/17, 9/21 and 25/18.

"Spiritual Growth in CFM," and "The Role of the Layman in the Church," August 28, 1960, lectures, Regional CFM Convention, St. Joseph College, South Portland, Maine. UNDA, CMRH 32.

"The Social Implications of the Mass." September 6, 1960, lecture, YCS Midwest Regional Study Week, Marycrest Farm, Elgin, Illinois, UNDA, CMRH 13/24

"The Lay Apostle Looks at the World." November 13, 1960, lecture, Third Family Life Conference, Family Life Bureau of NCWC and New York Area CFM, Fordham University. UNDA, CMRH 32.

"The Role of the Chaplain." November 14, 1960, lecture, New York area CFM Chaplains Study Day, New York. UNDA, CMRH 10/11.

"Some Reflections on Art." November 16, 1960, lecture, Sacred Heart Church Council of Catholic Women, Hubbard Woods, Illinois. UNDA, CMRH 21/18.

1961

"St. Peter and Christ." January 20, 1961, lecture, Coordinating Committee Meeting, Fatima Retreat House, Notre Dame. UNDA, CMRH 9/27.

"Ecumenical Cooperation among the Churches." March 3, 1961, lecture, Interseminary Movement, Mid-Winter Conference, Ecumenical Institute, Evanston, Illinois. UNDA, CMRH 32 and 36.

"Lay Spirituality." April 13, 1961, lecture, CFM Program Committee Meeting, Chicago. UNDA, CMRH 10/19, 11/28, and 14/5. Excerpts appeared as "The Spirituality of the Lay Apostle" in *Chaplain's Notes* (June 1961), pp. 1–2.

"The Lay Apostolate." May 4, 1961, lecture, National Council of Catholic Men National Convention, Pittsburgh, Pennsylvania. UNDA, CMRH 8/22.

"The Social Doctrine of the Mystical Body and Economic Life." June 9, 1961, lecture, College YCS National Study Week, St. Procopius College, Lisle, Illinois. UNDA, CMRH 13/24.

"What is CFM?" and "Spirituality of the Layman." July 28–29, 1961, lectures, Priest's Night and Couples Study Day, Boston Federation of CFM, Boston, Massachusetts. UNDA, CMRH 32.

"International Life" (also titled "Pius XII and International Life"). July 31, 1961, lecture, Coordinating Committee meeting, Regis College, Denver, Colorado. UNDA, CMRH 8/5, 9/21, and 9/27.

"The Spirituality of the Lay Apostolate." August 9, 1961, lecture, YCW Priests' Study Week, St. Joseph College, Collegeville, Indiana. UNDA, CMRH 14/8.

"Fundamentals of CFM." August 14, 1961, paper presented to Coordinating Committee Meeting, Fatima Retreat House, Notre Dame. UNDA, CMRH 9/4 and 9/27.

"Doctrine of the Church on the Formation of Lay Apostles." August 21, 1961, lecture, Chaplain's Study Week, Notre Dame. UNDA, CMRH 9/2 and 10/28.

"Spiritual Direction by the Chaplain." August 25, 1961, lecture, Chaplains' Meeting, CFM Convention, Notre Dame UNDA, CMRH 9/17 and 10/28.

"The Chaplain's View" and "Our Lady and the International Life Program." August 26, 1961, lectures, CFM National Convention, Notre Dame. UNDA, CMRH 9/14, 10/19, and 11/28. Excerpts of "The Chaplain's View" in "The Thirty Years of the Lay Apostolate." *Act* 15 (1961), pp. 2, 8, 15–16.

"The Lay Apostolate." August 28, 1961, lecture on WBBM Radio. UNDA, CMRH 8/15.

"You and the Mystical Body." September 3, 1961, lecture on the "Church of the Air," CBS Radio, in cooperation with the National Council of Catholic Men, UNDA, CMRH 8/5, 24/14, 28/26, and 30/33.

"Catholic Social Principles" and "The Church's Teaching on International Affairs." September 1–8, 1961, lectures, Seminar on International Affairs, Commission for International Development (CID) of the YCW, Columbia University, New York, UNDA, CMRH 13/1.

"Characteristic Qualities of Lay Spirituality." December 10, 1961, lecture, Pittsburgh Diocesan Union of Holy Name Societies Holy Name Day, Pittsburgh, Pennsylvania. UNDA, CMRH 36 and 37.

1962

"Art and the Liturgy," *New City* 1 (192), pp. 4–1. Reprinted in *Catholic Mind* 60 (1962), pp. 41–47. Excerpts in *Act* 16 (1962), pp. 4–6. UNDA, CMRH 21/13, 28/2, 29/12, 29/17, 38.

"The Lay Apostolate." January 1962 lecture, Coordinating Committee Meeting, Fatima Retreat House, Notre Dame. UNDA, CMRH 11/28.

"Reason for Participation in the Mass." February 26, 1962, lecture, Tri-State Liturgical Conference. UNDA, DMRH 24/22.

"Mater et Magistra." March 11, 1962, lecture, Rochester Diocese Christian Family Day, Rochester, Minnesota. UNDA, CMRH 36.

"Christian Art and the Liturgy." April 3, 1962, lecture, Fine Arts Series on Church Art, Loyola University, Chicago. UNDA, CMRH 36.

"Mass and the Life of the Parish." April 12, 1962, lecture, Loyola University, Chicago. UNDA, CMRH 24/22 & CMRH 36.

"CFM—What Is It, What Is It Doing, Where Is It Going?" May 27, 1962, lecture, CFM Convention, Archdiocese of Montreal, Quebec, Canada. UNDA, CMRH 9/14 and CMRH 35.

"The International Doctrine of the Church" and "The Mass as the Source and Center of the Lay Apostolate." June 6, 1962, lectures, College YCS National Study Week, St. Procopius College, Lisle, Illinois. UNDA, CMRH 13/27.

"The Priest's Spirituality." August 6, 1962, lecture, YCW Priests' Study Week, St. Joseph College, Collegeville, Indiana. UNDA, CMRH 14/8.

"The Work of the Apostolate." August 18, 1962, lecture, CFM Area Convention, Norman, Oklahoma. UNDA, CMRH 9/24.

"Christianity and Social Progress: A Review of Pope John's Encyclical." August 25, 1962, lecture, Milwaukee Area CFM Convention, Marquette University, Milwaukee, Wisconsin. UNDA, CMRH 36.

"The Complexity of the Communist Challenge." September 17, 1962, lecture, Freedom Forum, Thomas More Adult Education Centers, Batavia, Illinois. UNDA, CMRH 36.

"What Is the Mass?" September, 1962, lecture, Day of Recollection, Niles College Seminary, Niles, Illinois. UNDA, CMRH 24/22.

"The Theology of the Apostolate." October 15–19, 1962, lectures, Immaculate Heart College, Los Angeles, California, for Superiors and Directors Formation Programs, Sisters' Formation Conference. UNDA, CMRH 36.

"Spiritual Growth through Participation in the Liturgy." November 3, 1962, lecture, Dominican Sisters Forum, St. Mary's Parish, Evanston, Illinois. UNDA. CMRH 24/22.

"Abbot Marmion and Liturgical Renewal." November 25, 1962, lecture, Marmion Abbey, Aurora, Illinois. UNDA, CMRH 36. Appears as "Marmion and the Liturgical Renewal," *American Benedictine Review* 39 (1963), pp. 1–8.

"Spirituality of the YCS Member." December 27, 1962, lecture, Winter High School YCS Meeting, Notre Dame. UNDA, CMRH 12/16.

1963

"The Spirituality of the Layman." January 18, 1963, lecture, Coordinating Committee Meeting, CFM Headquarters, Chicago. UNDA, CMRH 8/5, 9/22, and 10/19. Reprinted in *Catholic Reporter*, the diocesan newspaper of Kansas City, Missouri (February 15, 1963). Also published as a Booklet by CFM, YCS, and YCW. *The Spirituality of the Layman.* Chicago: CFM, YCS, YCW, 1963.

"A Layman's Origin Is in the World." *Act* 16 (1963), pp. 4–6. Excerpts from January 18, 1963, lecture, Coordinating Committee Meeting, CFM Headquarters, Chicago.

"The Spirituality of the Lay Apostle." *Act* 16 (1963), pp.2, 11–12.

"Catholic Action in the United States." May 1, 1963, unpublished article for *Catholic Youth Encyclopedia.* UNDA. CMRH, 8/5 and 10/16.

"The Doctrine of the Church on Political Life." June 5, 1963, lecture, College YCS National Study Week, Barat College, Lake Forest, Illinois. UNDA, CMRH 13/28.

"CFM, YCS, YCW Chaplain's Training Course." June 11–21, 1963, course, St. Joseph College, Collegeville, Indiana. UNDA, CMRH 10/19, 14/8.

"The Clergy's Understanding of the Lay Apostolate." June 28, 1963, lecture, CFM Chaplains' Meeting, M.W. Area CFM Convention, Portland, Oregon. UNDA, CMRH 9/17.

"The Lay Apostolate." June 29, 1963, lecture, N.W. Area CFM Convention, Portland, Oregon. UNDA, CMRH 9/17. Tape also available. Excerpts appear as "The Spirituality of the Lay Apostle" in *Act* 16 (1963) pp. 2, 11–12. Also reprinted in *Our Lady of the Sacred Heart Magazine* (August 29, 1963).

"The Doctrine of the Church on the Parish." August 6, 1963, lecture, YCW National Study Week, St. Joseph College, Collegeville, Indiana. UNDA, CMRH 14/8.

"The Doctrine of the Church on the Formation of Lay Apostles." August 21, 1963, lecture, CFM Chaplains' Study Week, Notre Dame. UNDA, CMRH 9/23 and 11/19.

"International Life." August 22, 1963, lecture, YCS Study Week, St. Joseph College, Collegeville, Indiana. UNDA, CMRH 12/29.

"The Parish–The Leaven of the Community." August 23, 1963, lecture, CFM National Convention, Notre Dame. UNDA, CMRH 9/14 and 11/19.

"Mater et Magistra." August 24, 1963, lecture, CFM National Convention, Notre Dame. Tape also available. UNDA, CMRH 9/24.

"The Theologies of the Apostolate." October 1963 course, House of Studies, Sisters of the Juniorate Community, Los Angeles, California. UNDA, CMRH 9/6.

"The Importance of Active Participation in the Mass." October 1963 tape available. UNDA.

"Economic Life." October 11, 1963, lecture, YCW National Training Course, Marillac House, Chicago. UNDA, CMRH 21/9.

"The Role of the Layman in the Work of the Apostolate." October 14, 1963, lecture, CFM Regional Evening of Recollection, Sacred Heart Church, Lombard, Illinois. UNDA, CMRH 9/24.

"Papal Teaching on International Life." October 25, 1963, lecture, YCW National Training Course, Marillac House, Chicago. UNDA, CMRH 21/9.

"The Parish" and "The Role of the High School Layman." December 27, 1963, lectures, Winter Meeting of High School YCS, Fatima Retreat House, Notre Dame. UNDA, CMRH 12/12.

1964

"Appraisal of the U.S. Priesthood." January 15, 1964, lecture, YCW Priests' Winter Meeting, Chicago. UNDA, CMRH 9/2.

"The Layman's Role after Vatican II" and "Present State of the Movement: A View of the Past and the Future." January 31 and February 2, 1964, lectures, Executive Committee Meeting, Oconomowoc, Wisconsin. UNDA, CMRH 10/6 and 10/7.

"The Specialized Lay Apostolate." Unpublished article submitted on February 12, 1964, to Msgr. John H. Harrington, Editor, *Catholic Youth Encyclopedia*. New York: NCWC, 1964. UNDA, CMRH 9/18 and CMRH 37.

"High School Young Christian Students." Unpublished article submitted to the 1964 *Catholic Encyclopedia for School and Home*. UNDA, CMRH 12/10.

"Politics and Church Doctrine" and "The Inquiry Method." June 7 and 9, 1964, lectures, YCS National Study Week, St. Porcopius College, Lisle, Illinois. UNDA, CMRH 13/6 and 13/28.

"The Theology of Work." July 1964 lecture, Victorian Theological Association Convention, Chicago. UNDA, CMRH 9/5.

"The Church's Doctrine on Political Activity." August 1, 1964, lecture, CFM Coordinating Committee Meeting and Chaplains' Meeting, Marist College, Poughkeepsie, New York. UNDA, CMRH 10/1 and 10/8.

"The Role of the Catholic High School in Developing the Committed Christian." August 29, 1964, lecture, St. George High School Faculty, Evanston, Illinois. UNDA, CMRH 37.

"Sacred Art and the Spirit of the Liturgy." October 12, 1964, lecture, Cincinnati Archdiocese Liturgical Arts Commission, Cincinnati, Ohio. UNDA, CMRH 37. Excerpts published in *Catholic Telegraph* (October 1964).

"The Doctrinal Presentation of the Directory." November 13, 1964, talk, Liturgical Commission Meeting, Archdiocese of Chicago. UNDA, CMRH 7 and 22/6.

"Recommended Changes in the Mass." November 13, 1964, talk, Liturgical Commission Meeting, Archdiocese of Chicago. UNDA, CMRH 22/7.

"The New Constitution on the Liturgy," "The Mass," "Christ and the Formation of His Apostles," and "The Spirituality of the Layman." December 27, 29, 30, and 31, 1964, lectures, Winter YCS National Committee Meeting, Ecumenical Institute, Chicago. UNDA, CMRH 12/16, 12/31, 13/10, and 13/16.

1965

"Christ, the Center of the Apostolate." January 21, 1965, lecture, YCS College Area Chaplains' and Moderators' Meeting, Fatima Retreat House, Notre Dame. UNDA, CMRH 10/8 and 13/7.

"Mass and Community." April 9, 1965, lecture, CFM group, St. Mary's Church, Evanston, Illinois. UNDA, CMRH 24/22.

"Chaplains' Training Course on the Lay Apostolate." June 1965 course, St. Joseph College, Collegeville, Indiana. UNDA, CMRH 7.

"Today's Missions: Catholic Viewpoint on the Lay Apostolate." August 3, 1965, lecture, Northwestern University, Evanston, Illinois. UNDA, CMRH 9/2.

"The Doctrine of the Church on the Parish." August 6, 1965, lecture, YCW Chaplains Study Weeks, St. Joseph College, Collegeville, Indiana. UNDA, CMRH 14/8.

"The 1965 Inquiry Program." August 26, 1965, lecture, Coordinating Committee, Notre Dame. UNDA, CMRH 11/22.

"The Priest, the Layman in CFM." August 27, 1965, lecture, Chaplains' Meeting, CRM National Convention, Notre Dame. UNDA, CMRH 11/20.

"International Life and the Creative Use of Leisure Time" (also titled "The Use of Leisure Time"). August 28, 1965, lecture, CFM National Convention, Notre Dame. UNDA, CMRH 10/8 and 11/20.

"The Ideas that Animate Us, Our National Chaplain Defines the Basic Ideas of the
    Christian Family Movement." *Act* 18 (August, 1965), pp. 6–1.
"Spiritual Direction of the Laity." October 6, 1965, lecture, CF Chaplains' Meeting,
    Monte Alverno Retreat House, Appleton, Wisconsin. UNDA, CMRH 10/2
"A Look at Pleasure." *Act* 18 (1965), pp. 5–6.
"The Reasons for Singing." October 25, 1965, lecture, Sacred Heart Church,
    Hubbard Woods, Illinois. UNDA, CMRH 7 & 22/8.

1966

"The Role of Chaplain." February 10, 1966, lecture, Executive Committee Meeting,
    Villa Redeemer Retreat House, Glenview, Illinois. UNDA, CMRH 7.
"The Spirituality of CFM, Parts I, II, II." February 11, 1966, lectures, Executive
    Committee Meeting, Villa Redeemer Retreat House, Glenview, Illinois.
    UNDA, CMRH 10/19.
"YCS Chaplain's Training Course." June 13–17, 1966, course at St. Joseph College,
    Rensselear, Indiana. Tapes of this course were used in training sessions for
    Chaplains and Moderators across the United States. UNDA, CMRH 9/29
    & 11/22.
Forty Hours Devotion. Chicago: YCW, 1966. UNDA, CMRH 22/16.
"The Parish Is Christ." August 9, 1966, lecture, YCM Study Week, St. Joseph
    College, Rensselear, Indiana. UNDA, CMRH 9/1 and 24/13.
"Leisure Time." December 31, 1966, lecture, Midwest Regional YCS Meeting,
    Notre Dame. UNDA, CMRH 13/10.

1967

"Teilhard de Chardin and YCM." January 15, 1967, lecture, YCM Council, Chicago.
    UNDA, CMRH 24/28.
"Evolution: The Chardinian View." January 1967 lecture, YCM Full Timers Retreat,
    Chicago. UNDA, CMRH 24/28.
"YCS Training Course." March 1967 course, Ecumenical Institute, Chicago. UNDA,
    CMRH 7.
"The Coming Age of Leisure" and "Political Doctrine of Church in the Light of
    Vatican II." August 5 and 7, 1968, lectures, YCM National Study Week and
    CFM Convention, St. Joseph Seminary, Oakbrook, Illinois, UNDA, CMRH
    12/1 and 21/9.
"The Year of Faith." August 27, 1967, lecture, CFM National Convention,
    Notre Dame. UNDA, CMRH 10/9.

1969

"Christ Today and Hope." February 11, 1969, lecture, YCS, Chicago, and February 16,
    1969, YCM, Chicago. UNDA, CMRH 8/6.
"The Church Today and Hope for the Future." March 11, 1969, lecture, Sacred Heart
    Church, Hubbard Woods, Illinois. UNDA, CMRH 24/25.

1972

"The Main Themes of Vatican II." October 1, 1972, lecture, Sacred Heart Church,
Hubbard Woods, Illinois. UNDA, CMRH 25/20.
"The Anointing of the Sick." November 12, 1972, lecture, Sacred Heart Church,
Hubbard Woods, Illinois. UNDA, CMRH 22/14.
"Man and Forgiveness." December 6, 1972, lecture, Sacred Heart Church, Hubbard
Woods, Illinois. UNDA, CMRH 25/20.

1973

"What Is the Mass?" November 1973 Position Paper presented to the Sacred Heart
School Board on Children's Participation in the Mass. UNDA, CMRH 22/8.
"CFM Lives." July 22, 1974, lecture, CFM twenty-fifth nniversary Banquet, Barat
College, Lake Forest, Illinois. UNDA, CMRH 12/1.
"The New Rite of the Anointing of the Sick." August 18, 1974, lecture, Sacred Heart
Church, Hubbard Woods, Illinois. UNDA, CMRH 22/41.

SECONDARY SOURCES

Hillenbrand's many lectures and writings fall into certain categories,
which have inspired the divisions of this bibliography: Divine Life,
Hillenbrand Activities, Lay Apostolate, Leo XIII, Liturgical
Movement, Liturgy and Sacraments, Mystical Body, Pius X, Pius XI,
Pius XII, Roman Catholicism and American Society, Roman
Catholicism in Chicago, and Social Justice.

Divine Life

Aquinas, Thomas. *Aquinas on Nature and Grace.* Trans. A. M. Fairweather.
Philadelphia: Westminster Press, 1954.
Everett, Lawrence P. *The Nature of Sacramental Grace.* Washington, D.C.:
Catholic University of America, 1948.
Fortmann, Edmund J. *The Theology of Man and Grace: Commentary.* Milwaukee:
Bruce Publishing Company, 1966.
Haight, Roger. *The Experience and Language of Grace.* New York: Paulist Press, 1979.
Hopper, Jeffrey. *Understanding Modern Theology II: Reinterpreting Christian Faith for
Changing Worlds.* Philadelphia: Fortress Press, 1987.
Marmion, Columba. *Christ in His Mysteries.* Trans. Mother M St. Thomas. London:
Sands & Company, 1939.
——. *Christ the Life of the Soul.* Trans. A Nun of Tyburn Convent. St. Louis:
B. Herder Book Company, 1922.
Reinhold, H. A. "Nature Mirrors Supernature." *Orate Fratres* 16 (1941), pp. 80–82.
Rondet, Henri. *The Grace of Christ, A Brief History of the Theology of Grace.* Trans. Tad
W. Guzie. New York: Newman Press, 1967.

Scheeben, Matthias Joseph. *The Glories of Divine Grace*. Trans. Benedictine Monk of
   St. Meinrad's Abbey. New York: Benziger Brothers, 1898.
———. *The Mysteries of Christianity*. Trans. Cyril Vollert. St. Louis: B. Herder Book
   Company, 1946.
———. *Nature and Grace*. Trans. Cyril Vollert. St. Louis: B. Herder Book Company, 1954.

Hillenbrand Activities

"Ordination of Seven Priests and Dedication of New Rectory Mark Cardinal's
   Anniversary; Ordination of Seven Young Men to the Priesthood, Saturday."
   New World 37 (September 20, 1929), p. 1.
"Closing Exercises at the Seminary." *New World* 39 (June 19, 1931), p. 5.
"Chicago Priests to Take Advanced Studies Abroad." *New World* 39 (June 26, 1931),
   p. 5.
"Jubilee Mission Band Formed; Program nears Completion, Mission in Every Parish
   in Diocese to Mark Silver Jubilee Year of Episcopal Consecration of His
   Eminence George Cardinal Mundelein, Archbishop of Chicago." *New World*
   41 (July 28, 1933), pp. 1, 3.
"Rev. R. Hillenbrand is Rector of Seminary, Mundelein, Brilliant Alumnus, Noted
   Preacher in New Office." *New World* 44 (April 19, 1936), p. 1.
Chronicle of the House of Philosophy: 1936–1944. Mundelein: St. Mary of the Lake
   Seminary, 1936–1944.
Tanner, Paul. "The Summer School of Social Action for the Clergy." *Salesianum* 32
   (1937), pp. 169–173.
McGowan, Raymond. "Clergy Hail Schools of Social Action." *Catholic Action* 19
   (1937), pp. 16–17.
Tanner, Paul. "The First National Catholic Social Conference." *Salesianum* 33 (1938),
   pp. 115–122.
McGowan, Raymond. "Clergy Social Action in Buffalo and Chicago." *Catholic Action*
   20 (1938), p. 20.
Hillenbrand, Reynold, ed. *Summer School of Social Action for Priests, July 18–August 12,
   1938, Four Volumes*. Mundelein: St. Mary of the Lake Seminary, 1938.
"Free Labor Schools Open Here, November 7, True Teaching of The Church to
   Equip Workingmen to Meet Present Problems." *New World* 46 (October 28,
   1938), p. 3.
"Priests' Summer School Opens July 17, Noted Authority to be Lecturer on Social
   Action, Rev. R. A. McGowan on Faculty at Summer School for Priests."
   New World 47 (June 30, 1939), p. 1.
"Monsignor Hass Will Teach at Priests' Summer School of Social Action, Outstanding
   Authority on Social Questions of the day to teach class on Labor Legislation in
   the Light of Church Doctrine, Sessions: July 17–28 at St. Mary of the Lake
   Seminary." *New World* 47 (June 30, 1939), p. 1.
"Labor Problems Studied by Clergy, Students from 16 Dioceses at Seminary."
   New World 47 (July 21, 1939), p. 1.
"McGowan, Raymond. "Social Action Schools for the Clergy." *Catholic Action* 21
   (1939), p. 21.
Ellard, Gerald. "Progress of the Dialogue Mass in Chicago." *Orate Fratres* 14 (1940),
   pp. 19–25.

——. "Black or the Color of the Day." *Orate Fratres* 14 (1940), pp. 161–165.
"Institute Opens Labor Sessions July 8, Chicago Priests Gather for Study Next Week." *New World* 48 (July 5, 1940), pp. 1–2.
"Liturgical Congress Opens October 21, Leaders Will Gather for Big Program, Lectures to be at Cathedral." *New World* 48 (October 18, 1940), pp. 9, 13.
"National Liturgical Week Successful, Archbishop Stresses Corporate Worship." *New World* 48 (November 1, 1940), p. 13.
Ducey, Michael. "The Liturgical Week, October 21–25, Chicago." *Orate Fratres* 14 (1940), pp. 369–372.
"Priests' Liturgy School Opens Monday, Prominent Liturgists to Lecture, Enroll from 15 Dioceses." *New World* 49 (July 11, 1941), pp. 9, 13.
"Liturgy School for Priests Opens at Seminary, 25 Dioceses in U.S. Represented." *New World* 49 (July 18, 1941), p. 1.
"Integrating at Aquinas High." *Orate Fratres* 16 (1941), pp.39–42.
"Our Part in World Peace to Be Subject of Mercy Forum Panel Discussion, December 12." *New World* 51 (1943), p. 10.
"Catholic Forum on Industrial Problems Opens Here Monday, Speakers from East, Midwest to Address Two Day Meeting, Business, Labor, and Education Leaders Take Part in Program." *New World* 52 (February 18, 1944), p. 1.
"Industrialists Plan for Post War Reorganization of Labor, Bishop Haas asks Guarantee of Return to Jobs for all, Msgr. Ryan urges adoption of Bishops 'Social Program'." *New World* 52 (February 25, 1944), p. 1.
"Appoint Seminary Head to Hubbard Woods." *New World* 52 (July 28, 1944), p. 1.
Fleming, Helen. "Parish Flock Joins in Latin of Mass. *Daily News* (October 31, 1949), p. 48.
Senser, Robert. "How a Parish Came to Sing." *Orate Fratres* 26 (1952), pp. 257, 259.
Conley, Thomas P. "I Hear Whole Congregations Singing," In: *National Liturgical Week 1952*, pp. 49-56. Elsberry, Mo.: The Liturgical Conference, 1953.
Ducey, Michael. "The National Liturgical Weeks and American Benedictines." *American Benedictine Review* 6 (1955), pp. 156–167.
Bauer, Pam. "Hillenbrand Anticipated Vatican II." *National Catholic Reporter* 15 (June 1, 1979), p. 9.
Cantwell, Daniel. "Homily Preached at the Eucharist Celebrating the Life and Passing of Msgr. Reynold Hillenbrand." *Liturgy 70* 10 (1979), pp. 204.
Diekmann, Godfrey. "Msgr. Reynold Hillenbrand." *Liturgy 70* 01 (1979), p. 2.
McClory, Robert. "Hillenbrand: U.S. Moses." *National Catholic Reporter* 15 (September 7, 1979), pp. 3, 38–39.

Lay Apostolate

De la bedoyere, Michael. *The Cardijn Story, A Study of the Life of Mgr. Joseph Cardijn and the Young Christian Workers' Movement Which He Founded.* London: Longmans, Green, & Company, 1958.
——. *The Layman in the Church.* London: Burns & Oates, 1954.
Brown, Alden Vincent. *The Grail Movement in the United States, 1940–1972: The Evolution of an American Catholic Laywoman's Community.* Unpublished Ph.D. Dissertation. New York: Union Theological Seminary, 1982.

Burns, Jeffrey Mark. *American Catholics and the Family Crisis 1930–1962, the Ideological and Organizational Response.* Unpublished Ph.D. Dissertation. Notre Dame: University of Notre Dame, 1982.

———. *The Christian Family Movement.* Notre Dame: Center for the Study of American Catholicism, 1982.

Callahan, Daniel. *The Mind of the Catholic Layman.* New York: Charles Scribner's Sons, 1963.

Cardijn, Joseph. *Challenges to Action.* Ed. Eugene Langdale. Chicago: Fides Publishers, 1955.

———. *Laymen into Action.* Trans. Anne Heggie. London: Geoffrey Chapman, 1964.

Civardi, Luigi. *A Manual of Catholic Action.* Trans. C.C. Martindale. New York: Sheed & Ward, 1943.

Coles, Robert. *A Spectacle unto the World: The Catholic Worker Movement.* New York: Viking Press, 1973.

Congar, Yves M. J. *Christians Active in the World.* Trans. P.F. Hepburne-Scott. New York: Herder & Herder, 1968.

———. *Faith and the Spiritual Life.* Trans. A. Manson & L.C. Sheppard. New York: Herder & Herder, 1968.

———. *A Gospel Priesthood.* Trans. P. F. Hepburne-Scott. New York: Herder & Herder, 1967.

———. *Laity, Church, and World.* Trans. Donald Attwater. Baltimore: Helicon Press, 1960.

———. *Lay People in the Church, A Study for a Theology of the Laity.* Trans. Donald Attwater. Westminster: Newman Press, 1957.

———. *The Wide World, My Parish, Salvation, and Its Problems.* Trans. Donald Attwater. Baltimore: Helicon Press, 1961.

Cunningham, Jim. "Specialized Catholic Action." In: *The American Apostolate, American Catholics in the Twentieth Century*, pp. 41–65. Ed. Leo R. Ward. Westminster: Newman Press, 1952.

Day, Dorothy. *House of Hospitality.* New York: Sheed and Ward, 1939.

———. *The Long Loneliness, an Autobiography of Dorothy Day.* New York: Harper & Row, 1952.

Doohan, Leonard. *Laity's Mission in the Local Church, Setting a New Direction.* San Francisco: Harper & Row, 1986.

———. *The Lay-Centered Church, Theology, and Spirituality.* Minneapolis: Winston Press, 1984.

Durrwell, Francis X. *The Apostolate and the Church.* Trans. Edward Quinn. Denville, New Jersey: Dimension Books, 1973.

Ellinger, Rory V. "Decline and Fall of a Student Movement." *Commonweal* 89 (January 30, 1969), p. 346.

Fitzsimons, John & McGuire, Paul, eds. *Restoring All Things: A Guide to Catholic Action.* New York: Sheed & Ward, 1938.

Fundamentals of the YCW. Chicago: YCW, 1963.

Geaney, Dennis. *You Are Not Your Own.* Chicago: Fides Publishers, 1954.

Geissler, Eugene S. *An Introduction to Catholic Action and an Exposition of the Jocist Technique.* South Bend, Indiana: Apostolate Press, 1945.

Greeley, Andrew. "A Sociologist Looks at the CFM." This article was written for the October 1963 issue of *Marriage* magazine, but never printed due to the protest of the Archdiocese of Chicago. In: UNDA, CMRH 10/17.

Giese, Vincent J. *The Apostolic Itch*. Chicago: Fides Publishers, 1954.

Hesburgh, Theodore. *The Theology of Catholic Action*. Notre Dame: Ave Maria Press, 1946.

Kotre, John N. *Simple Gifts, the Lives of Pat and Patty Crowley*. New York: Andrews and McMeel, Inc., 1979.

Kraemer, Hendrick. *A Theology of the Laity*. Philadelphia: Westminster Press, 1958.

Leaders' Bulletin, Catholic Action Students, University of Notre Dame. Notre Dame: University of Notre Dame, 1940–1950.

De Lubac, Henri. *The Splendor of the Church*. Trans. Michael Mason, Glen Rock, New Jersey: Paulist Press, 1956.

Lucey, Rose Marciano. *Roots and Wings, Dreamers and Doers of the Christian Family Movement*. San Jose: Resource Publications, 1987.

Lyonnet, Stanislaus. "La rédemption de l'univers." *Lumière te Vie* 48 (1960), pp. 43–62.

De Margerie, B. "Le Christ, la sécularisation et la consécration du monde." *Nouvelle Revue Théologique* 91 (1969), pp. 370–395.

McBrien, Richard P. "A New Theology of the Laity." *American Ecclesiastical Review* 160 (1969), pp. 73–86.

Metz, Johannes-Baptist & Schillebeeckx, Edward, eds. *Concilium 180: The Teaching Authority of Believers*. Edinburgh: T. & T. Clark, 1985.

Meyer, Bernard F. *The Mystical Body in Action: A Workbook of Parish Catholic Action*. Herman, Penn.: Center for Men of Christ the King, 1947.

Michel, Virgil. "The Layman in the Church." *Commonweal* 12 (1930), pp. 123–125.

Newman, Jeremiah. *What is Catholic Action? An Introduction to the Lay Apostolate*. Westminster: Newman Press, 1958.

O'Malley, Joseph M. *Canon Joseph Cardijn, the Workers' Apostle*. Montreal: Editions Ouvrieres, 1947.

Philips, Gerard. *Achieving Christian Maturity*. Trans. Eileen Kane. Chicago: Franciscan Herald Press, 1966.

——. *The Role of the Laity in the Church*. Trans. John R. Gilbert and James W. Moudry. Chicago: Fides Publishers, 1956.

Putz, Louis J. *The Modern Apostle*. Notre Dame: Fides Publishers, 1957.

Quigley, Martin Jr. and Connors, Edward M. *Catholic Action in Practice: Family Life, Education, International Life*. New York: Random House, 1963.

Robb, Dennis Michael. *Specialize Catholic Action in the United States, 1936–1949: Ideology, Leadership, and Organization*. Unpublished Ph.D. Dissertation. Lubbock, Texas: Texas Tech University, 1977.

Seasoltz, R. Kevin. "Contemporary American Lay Movements in Spirituality." *Communio* 6 (1979), pp. 339–364.

Sicius, Francis Joseph. *The Chicago Catholic Worker Movement, 1936 to the Present*. Unpublished Ph.D. Dissertation. Chicago: Loyola University, 1979.

Suhard, Emmanuel. *Growth or Decline? The Church Today*. Trans. James J. Corbett. Chicago: Fides Publishers, 1948.

Ward, Leo R. *Catholic Life, U.S.A., Contemporary Lay Movements*. St. Louis: B. Herder Book Company, 1959.

——. *The American Apostolate*. Westminster: Newman Press, 1952.

Wendell, Francis N. *The Formation of a Lay Apostle*. New York: Third Order of St. Dominic, 1944.

Young Christian Students. South Bend, Indiana: Fides Publishers, 1950.

Young Christian Students, Student Social Responsibility. Chicago: Young Christian
    Students, 1949.

Leo XIII

Gargan, Edward T., ed. *Leo XIII and the Modern World.* New York: Sheed & Ward,
    1961.
Leo XIII. *Rerum Novarum, The Condition of Labor.* Trans. authorized by the Holy See.
    Washington: National Catholic Welfare Conference, 1942.
Leo XIII. *The Church Speaks to the Modern World, The Social Teachings of Leo XIII.*
    Ed. Etienne Gilson. New York: Image Books, 1954.
De T'Seracles, Charles and Egan, Maurice F. *The Life and Labor of Pope Leo XIII.*
    Chicago: Rand, McNally, & Company, 1903.

Liturgical Movement

Barrett, Noel H. *The Contribution of Martin B. Hellriegel to the American Liturgical
    Movement.* Unpublished Ph.D. Dissertation. St. Louis: St. Louis University,
    1976.
Beauduin, Lambert. "Dom Marmion and the Liturgy." In: *More About Marmion*, pp.
    60–13. Trans. by Earl of Wicklow. St. Louis: B. Herder Book Company, 1949.
——. "L'espirit paroissial dans la tradition." *Les Questions Liturgiques* II (1911–1912),
    pp. 16–26, 80–90, 305–311.
Bouyer, Louis. *Liturgical Piety.* Notre Dame: University of Notre Dame Press, 1955.
Casel, Odo. "The Liturgical Movement in the Catholic Church." In: *Twentieth-Century
    Theology in the Making, Vol. III: Ecumenicity and Renewal.* Ed. Jaroslav Pelikan
    and trans. R. A. Wilson. New York: Harper & Row, 1971.
Ducey, Michael. "The National Liturgical Weeks and American Benedictines."
    American Benedictine Review VI (1955): 156–167.
Garner, Joel Patrick. *The Vision of a Liturgical Reformer: Hans Ansgar Reinhold,
    American Catholic Educator.* Unpublished Ph.D. Dissertation. New York:
    Columbia University, 1972.
Hall, Jeremy. *The Full Stature of Christ, the Ecclesiology of Virgil Michel.* Collegeville:
    Liturgical Press, 1976.
Hellriegel, Martin B. "The Liturgical Movement and the Sacraments." *Orate Fratres*
    10 (1936), pp. 504–505.
Jungmann, Joseph A. *Liturgical Renewal, In Retrospect and Prospect.* With a Chapter
    on the Liturgical Movement in the British Isles by J. B. O'Connell. London:
    Burns & Oates, 1965.
Kennedy, Robert J. *Michael Mathis: American Liturgical Pioneer.* Washington: Pastoral
    Press, 1987.
Koenker, Benjamin. *The Liturgical Renaissance in the Roman Catholic Church.* Chicago:
    University of Chicago Press, 1954.
Klein, Leo J. *The Role of Gerald Ellard (1894–1963) in the Development of
    the Contemporary American Catholic Liturgical Movement.* Unpublished
    Ph.D. Dissertation. New York: Fordham University, 1971.

La Farge, John. "Progress and Rhythm in the Liturgical Movement." In: *Liturgy for the People, Essays in Honor of Gerald Ellard, 1894–1963*. Ed. William J. Leonard. Milwaukee: Bruce Publishing Company, 1963.

Madden, Lawrence J. *The Liturgical Conference of the U.S.A.: Its Origins and Development: 1940–1968*. Unpublished Ph.D. Dissertation. Trier: University of Trier, 1969.

Marx, Paul. *Virgil Michel and the Liturgical Movement.* Collegeville: Liturgical Press, 1957.

McManus, Frederick R. "American Liturgical Pioneers." In: *Catholics in America, 1776–1976*. pp. 155–158. Ed. Robert Trisco. Washington: NCCB Committee for the Bicentennial, 1976.

———. *The Revival of the Liturgy.* New York: Herder & Herder, 1963.

———. ed. *Thirty Years of Liturgical Renewal: Statements of the Bishops' Committee on the Liturgy.* Washington: United States Catholic Conference, 1987.

Michel, Virgil. "The Liturgical Movement and the Future." *America* 54 (1935), pp. 6–1.

———. "The Scope of the Liturgical Movement." *Orate Fratres* 10 (1936), pp. 485–490.

———. "The Significance of the Liturgical Movement." *NCWC Bulletin* 10 (1929), pp. 6–8, 26.

Murray, Jane Marie and Marx, Paul. "The Liturgical Movement in the United States." In: *The Catholic Church, U.S.A.*, pp. 301–314. Ed. Louis J. Putz. Chicago: Fides Publishers Association, 1956.

O'Shea, William. "Liturgy in the United States 1889–1964." *America Ecclesiastical Review* CL (1964): 176–196.

Quitslaund, Sonya A. *Beaudin: A Prophet Vindicated.* New York: Newman Press, 1973.

Rousseau, Oliver. *The Progres of the Liturgy: An Historical Sketch from the Beginning of the Nineteenth Century to the Pontificate of Pius X.* Trans. Westminster Priory Benedictines. Westminster: Westminster Priory, 1951.

"Vernacular Society to Merge with the Liturgical Conference." *Liturgy* 10 (1965), p. 4.

What Is the Liturgical Movement? Boston: Liturgical Conference, 1948, revised and enlarged, 1956.

White, Susan J. *The Liturgical Arts Society (1921–1972): Art and Architecture in the Agenda of the American Roman Catholic Liturgical Renewal.* Ph.D. Dissertation. Notre Dame: University of Notre Dame Press, 1987.

Wiethoff, William. *Popular Rhetorical Strategy in the American Catholic Debate Over Vernacular Reform 1953–1968.* Unpublished dissertation. Michigan: University of Michigan, 1974.

Liturgy and Sacraments

Abbott, Walter M., ed. *The Documents of Vatican II.* Chicago: Geoffrey Chapman, 1966.

Anson, Peter F. *Churches, their Plan and Furnishing.* Eds. Thomas F. Croft-Fraser and H. A. Reinhold. Milwaukee: Bruce Publishing Company, 1948.

Beauduin, Lambert. *Liturgy the Life of the Church.* Trans. Virgil Michel. Collegeville: The Liturgical Press, 1929.

Berger, Teresa. "*Sacrosanctum Concilium* and Worship and the Oneness of Christ's Church: Twenty-Five Years Later." *Worship* 62 (1988), pp. 299–316.

Boberick, Aurelius. "Liturgy and Spiritual Growth." In: *National Liturgical Week 1961*, pp. 91–105. Washington: The Liturgical Conference, 1962.

Boularand, Ephrem. "The Christocentric Quality in Dom Marmion." In: *More About Marmion*, pp. 89–110. Trans. by the Earl of Wicklow. St. Louis: B. Herder Book Company, 1949.

Brasso, Gabriel M. *Liturgy and Spirituality.* Trans. Leonard J. Doyle. Collegeville: The Liturgical Press, 1971.

Broccolo, Gerard T. "The Eucharist as Sacrifice." Unpublished paper. Chicago: Archdiocesan Liturgical Commission, 1968. UNDA, CMRH 28/11.

———. *Prophetic Fellowship, The Ecclesial Dynamic of Christian Liturgy.* S.T.D. Dissertation. Roma: Pontificium Anthenaeum Anselmianum, 1970.

Cabrol, Ferdinand. *The Holy Sacrifice, A Simple Explanation of the Mass.* Trans. C. M. Anthony. London: Burns, Oates, & Washbourne, 1937.

Caronti, Emmanuele. *The Spirit of the Liturgy.* Trans. Virgil Michel. Collegeville: The Liturgical Press, 1926.

Casel, Odo. *The Mystery of Christian Worship, and Other Writings.* Ed. Burkhard Neunheuser. Westminster: Newman Press, 1962.

Cellier, Frank Stephen, ed. *Liturgy Is Mission.* New York: Seabury Press, 1964.

Chinnici, Joseph P. "Virgil Michel and the Tradition of Affective Prayer." *Worship* 62 (1988), pp. 225–236.

Cirrincione, Joseph. "The Possibilities of Liturgical Life in City Parishes." In: *National Liturgical Week 1944.* pp. 81–1. Chicago: The Liturgical Conference, 1945.

Devine, Arthur. *The Sacraments Explained According to the Teaching and Doctrine of the Catholic Church.* New York: Benziger Brothers, 1905.

Diekman, Godfrey. "First Born from the Dead." In: *National Liturgical Week 1962,* pp. 16–28. Washington: The Liturgical Conference, 1963.

———. "The Full-Sign of the Eucharist." In: *National Liturgical Week 1964,* pp. 86–94. Washington: The Liturgical Conference, 1964.

———. "Sunday Morning: Retrospect and Prospect." In: *Sunday Morning: A Time for Worship.* Ed. Mark Searle. Collegeville: Liturgical Press, 1982.

Egan, John J. *Liturgy and Justice: An Unfinished Agenda.* Collegeville: The Liturgical Press, 1984.

Ellard, Gerald. *Christian Life and Worship, Revised and Enlarged Edition.* Milwaukee: Bruce Publishing Company, 1940.

———. *Men at Work at Worship: America Joins the Liturgical Movement.* New York: Longmans, Green, & Company, 1940.

———. *The Mass in Transition.* Milwaukee: Bruce Publishing Company, 1956.

———. *The Mass of the Future.* Milwaukee: Bruce Publishing Company, 1948.

———. "The New Easter Light and Its Growing Vision." In: *National Liturgical Week 1952,* pp. 9–22. Elsberry, Missouri: The Liturgical Conference, 1953.

Glen, Jennifer. "Twenty Years Later: A Reflection on the Liturgical Act." *Assembly* 12 (1986), pp. 325–328.

Govert, Henry. "The Eucharist: A Sacrament of a Sacrifice." in: *Let Us Give Thanks: Explanation and Texts of the New Eucharistic Prayers.* Gerard Broccolo and Mary Jo Tully, Eds. Chicago: Liturgy Training Program, 1968.

Guardini, Romano. "A Letter form Romano Guardini." *Assembly* 12 (1986), pp. 322–324.

———. *The Church and the Catholic* and *The Spirit of the Liturgy.* Trans. Ada Lane. New York: Sheed & Ward, 1953.

——. *The Lord*. Trans. Elinor Castendyk Briefs. Chicago: Henry Regnery Company, 1954.

Hellriegel, Martin B. "A Pastor's Description of Liturgical Participation in His Parish." In: *National Liturgical Week 1941*, pp. 82–90. Newark: Benedictine Liturgical Conference, 1942.

——. *How to Make the Church Year a Living Reality*. Notre Dame: University of Notre Dame, 1955.

—— and Jasper, A. J. *The True Basis of Christian Solidarity*. Trans. William Busch. St. Louis: Central Bureau of the Central Verein, 1947.

Herwegen, Ildefons, *The Art Principle of the Liturgy*. Trans. William Busch. Collegeville: The Liturgical Press, 1931.

Himes, Kenneth R. "Eucharist and Justice: Assessing the Legacy of Virgil Michel." *Worship* 62 (1988), pp. 201–224.

Hovda, Robert. "The Paschal Mystery and the Liturgical Year." In *National Liturgical Week 1964*, pp. 51–66. Washington: The Liturgical Conference, 1964.

Irwin, Kevin W. *Liturgy, Prayer, and Spirituality*. New York: Paulist Press, 1984.

——. "The Constitution on the Sacred Liturgy, *Sacrosanctum Concilium* (4 December 1963)." In: *Vatican II and its Documents, an American Reappraisal*, pp. 9–38. Ed. Timothy O'Connell. Wilmington: Michael Glazier, 1986.

Jungmann, Joseph A. "Constitution on the Sacred Liturgy." In *Commentary on the Documents of Vatican II*, pp. 1–104. Ed. Herbert Vorgrimler. New York: Herder & Herder, 1967.

——. *Liturgical Worship*. Trans. Monk of St. John's Abbey. Collegeville: The Liturgical Press, 1941.

——. *Pastoral Liturgy*. Trans. Challoner Publications. New York: Herder and Herder, 1962.

——. *The Eucharistic Prayer: A Study of the Canon of the Mass*. Trans. Robert L. Batley. London: Burns & Oates, 1956.

——. *The Liturgy of the Word*. Trans. H. E. Winstone. Collegeville: Liturgical Press, 1966.

——. *The Mass of the Roman Rite, Its Origins and Development (Missarum Sollemnia)*. Trans. Francis A. Brunner. Westminster: Christian Classics, 1986.

——. *The Mass, An Historical, Theological, and Pastoral Survey*. Trans. Julian Fernandez, Ed. Mary Ellen Evans. Collegeville: The Liturgical Press, 1976.

——. *The Sacrifice of the Church, the Meaning of the Mass*. Trans. Clifford Howell. Collegeville: The Liturgical Press, 1956.

Kilmartin, Edward J. *Christian Liturgy: Theology and Practice*. New York: Sheed & Ward, 1988.

——. "Theology of the Sacraments: Toward a New Understanding of the Chief Rites of the Church of Jesus Christ." In *Alternative Futures for Worship, Vol. I: General Principles*, pp. 123–174. Ed. Regis A. Duffy. Collegeville: The Liturgical Press, 1987.

King, James W. *The Liturgy of the Laity*. Westminster: Newman Press, 1963.

Marshall, Romey P. and Taylor, Michael J. *Liturgy and Christian Unity*. Englewood Cliffs: Prentice-Hall, 1965.

Megivern, James J. *Official Catholic Teachings, Worship and Liturgy*. Wilmington: McGrath Publishing Company, 1978.

Michel, Virgil. "Advertising Our Wares." *Orate Fratres* 4 (1930), pp. 122–126.

———. *The Christian in the World.* Collegeville: The Liturgical Press, 1939.

———. "Liturgy and Catholic Life." *Catholic Action* 16 (1934), pp. 115–128.

———. *The Liturgy of the Church according to the Roman Rite.* New York: Macmillan Company, 1937.

———. "The Liturgy: The Basis of Social Regeneration." *Orate Fratres* 9 (1935), pp. 536–545.

———. *My Sacrifice and Yours, Second Edition.* Collegeville: The Liturgical Press, 1927.

———. *Our Life in Christ.* Collegeville: The Liturgical Press, 1939.

———. "The True Christian Spirit." *Ecclesiastical Life* 82 (1930), pp. 128–142.

Mick, Lawrence E. *To Live as We Worship.* Collegeville: The Liturgical Press, 1984.

Miller, John H. *Fundamentals of the Liturgy.* Notre Dame: Fides, 1959.

———. "Liturgical Studies." In *Theology in Transition: A Biographical Evaluation of the "Decisive Decade," 1954–1964*, pp. 174–211. Ed. Elmer O'Brien. New York: Herder & Herder, 1965.

O'Meara, Thomas F. *The Future of Catholicism.* Notre Dame: University of Notre Dame, 1986.

Parsch, Pius. *Study the Mass.* Trans. William Busch. Collegeville: The Liturgical Press, 1941.

———. *The Liturgy of the Mass.* Trans. Frederic C. Eckhoff. St. Louis: B. Herder Book Company, 1936.

Philipon, M.M. *The Sacraments in the Christian Life.* Trans. John A. Otto. Westminster: Newman Press, 1954.

Power, David N. *The Sacrifice We Offer: The Tridentine Dogma and its Reinterpretation.* New York: Crossroad, 1987.

Rahner, Hugo, ed. *The Parish, from Theology to Practice.* Trans. Robert Kress. Westminster: Newman Press, 1958.

Rahner, Karl. "Theology and Anthropology." In T. Patrick Burke, Ed. *The Word in History: St. Xavier Symposium,* New York: Sheed & Ward, 1966. pp. 1–23.

Reinhold, H.A. *The American Parish and the Roman Liturgy: An Essay in Seven Chapters.* New York: Macmillan Company, 1958.

———. *The Dynamics of the Liturgy.* New York: Macmillan Company, 1961.

———. "More or Less Liturgical." *Orate Fratres* 13 (1939), pp. 152–155, 213–218, 251–263.

———. "A Social Leaven. *Orate Fratres* 26 (1951), pp. 515–519.

———. *Speaking of Liturgical Architecture.* Notre Dame: University of Notre Dame, 1952.

Roquet, A.M. *Christ Acts through the Sacraments.* Trans. Carisbrooke Dominicans. Collegeville: The Liturgical Press, 1957.

Saliers, Don E. *Worship and Spirituality.* Philadelphia: Westminster Press, 1984.

Schmemann, Alexander. *Liturgy and Life: Christian Development through Liturgical Experience.* New York: Dept. of Religious Education, Orthodox Church of America, 1974.

Schoof, Mark. *A Survey of Catholic Theology, 1800–1970.* Trans. N.D. Smith. New York: Paulist Newman Press, 1970.

Searle, Mark, ed. *Liturgy and Social Justice.* Collegeville: The Liturgical Press, 1980.

———. "On the Art of Lifting up the Heart: Liturgical Prayer Today." *Studies in Formative Spirituality* 3 (1982), pp. 399–410.

Sears, Robert T. "Trinitarian Love as Ground of the Church." In *Why the Church?*, pp. 108–135. Eds. Walter Burghardt & William Thompson. New York: Paulist Press, 1976.

Shands, Alfred R. *The Liturgical Movement and the Local Church.* London: SCM Press Ltd., 1959.

Sheppard, Lancelot, ed. *The People Worship, A History of the Liturgical Movement.* New York: Hawthorn Books, Inc. 1965.

Vitry, Ermin. "Restoration of the Parish High Mass and Vespers." In *National Liturgical Week 1944.* pp. 145–156. Chicago: The Liturgical Conference, 1945.

White, James F. *Sacraments as God's Self Giving.* Nashville: Abingdon Press, 1983.

Mystical Body

Adam, Karl. *The Spirit of Catholicism.* Trans. Justin McCann. New York: Macmillan Company, 1935.

Bluett, Joseph J. "Current Theology: The Mystical Body of Christ 1890–1940." *Theological Studies* III (1942): 261–282.

Day, Dorothy. *The Mystical Body of Christ.* East Orange, New Jersey: Thomas Barry, 1936.

Hellrigel, Martin B. *Vine and Branches.* St. Louis: Pio Decimo Press, 1948.

Jurgenmeier, Frederich. *The Mystical Body of Christ as the Basic Principle of Spiritual Life.* Trans. Harriet G. Strauss. New York: Sheed & Ward, 1954.

Leen, Edward. *The True Vine and Its Branches.* New York: P. J. Kenedy & Sons, 1938.

Lord, Daniel Aloysius. *Our Part in the Mystical Body.* St. Louis: The Queen's Work, 1935.

Mersch, Emile. *The Whole Christ: The Historical Development of the Doctrine of the Mystical Body in Scripture and Tradition.* Trans, John R. Kelly. Milwaukee: Bruce Publishing Company, 1938.

Plus, Raoul. *In Chris Jesus.* Trans. Peter Addison. Westminster: Newman Bookshop, 1948.

Sheen, Fulton J.. *The Mystical Body of Christ.* New York: Sheed & Ward, 1935.

Pius X

Diekmann, Godfrey. "Lay Participation in the Liturgy of the Church." In: *A Symposium on the Life and Work of Pope Pius X*, pp. 137-158. Washington: Confraternity of Christian Doctrine, 1946.

Huber, Raphael M. "Biographical Sketch of Pope Pius X." In: *A Symposium of the Life and Work of Pop Pius X,* pp. 1-49. Washington: Confraternity of Christian Doctrine, 1946.

Pius XI

Brown, Francis J. *Social Justice in the Modern World, Encyclical Letter of Pope Pius XI (Quadragesimo Anno) with Outline and Index.* Chicago: Outline Press, 1947.

Bruehl, Charles P. *The Pope's Plan for Social Reconstruction, A Commentary on the Social Encyclicals of Pius XI.* New York: Devin-Adair Company, 1939.

Fitzsimmons, John &McGuire, Paul. *Restoring All Things, A Guide to Catholic Action.* New York: Sheed & Ward, 1938.

Hughes, Philip. *Pope Pius the Eleventh*. London: Sheed & Ward, 1938.

McGowan, R. A. *Toward Social Justice: A Discussion and Application of Pius XI's "Reconstructing the Social Order"*. New York: Paulist Press, 1931.

Michel, Virgil. *Christian Social Reconstruction: Some Fundamentals of Quadragesimo Anno*. Milwaukee: Bruce Publishing Company, 1937.

Nell-Breuning, Oswald von. *Reorganization of the Social Economy, The Social Encyclical Developed and Explained*. Ed. Vernard W. Dempsey. Milwaukee: Bruce Publishing Company, 1936.

Pius XI. *Quadragesimo Anno, On Reconstructing the Social Order*. Trans. authorized by the Holy See. Washington: National Catholic Welfare Conference, 1942.

Pius XI. *Sixteen Encyclicals of Pope Pius XI*. Washington, D.C.: National Catholic Welfare Conference, 1938.

Pius XI. *The Encyclicals of Pius XI*. Trans. James H. Ryan. St. Louis: B. Herder Book Company, 1927.

Pius XII

Bagiackas, Joseph J. W. *Pope Pius XII and Lay Responsibility in Public Life*. Unpublished master's thesis. Notre Dame: University of Notre Dame, 1950.

Kelly, John E. "The Encyclical, *Mediator Dei*." In: *National Liturgical Week 1948*, pp. 9–14. Conception, Mo.: The Liturgical Conference, 1949.

Pius XII. *Christ, the Center of the Church's Liturgy, Address by His Holiness, Pope Pius XII, to the Delegates of the First International Congress of Pastoral Liturgy, Assembled in Vatican City, September 22, 1956*. Trans. Vatican Press Office. Clyde, Missouri: Benedictine Convent of Perpetual Adoration, 1957.

Pius XII. *Guide for Living, An Approved Selection of Letters and Addresses of His holiness Pope Pius XII*. Ed. Maurice Quinlan. New York: Longmans, Green, & Company, 1960.

Pius XII. *Mediator Dei, Encyclical Letter of Pope Pius XII on the Sacred Liturgy*. Trans. Vatican Library. Washington: National Catholic Welfare Conference, 1947.

Pius XII. *Pius XII Speaks on the Lay Apostolate*. Rome: Permanent Committee for International Congresses on the Apostolate of the Laity, 1955.

Pius XII. *Selected Letters and Addresses of Pius XII*. Ed. G. D. Smith. London: Catholic Truth Society, 1949.

Pius XII. *The Pope Speaks: The Teaching of Pope Pius XII*. Ed. Michael Chinigo. New York: Pantheon Books, 1957.

Pius XII. *The Pope Speaks: The Words of Pius XII*. With a biography by Charles Rankin. New York: Harcourt, Brace, & Company, 1940.

Roman Catholicism and American Society

Abell, Aaron, I. and others. *A History of the United States of America*. New York: Forham University Press, 1952.

Ahlstrom, Sydney E. *A Religious History of the American People*. New Haven: Yale University, 1972.

Barry, Colman J. *The Catholic Church and German Americans*. Milwaukee: Bruce Publishing Company, 1953.

Bernstein, Irving. *A History of the American Worker 1920–1933: The Lean Years.* Boston: Houghton Mifflin Company, 1960.

Brophy, Don & Westenhaver, Edythe, eds. *The Story of Catholics in America.* New York: Paulist Press, 1978.

Cogley, John. *Catholic America.* New York: Dial Press, 1973.

—— and Von Allen, Roger. *Catholic America, Expanded and Updated.* Kansas City: Sheed & Ward, 1986.

Dolan, Jay P. *An American Catholic Church: Essays on the Americanization of the Catholic Church.* Moraga, Cal.: St. Mary's College of California, 1979.

——. *The American Catholic Experience: A History from Colonial Times to the Present.* New York: Doubleday & Company, 1985.

——. "The American Catholic Parish: An Historical Perspective, 1820–1980." In: *The Parish in Transition, Proceedings of a Conference on the American Catholic Parish,* pp. 33–46. Ed. David Byers. Washington: USCCB, 1986.

——. ed. *The American Catholic Parish: A History from 1850 to the Present, Two Volumes.* New York: Paulist Press, 1987.

Eberhardt, Newman C. *A Survey of American Church History.* St. Louis & London: B. Herder Book Company, 1964.

Ellis, John Tracy. *American Catholicism, Second Edition, Revised.* Chicago: University of Chicago, Press, 1969.

Gleason, Philip. *The Conservative Reformers, German-American Catholics and the Social Order.* Notre Dame: University of Notre Dame Press, 1968.

Gleason, Philip. *Catholicism in America.* New York: Harper & Row, 1970.

Greeley, Andrew M. *The Catholic Experience: An Interpretation of the History of American Catholicism.* New York: Doubleday & Company, 1967.

Hennessey, James. *American Catholics: A History of the Roman Catholic Community in the United States.* New York: Oxford University Press, 1981.

Hudson, Winthrop S. *Religion in America, An Historical Account of the Development of American Religious Life, Third Edition.* New York: Charles Scribner's Sons, 1981.

McAvoy, Thomas T., ed. *Roman Catholicism and the American Way of Life.* Notre Dame: University of Notre Dame Press, 1960.

——. *A History of the Catholic Church in the United States.* Notre Dame: University of Notre Dame Press, 1969.

Putz, Louis J., ed. *The Catholic Church U.S.A.* Chicago: Fides Publishers Association, 1956.

Shaw, Stephen J. *Chicago's Germans and Italians, 1903–1939: The Catholic Parish as a Way-Station of Ethnicity and Americanization.* Unpublished Ph.D. dissertation. Chicago: University of Chicago, 1981.

Roman Catholicism in Chicago

Avella, Steven M. *Meyer of Milwaukee: The Life and Times of a Midwestern Archbishop.* Unpublished Ph.D. dissertation. Notre Dame: University of Notre Dame, 1984.

Buehrle, Marie Cecilia. *The Cardinal Stritch Story.* Milwaukee: Bruce Publishing Company, 1959.

Brocoolo, Gerard. "The Chicago Parish: Gathering Us into Ministry." September 24, 1978, lecture at the 1978 Archdiocesan Liturgical Conference. NCR Cassettes.

Geaney, Dennis J. "The Chicago Story." *Chicago Studies* 2 (1963), pp. 281–300.

Giese, Vincent J. "The Lay Apostolate in Chicago." In: *The Catholic Church, U.S.A.*
    pp. 358–376. Ed. Louis J. Putz. Chicago: Fides Publishers Association, 1956.
"The Great Congress and What It Stands for Arranged in Catechism Form for
    Convenience." *New World* 34 (June 20, 1926, pp. 4–5.
Kantowicz, Edward R. *Corporation Sole: Cardinal Mundelein and Chicago Catholicism.*
    Notre Dame: University of Notre Dame Press, 1983.
Koenig, Harry C., ed. *Caritas Christi Urget Nos: A History of the Parishes of the*
    Archdiocese of Chicago, Two Volumes. Chicago: Archdiocese of Chicago, 1980.
Koenig, Harry C., ed. *Caritas Christi Urget Nos: A History of the Institutions of the*
    Archdiocese of Chicago, Two Volumes. Chicago: Archdiocese of Chicago, 1980.
Martin, Paul R. *The First Cardinal of the West: The Story of the Church in the Archdiocese*
    of Chicago under the Administration of his Eminence, George Cardinal Mundelein,
    Third Archbishop of Chicago and First Cardinal of the West. Chicago: New World
    Publishing Company, 1943.
Mayer, Harold M. & Wade, Richard C. *Chicago, Growth of a Metropolis.* Chicago:
    University of Chicago Press, 1969.
Newell, Barbara Warne. *Chicago and the Labor Movement, Metropolitan Unionism in the*
    1930s. Urbana: University of Illinois Press, 1961.
"The Official Program of the 28th International Eucharistic Congress." *New World* 34
    (June 18, 1926), pp. 2–3.
Quigley Preparatory Seminary North, Seventy-fifth Jubilee: 1905–1980. Chicago:
    Archdiocese of Chicago, 1980.
Sanders, James W. *The Education of an Urban Minority: Catholics in Chicago 1835–1965.*
    New York: Oxford University Press, 1977.
Shanabruch, Charles. *Chicago's Catholics: The Evolution of an American Identity.*
    Notre Dame: University of Notre Dame Press, 1981.
100 Years, the History of the Church of the Holy Name. Chicago: Cathedral of the Holy
    Name, 1949.

Social Justice

Abell, Aaron I. *American Catholicism and Social Action: A Search for Social Justice,*
    a Comprehensive Study of the Catholic Social Movement in the United States from
    1865–1950. Notre Dame: University of Notre Dame Press, 1963.
——. ed. *American Catholic Though on Social Questions.* New York: Bobbs-Merrill, 1968.
Blantz, Thomas E. *A Priest in Public Service, Francis J. Hass and the New Deal.*
    Notre Dame: University of Notre Dame, 1982.
Broderick, Francis L. *Right Reverend New Dealer, John A. Ryan.* New York: MacMillan
    Company, 1963.
Calvez, Jean-Yves & Perrin, Jacques. *The Church and Social Justice: The Social Teachings*
    of the Popes from Leo XIII to Pius XII (1878–1958). Chicago: Henry Regnery
    Company, 1961.
Camp, Richard L. *The Papal Ideology of Social Reform: A Study in Historical*
    Development, 1878–1967. Leiden: E.J. Brill, 1969.
Cronin, John F. *Catholic Social Principles: The Social Teaching of the Catholic Church*
    Applied to American Economic Life. Milwaukee: Bruce Publishing Company, 1950.
——. *Social Problems and Economic Life, Revised Editon.* Milwaukee: Bruce Publishing
    Company, 1964.

Drummond, William F. *Social Justice*. Milwaukee: Bruce Publishing Company, 1955.

Fox, Mary Maritta. *Peter E. Dietz, Labor Priest*. Notre Dame: University of Notre Dame Press, 1953.

Fremantle, Anne. *The Social Teachings of the Church*. New York: Mentor-Omega Books, 1963.

———, ed. *The Papal Encyclicals in their Historical Context*. New York: American Book Company, 1963.

Harte, Thomas J. *Papal Social Principles: A Guide and Digest*. Gloucester, Mass.: Bruce Publishing Company, 1956.

Mainelli, Vincent. *Social Justice*. Wilmington: Consortium Books, 1978.

Proceedings, First National Catholic Social Action Conference, Milwaukee, Wisconsin, May 1–4, 1938. Washington: National Catholic Welfare Conference, 1938.

Shields, Leo W. *The History and Meaning of the Term Social Justice*. Notre Dame: University of Notre Dame Press, 1941.

Index

Books/Documents/Magazines

Events

Robert Tuzik, PHD, is a priest of the Archdiocese of Chicago. He holds an STL from the University of St. Mary of the Lake and a PHD in liturgical studies from the University of Notre Dame. He has been an associate pastor of five parishes in Chicago and is currently special projects coordinator for the Office of Divine Worship of the Archdiocese of Chicago. He also serves as liturgical consultant to his Eminence, Cardinal Francis George. He has served as special consultant to ICEL and the BCL and is a member of the Society for Catholic Liturgy and Region VII of the FDLC. He has served as an adjunct professor of liturgy at the University of St. Mary of the Lake and as a lecturer at Loyola University of Chicago. He has published numerous articles in *Pastoral Liturgy, Liturgical Ministry, Modern Liturgy, Assembly,* and *Antiphon.*

About the Liturgical Institute

The Liturgical Institute, founded in 2000 by His Eminence Francis Cardinal George of Chicago, offers a variety of options for education in Liturgical Studies. A unified, rites-based core curriculum constitutes the foundation of the program, providing integrated and balanced studies toward the advancement of the renewal promoted by the Second Vatican Council. The musical, artistic, and architectural dimensions of worship are given particular emphasis in the curriculum. Institute students are encouraged to participate in its "liturgical heart" of daily Mass and Morning and Evening Prayer. The academic program of the Institute serves a diverse, international student population—laity, religious, and clergy—who are preparing for service in parishes, dioceses, and religious communities. Personalized mentoring is provided in view of each student's ministerial and professional goals. The Institute is housed on the campus of the University of St. Mary of the Lake/Mundelein Seminary, which offers the largest priestly formation program in the United States and is the center of the permanent diaconate and lay ministry training programs of the Archdiocese of Chicago. In addition, the University has the distinction of being the first chartered institution of higher learning in Chicago (1844), and one of only seven pontifical faculties in North America.

For more information about the Liturgical Institute and its programs, contact: usml.edu/liturgicalinstitute. Phone: 847-837-4542. E-mail: litinst@usml.edu.